SONGS OF THE GREAT AMERICAN WEST

Compiled and Edited by
IRWIN SILBER

Music Annotated, Edited and Arranged by
EARL ROBINSON

DOVER PUBLICATIONS, INC.
New York

I should like to thank the following for giving me permission to use various materials in this book: Howard S. Richmond and Al Brackman of The Richmond Organization for permission to use songs from the Lomax collections, plus other copyrighted material; Folkways Records for various songs as performed on several LPs recorded by L. M. Hilton, Pete Seeger, Rosalie Sorrels, and others; The Texas Folklore Society for permission to reproduce songs from various publications; Margaret Larkin for permission to include a number of songs from her book, *Singing Cowboy*; Sanga Music for permission to include their copyrighted song "Ludlow Massacre"; Stormking Music for permission to include the copyrighted song "Jesse James" (II); Oak Publications for permission to reprint "The Preacher and the Slave" from *Songs of Joe Hill*; the publication *Heritage of Kansas* for permission to reprint material from various issues; *Western Folklore* for permission to reprint the song "Root Hog, or Die"; Harcourt, Brace and World Publishing Co. for permission to reprint various selections from *The American Songbag* by Carl Sandburg; and Indiana University Press for permission to reprint "Mountain Meadows Massacre" from *Saints of Sage and Saddle* by Austin and Alta Fife.

Copyright

Published in Canada by General Publishing Company, Ltd., 30 Lesmill Road, Don Mills, Toronto, Ontario.

Published in the United Kingdom by Constable and Company, Ltd., 3 The Lanchesters, 162–164 Fulham Palace Road, London W6 9ER.

Bibliographical Note

This Dover edition, first published in 1995, is an unabridged republication of the work first published by The Macmillan Company, New York, 1967. A new editorial note on p. 328 updates information about the book's Discography.

Library of Congress Cataloging-in-Publication Data

Songs of the great American west / compiled and edited by Irwin Silber ; music annotated, edited, and arranged by Earl Robinson.
     p. of music.
  In part for voice and piano; in part unacc.; includes chord symbols and guitar chord diagrams.
    Reprint. Originally published: New York : Macmillan, 1967.
    Includes bibliographical references (p.   ) and indexes.
    Discography: p.
    ISBN 0-486-28704-1 (pbk.)
    1. Folk music—West (U.S.) 2. Folk songs, English—West (U.S.) 3. Ballads, English—West (U.S.) I. Silber, Irwin, 1925– . II. Robinson, Earl, 1910– .
M1629.6.W5S58   1995   95-17334
                                                                    CIP
                                                                                 M

Manufactured in the United States of America
Dover Publications, Inc., 31 East 2nd Street, Mineola, N.Y. 11501

For Joshua and Fred

ACKNOWLEDGMENTS

THE HEART and soul of this book is the work of men and women long since gone, the ballad makers of another age who memorialized their lives and times in song. We know the names of a handful of these gifted minstrels—John Stone, "Doc" Robinson, Mart Taylor, the Hutchinson Family Singers, N. Howard Thorp, Joe Hill—but for the most part their individual identities are lost in the giant cauldron of history, their only epitaphs these songs which are now a part of the fabric of the American heritage.

Who were they—these '49ers, long-tom toters, lousy miners, Missouri Pikers, Mormon Saints and co-habs, handcart pioneers, homesteaders, nesters, sod-busters, hayseeds, Lane County bachelors, ladies of the line; these greenhorns, tenderfoot cowboys, range riders, *vaqueros,* buffalo skinners, gun slingers, lumberjacks, railroaders, bindlestiffs, hokey boys, Wobblies—and all the girls they left behind?

They were people—ordinary people, the writers, the singers, and those they sang about. They were seekers and searchers—looking for a home, a job, a fortune, a wife, a chance for a good time and an even break. In their search they conquered and settled almost half a continent.

In the most fundamental sense, this is their book. To acknowledge their contribution would be presumptuous. All we can say to them is, "We're glad you walked across the path of our history and left us these keepsakes of your time."

My work in compiling and editing this collection, and providing some historical setting for the songs, was aided immeasurably by a number of institutions and individuals. The following libraries provided me with a great wealth of rare source material: The Music Division of the Library of Congress, The Archive of Folk Song in the Library of Congress, The Library of the Society of California Pioneers in San Francisco, The Bancroft Library at the University of California in Berkeley, The New York Public Library, The San Francisco Public Library, The California State Library in Sacramento, The Los Angeles Public Library, The Library at the University of California in Los Angeles, The Library of the Juilliard School of Music in New York City, and the Chicago Public Library.

Many scholars, folklorists and singers were most generous in allowing me the use of their researches and in taking time to give advice, suggestions, and comments on my efforts. Among these I particularly want to thank Dr. John D. Robb, whose work in collecting and transcribing the folk music of the Spanish Southwest has been an outstanding contribution to our knowledge of this significant tradition; Alan Lomax, who has freely made available to me the product of years of pioneering research by his father, John A. Lomax, and himself, and whose own appreciation of our folk heritage was one of my earliest inspirations; Pete Seeger, who first made me aware of the living vitality of folk music;

and Moses Asch, whose monumental library of folk music on Folkways Records is one of the wondrous achievements of our time.

It would not be possible to list all of the singers, writers, friends, and associates who helped me with songs, ideas, encouragement, and criticism. But the following merit particular mention: J. Frank Dobie, Jenny Vincent, J. Barre Toelken, Edith Fowke, Elena Paz, Wayland Hand, Tony Kraber, Carol Lewis, Arthur Kevess, Rosalie Sorrels, Waldemar Hille, B. A. Botkin, José Carlos Santos, and Gail Gardner.

I was fortunate to have working with me in the capacity of music editor for the collection one of the musical pioneers of our generation, Earl Robinson, whose songs and cantatas comprise a great living tribute to the genius of our American heritage.

I. S.

CONTENTS

THOUGHTS ON THE MUSIC   xiii

INTRODUCTION   xv

Part 1   *"Ho! For California!"*

THE RACE TO CALIFORNIA   5

HO! FOR CALIFORNIA   9

SACRAMENTO   12

SWEET BETSY FROM PIKE   14

JOE BOWERS   18

CROSSING THE PLAINS   23

COMING AROUND THE HORN   27

WE'LL GIVE 'EM JESSIE   30

SIOUX INDIANS   33

A LA RU   36

SONG OF HAPPINESS   38

THE PACIFIC RAILROAD   39

Part 2   *"On the Plains of Mexico"*

REMEMBER THE ALAMO!   47

GREEN GROW THE LILACS   49

SANTY ANNO   52

THE MAID OF MONTEREY   55

BUENA VISTA   57

MUSTANG GRAY   60

CLARÍN DE CAMPAÑA   62

EL TECOLOTE   64

Part 3 "Come, Come, Ye Saints!"

COME, COME, YE SAINTS   73
SEA GULLS AND CRICKETS   75
THE MOUNTAIN MEADOWS MASSACRE   77
THE HANDCART SONG   80
BRIGHAM YOUNG   83
ECHO CANYON   89

Part 4 "The Days of '49"

THE DAYS OF FORTY-NINE   96
THE GOOD OLD DAYS OF '50, '1, AND '2   99
WHEN I WENT OFF TO PROSPECT   100
LIFE IN CALIFORNIA   104
SEEING THE ELEPHANT   107
I OFTEN THINK OF WRITING HOME   111
CALIFORNIA AS IT IS   114
THE LOUSY MINER   117
POKER JIM   120
HANGTOWN GALS   123
HUMBUG STEAMSHIP COMPANIES   125
CALIFORNIA STAGE COMPANY   130
WE ARE ALL A-PANNING   132
CORRIDO DE JOAQUÍN MURIETA   135
TWELVE HUNDRED MORE   138
ROOT HOG, OR DIE   142
I'M OFF TO BOISE CITY   145
THE DREARY BLACK HILLS   149
THE OLD SETTLER'S SONG   153

Part 5 "Ride Around Little Dogies"

I RIDE AN OLD PAINT   161
THE OLD CHISHOLM TRAIL   164
THE BUFFALO SKINNERS   169
GIT ALONG, LITTLE DOGIES   173
COWBOY'S GETTIN'-UP HOLLER   177
GOOD-BYE OLD PAINT   179

CORRIDO DE KANSAS   181
DONEY GAL   184
THE TRAIL TO MEXICO   187
COWBOY'S LIFE IS A DREARY, DREARY LIFE   192
THE GAL I LEFT BEHIND ME   195
UTAH CARROLL   197
BURY ME NOT ON THE LONE PRAIRIE   200
SPANISH IS THE LOVING TONGUE   203
LITTLE JOE, THE WRANGLER   206

Part 6 "The Farmer Is the Man"

THE HOMESTEAD OF THE FREE   213
UNCLE SAM'S FARM   215
THE LITTLE OLD SOD SHANTY ON MY CLAIM   218
WESTERN HOME   221
THE LANE COUNTY BACHELOR   224
KANSAS BOYS   229
THE WYOMING NESTER   231
DAKOTA LAND   233
THE KANSAS FOOL   235
THE FARMER IS THE MAN   236
THE HAYSEED   240
THE INDEPENDENT MAN   243
THE PEOPLE'S JUBILEE   245

Part 7 "Come All You Bold Fellers"

JESSE JAMES   252
SAM BASS   257
BILLY THE KID   260
THE ZEBRA DUN   262
EL TORO MORO   265
CORRIDO DE HERACLIO BERNAL   270
CUSTER'S LAST CHARGE   273
ROY BEAN   276
THE STREETS OF LAREDO   279
TYING TEN KNOTS IN THE DEVIL'S TAIL   283

Part 8 "Roll On, Columbia"

THE BIG ROCK CANDY MOUNTAIN   291
THE LUDLOW MASSACRE   296
THE PREACHER AND THE SLAVE   298
THE COMMONWEALTH OF TOIL   302
TOO REE AMA   304
THE FROZEN LOGGER   306
FIFTY THOUSAND LUMBERJACKS   308
WHEN THE ICE WORMS NEST AGAIN   311
ROLL ON, COLUMBIA   314
BIBLIOGRAPHY   319
DISCOGRAPHY   328
SUBJECT INDEX   329
INDEX OF TITLES AND FIRST LINES   333

THOUGHTS ON THE MUSIC

ALL FOLK MUSIC is essentially creative. The original singer may have stolen tune or words from friends, acquaintances, or the air around him, but by virtue of his need to say musically and poetically what was on his mind he became a creator. As a member of the human race his song often struck universal chords. But as an individual, differing as we all do in special priceless ways from every other individual, he had to be original. And as the song is passed on from mouth to ear to mouth again, the creation and change go on.

It is through this oral method of communication and memory that the "folk process" comes into operation. A word or phrase is disremembered, or doesn't say it quite right. A line is added or subtracted—sometimes a whole new verse says better what the next singer feels. Then somehow the tune gets changed in transmission. Perhaps a lower voice can't reach some of the high notes. Or the tenor or soprano with a flare transposes a low note into a high flourish. A gang gets to singing it and three versions get going at once, then coalesce under the leadership of the strongest voice. Occasionally the deeply creative person, or perhaps the trained poet or musician, takes a hand. Then the song may get solidified and written down. But nothing really stops the folk process as long as the song meets a need of people.

The songs in this book, it is surmised, continue to meet such needs. Some of the words may seem archaic and not exactly "with it" in today's urban civilization. But the emotions expressed in humor and tragedy are with us still. The need to remember, feel, and understand our heritage is there still. The joy in singing a beautiful, a sad, a brave, and, above all, an honest song will be with us for some time to come—and so will the joy and need to be creative.

Therefore, the approach to the songs in this book, like the folk process itself, is a creative one. The original words and tunes have not been tampered with at all, except in those few cases where a composite text or melody has been used. In this way the feeling of the original men and women who sang these songs into life has been preserved. In many cases, as with the cowboy songs, these were sung without any accompaniment. You who will sing and use these songs can be certain that you are faithful to an original model simply by singing these songs as written. This in itself is a creative process. Or you may sing them your own way, without any accompaniment at all, the way you feel them—also a creative approach. Piano or guitar—banjo, accordian, concertina, autoharp—can, however, be very helpful. In suggesting chords and accompaniments for these instruments a basic and yet somewhat off-beat approach has been used. A few of the songs have been arranged quite traditionally, the expected chords in their expected places. But in the great majority of songs you may find surprises: a "wrong" chord, which after some inspection and replaying sounds right; an indicated bass line that plays against and enriches the melody; a change of accompaniment in the middle of the song from umpah to strong rhythmic chords, etc.

Frankly it was fun to make conscious use of the folk process while carefully preserving the basic character of the song. To search for the interesting and unexpected to replace the obvious is part of creation. But this is by no means either to confuse you or to inhibit your own creative ideas. Rather it is to indicate directions in which you can add your own ideas and feelings to the song. Make it live today for you and your friends.

Now to some of the specifics. The chords in parentheses serve two purposes. The main one is to allow you to be traditional and simple if you want. So most of the time the chords in parentheses are simpler or more obvious than the indicated one. You can't, however, always count on this. A few times I stated the obvious or simple chord first and put the more interesting or difficult one in parentheses. So there you are—try them both. And you may make up your own if you don't like these.

You will have noticed by now that the main instrumental direction is toward six-string guitar, tuned from bass to treble E A D G B E. This is because there are more guitars than anybody. There are bass runs indicated, um-pahs and um-pah-pahs and hammer-ons (designated by H). Page 242 describes how hammer-ons work on the D string. Other strings are similar.

The interesting variations gained by using chords in inversion have been understood by serious composers for centuries, and there is no reason why guitar players shouldn't partake of this advantageous technique. So read this part if you are interested in understanding those chords with the roman numerals under them, like this (A   C   E maj7).

                 V   III   VII

A simple basic chord is made up of the notes on 1, 3, and 5 of the scale. A seventh chord adds 7 to those three numbers. By definition the name of the chord is also number 1 so you can actually figure out the notes of practically any chord. Here is an example. To construct the C chord lay out the scale as follows: $C\ D\ E\ F\ G\ A\ B\ C$; 1, 3, and 5 give

$$1\ 2\ 3\ 4\ 5\ 6\ 7\ 8$$

you C, E, and G, which happen to be the notes in the C chord. To construct a seventh chord on G

$$1\ 2\ 3\ 4\ 5\ 6\ 7\ 8$$

$G\ A\ B\ C\ D\ E\ F\ G$, G being 1, the G7th chord is GBDF. Right? Right. In the root position of the chord the lowest note played (usually one of the three bass strings on the guitar) is number 1—also the letter name of the chord. In the first inversion

   A   D   G7

(III III III, etc.) the third is in the bass and the one up above somewhere. In the second inversion (E Bm, etc.) the fifth is in the bass. In the third

   V V

inversion the seventh might be in the bass. An extra nice effect is when a note *not in the chord* is in the bass. This is usually indicated as Gm7

                        (Cin bass).

Inversions give a feeling of movement. Many more can be used than are indicated in these songs. Try out your own. A song usually ends in the root position, however.

Now a word to piano players. The thirty-odd songs with piano accompaniment were designed to bring out the specific characteristics of these songs in a more interesting manner and are to have fun with. If occasionally they are a little difficult, they are all very playable and will become more enjoyable with just a little work. On the single-line melodies (lead sheets) play the tune with the right hand and do things to the chords with your left, i.e., um-pah, arpeggio, or just straight marching rhythm. Where the guitar part or a bass line is written out it is to be played down an octave.

If you have a mixed chorus of at least two men and two women—or if you can get together a barbershop quartet—there are several arrangements just made for you. Three songs have guitar tablature (tab) which indicates exactly how a song is to be played. There is a full discussion of Tab in my *Young Folk Song Book,* published by Simon & Schuster.

This is a wonderful collection of songs. Here's wishing you the best—to play, work, enjoy, and sing songs of the great American west.

EARL ROBINSON

INTRODUCTION

THERE ARE MANY WAYS of telling the story of an epoch. Historians, from the perspective of time, analyze social forces, political developments, and economic causes, and place the march of events in a logical sequence so that man may know something of the long road he has already traveled. Novelists, storytellers, playwrights can find much of the essence of the past in the tale of one person or a group of characters created in the mind but representative of their time and place. A poet may give an insight into an era with an image that suddenly makes yesterday as real as today. Antiquarians, cherishing the keepsakes of the past, help us to imagine the specifics and commonplaces of history.

But the people who have lived through great historical events have a way of telling their own story—and of keeping that story alive. In ballads, lullabies, battle cries, love songs, topical verse, children's singing games, and the like—passed on from one generation to another by memory and word of mouth—the people say to us, "This is the way it really was!" And we, in retrospect, call the sum total of this expression *folk song*.

Taken by themselves, such songs are, at best, a dubious method of recounting history. Fact and fancy intermingle freely in folk song, but the exactitude of dates, names, and places becomes increasingly less important the longer a song is sung. The unwary researcher, basing his information of an era on song alone, may mistake the passions or prejudices of a ballad for narrative fact, and overlook the deeper insight of emotional fact, without regard to particular circumstance. For these songs not only relate history, they themselves are part of the historical process.

The songs in this collection fulfill a threefold function. First of all, they are keepsakes of the past, forget-me-nots in rhyme and melody created and sung by people out of the experiences of their own lives and times. Taken as a body of literature, they provide us with a panorama of the morals, customs, prejudices, and social values of an era. Second, they are narratives (however inaccurate) of past events. Last, and perhaps most important, they are works of art with a continuing existence of their own, many of them still sung today, reminding us of the feelings, moods, and emotions which human beings of all ages hold in common.

The particular meeting ground of the songs in these pages is the story of the American West, a story which is in fact many stories, an episodic pageant played out on a giant stage over the course of three centuries. Many of these songs are the works of professional ballad makers; others come out of that great anonymous melting pot in which the identities of the authors have long been lost. All of them were originally known and sung by people whose lives were inexorably bound up with the conquest and settlement of the lands comprising the American West. The area covered in this collection of songs is bounded on the east by the Dakotas, Nebraska, Kansas, and western Texas —following the sun to the Pacific shore, and including portions of northern Mexico, western Canada, and Alaska.

A collection of this kind naturally reflects the views and values of its editor. A book, like any container, has limits—and the act of selection and categorization becomes thereby a value judgment. A word, therefore, concerning my own point of view.

My aim in compiling these songs has been to provide, through song, a representative picture of the main historical experiences which contributed to the winning of the West. This goal was somewhat limited by the availability of appropriate song material; certain significant periods are covered either inadequately, or in some cases not at all. (I was able to find very few songs, for example, concerning early western explorations, and had to settle for a Frémont political campaign song to illustrate this period.)

Basically, the events with which this book is concerned took place from the early 1840's on through the second half of the nineteenth century, spilling over into the first two decades of the twentieth century. These include the war with Mexico, the Mormon emigration, the great Gold Rush of 1849 and the westward movement which followed in its wake, the settlement of the plains, the era of the Texas longhorns and the cowboys who drove them along the dusty cattle trails. The final section includes songs of the twentieth century that reflect movements and trends of particular historical significance. Here are songs of the I.W.W. (the "Wobblies"), Alaska, the Grand Coulee Dam, and out of the more recent folklore of the West. I intended, originally, to have a section dealing with the songs of the Spanish Southwest, but the logic of this book seemed to call for integration of the Spanish songs in the appropriate topical groupings.

The documentary notes to the collection appear in the following manner. A brief historical essay providing background to the period and its social and political framework opens each section. Each song is then discussed in terms of its subject matter and its specific historical and cultural relevance. In some cases, Earl Robinson has added a special musical note of his own in the introduction to a song. These notes appear in italics. Finally, headnotes provide data on the origin and immediate source for the particular version that appears.

Throughout, I have tried to select versions of the songs which seemed to be closest to those sung by the people of those days. Many folk songs which have survived through oral tradition up to our own time were originally popular song creations by professional ballad makers. Wherever possible, I have chosen the original rather than the traditional version. For instance, I was fortunate enough to discover the original sheet music for *The Maid of Monterey,* and it appears in this collection in that version rather than as a folk variant collected decades later.

The songs in this book are of necessity only a small sampling of the music that was sung and played in the days of the opening and settling of the West. To get a truly complete picture, one should be familiar with all of the popular and religious music of the era. I have selected those songs whose subject matter and significance relate directly to the main theme of this collection.

Beyond this, an editor should let the songs tell their own story, which they can do far more eloquently.

I. S.

New York City
October, 1966

PART 1

"Ho! For California!"

I'm goin' out West next fall,
I'm goin' out West next fall,
I'm goin' out West whar times is best,
I'm goin' out West next fall:

THE MIGHTY SURGE of westward migration which swept mid-nineteenth-century America is one of the great dramatic epics of our age. And as befits a momentous stage in man's development, this awesome upheaval has been resoundingly celebrated in song and story.

By the 1830's, America's western frontier had reached as far as Independence, Missouri. Beyond that lay a handful of military outposts and lonely settlements, infinitesimal pinpricks on the great expanse of prairie and desert between Missouri and the mountains. Beyond the snowcapped peaks, a few adventurous Americans had found their way to the Pacific Ocean and the Mexican state of California.

Less than twenty years later, California was a state in the Union with a population energetically booming at a prodigious rate, while settlements were taking root in Kansas, Nebraska, Colorado, the vast Wyoming territories, and the great virgin lands of the Northwest. A war and an accident in the intervening years provided the causes for this phenomenal transformation.

The victorious war with Mexico added more than a million square miles to the national territory of the United States. California's independence was proclaimed with the raising of the Bear Flag at Sonoma on June 15, 1846. Two years later, even before the peace treaty with Mexico had confirmed

the accession of California by the United States, a New Jersey-born mechanic by the name of James W. Marshall accidentally discovered gold on the American River in the low Sacramento Valley.

The news of this discovery and of subsequent explorations which revealed an incredible golden wealth in the California soil swept across the country. Within a few months, the gold in California had become the number-one topic in the land. Gold-rush fever was a contagion that spread on the wings of rumor. Tales of gold strikes which turned paupers into millionaires overnight were on everyone's lips. The American dream, the promise of utopia on earth, was less than 3,000 miles away.

By the end of 1849, the population of California had been swelled by 100,000. From every section of the United States (and from Europe and Asia as well), the gold seekers came. From the great population centers of the eastern seaboard they came, in sailing ships around Cape Horn and up along the Pacific Coast to San Francisco. In primitive ocean steamers they came, sailing for Panama and the trek across the jungle wilderness at the narrowest point of the Isthmus, scrambling for places aboard the sea-worn vessels bound for the Golden Gate. In wagons and on foot they came, heading off from Pike County into a sketchily charted land of burning deserts and summer snows, a vision of shining gold driving them on to surmount incredible obstacles of hunger, thirst, disease, bone weariness, and hostile Indians. And many a man who set out in search of gold never saw the California soil.

The people died on every route, they sickened
    and died like sheep,
And those at sea, before they were dead, were
    launched into the deep;
And those that died while crossing the plains fared
    not so well as that,
For a hole was dug and they thrown in, along the
    miserable Platte.[1]

In the wake of this trek, a vast literature of song grew up, preserving the story in melody and rhyme. From the East came songs of departure and farewell, songs of yearning and utopia, songs reflecting the popular moods and sentiments of

[1] "The Fools of '49," from *Put's Original California Songster*.

back-home neighbors and friends. But most of the songs were products of the new and teeming world in which San Francisco seemed to be the center of the universe. The California songs were, by and large, the products of a small band of stage personalities who entertained in the saloons and music halls of the old Barbary Coast. "Doc" Robinson, Mart Taylor, Sam Wells, the mysterious Johnson, and, above all, that incredible genius of topical verse, "Old Put," these were the song makers who set the tone for the first generation of California popular music. Most of the songs entertained the audiences of their time and passed on to become historical curiosities. A few took hold and survived the passing of their age, drifting into the precious store of memories which man keeps alive by word of mouth from one generation to the next and which we call folk music.

The Race to California

(THE GOOD TIME'S COME AT LAST)

by R. V. Sankey

"A comic song written to a golden measure, and dedicated to the Master of the Mint by one of the Golden Fleece." Published in London, England, by Leoni Lee & Coxhead (n.d., circa 1849).

> Goodbye, my lads, goodbye,
> No one can tell me why
> I am bound to California
> To reap the shining gold.[1]

THE gold fever swept eastward from California. Ships from San Francisco bound for Atlantic ports carried the news in letters back east. From New York, Boston, and Philadelphia, the reports of fabulous gold strikes spread on the wings of fantasy and hope. Trans-Atlantic ships quickly brought the wild rumors and even wilder facts to England, where the news touched off a gold-fever epidemic.

The gold rush spawned songs and tales and wishful dreams of sudden wealth. A folklore of the gold rush became a part of the national idiom. They told the story of the old prospector who died and went to heaven. The place was so crowded that St. Peter told him to wait outside until the crush eased up. With a pioneer's instinct for action, the old prospector let an angel in "on the secret" that a fabulous gold strike had just taken place in hell. Within minutes, heaven was depopulated as angels headed for the nether regions in droves. Wistfully, the old prospector stood at the Pearly Gates and watched the great exodus. Suddenly, with a determined thrust of his jaw, the old miner turned and

started chasing the descending angels. "Hey," yelled St. Peter, "Where are you going? You can come into heaven, now. We've got plenty of room." The prospector waved his hand at Peter and said, "No thanks. I think I'll follow the crowd. There may be some truth in that rumor after all!"

This song was written and sung in England. It is typical of several popular music hall numbers of the day celebrating the discovery of gold in California. Even the school children sang of the great rush for gold in 1849:

> Come young and old,
> Come dig for gold,
> Come small and big,
> Come dig, dig, dig.[2]

For singing with guitar accompaniment, try this song with an eighth-note um-pah in the verses and solid strums on the main beats of the chorus. If too high for your voice, the easiest transposition is down to the key of C.

[1] From "Bound to California," capstan shanty, *A Book of Shanties*, C. Fox Smith.

[2] From "Dig! Dig! Dig!"—"A California two-part song and chorus as performed at Trinity School, New York, on occasion of the Examination, April 27, 1849." (From the original sheet music in the Library of Congress.)

THE RACE TO CALIFORNIA

1. Oh, the good time is come at last, and each suc-ceed-ing day, Sir, In-
ven-tions, cu-ri-os-i-ties, new nov-el-ties dis-play, Sir, But
pow'r of steam and light of gas, and e-lec-tri-ci-ty, Sir, Are
naught to Cal-i-for-nia's wealth, that great and last dis-cov-er-y

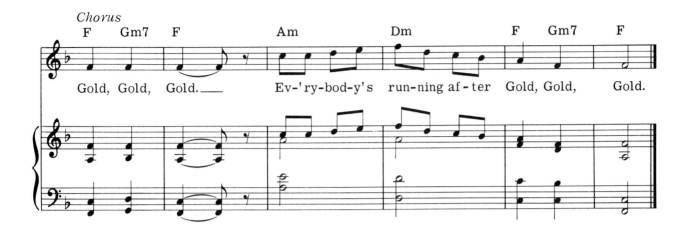

Chorus

F Gm7 F Am Dm F Gm7 F

Gold, Gold, Gold.___ Ev-'ry-bod-y's run-ning af-ter Gold, Gold, Gold.

Oh, the good time is come at last, and each succeeding day, Sir,
Inventions, curiosities, new novelties display, Sir;
But pow'r of steam and light of gas, and electricity, Sir,
Are nought to California's wealth that great and last discovery—

Chorus:

Gold, Gold, Gold.
Ev'rybody's runnng after Gold, Gold, Gold.

Ten thousand ships they're building now to cross the wide Atlantic,
And all are on their way to reach those golden shores romantic;
Butchers, bakers, leave their work, cobblers and "Navvies" too, Sir,
And even lawyers emigrate. Oh dear, what shall we do, Sir?

(Chorus)

The miser looks with wistful eye, the spendthrift hails with glee, Sir,
The golden scheme now set afloat by many a company, Sir.
In breathless haste they all set off and like the Gilpin chase, Sir,
All nations for the ingots rare to California race, Sir.

(Chorus)

Some travel by the aid of steam, some tramp upon their feet, Sir,
And some in ships, some in balloons, their voyages complete, Sir.
But all go with the same intent, the hope of gaining wealth, Sir,
Nor do they stop to eat or drink, regardless of their health, Sir.

(Chorus)

Soldiers desert, no wonder, since the means of getting rich, Sir,
Is open to the poorest man by scraping in a ditch, Sir.
Their officers now make their beds, and cook their meals we hear, Sir,
But soon they must betake themselves to scrape *there* too, we fear, Sir.

(Chorus)

7

'Tis true we have a *Silver Street,* and a *Golden Square,* Sir,
But still we must remember they've golden mountains *there,* Sir,
Now doubtless they will build their towns of gold or such like stuff, Sir,
And as we all are going *there,* they'll soon have "bricks" enough, Sir.

(Chorus)

Oh the glorious time has come at last, deny it who's so bold, Sir,
A pound of baked potatoes new, will bring its weight in gold, Sir,
While blankets, brandy, lucifers, and shoes and boots worn out, Sir,
Will rise, that every soul will wish, a "healing" time, no doubt, Sir.

(Chorus)

Instead of drinking pump water, or even Half-and-Half, Sir,
We all will live like jolly souls and port and sherry quaff, Sir,
In "spirits" we will keep ourselves, the mettle's coming in, Sir,
And not a man will now be found who'll say he wants for tin, Sir.

(Chorus)

Oh the good time has come at last, we need no more complain, Sir,
The rich can live in luxury, and the poor can do the same, Sir.
For the good time has come at last, and as we all are told, Sir,
We shall be rich at once now, with California gold, Sir.

(Chorus)

Ho! For California!

(THE CALIFORNIA GOLD DIGGERS)

WORDS: Jesse Hutchinson, Jr.
MUSIC: Adapted and arranged by Nathan Barker

From the original sheet music published by S. W. Marsh & Co., Boston, Mass., 1849. Additional verses from *The Hutchinson Family Wordbook*.

When the gold fever raged, I was doing very well,
With my friends all around, young and old;
'Twas a long time ago, and I bade them farewell,
And embarked for the land of gold.[1]

AMONG the tens of thousands who joined the great gold rush was a nameless band of fortune hunters from Massachusetts who set out overland in the spring of 1849. Their distinction, as a group, rests in the fact that their send off was attended by the most popular singing group of the day—the Hutchinson Family Singers.

In honor of the occasion, the famous singing family composed a song, borrowing portions of a Dan Emmett melody ("Boatman's Dance") for their refrain. It was a typical Hutchinson Family composition, with a good singing refrain and a rousing antislavery finale. (The Hutchinsons were as notorious for their outspoken abolitionism as they were popular for their rousing musical performances.)

The song spread, serving as an unofficial anthem for many a gold-hunting band. With California-bound ships transporting a huge number of these emigrants (particularly from Eastern seaboard ports), the second verse was added two years later. In time, American sailors whittled down the words, changed and rechanged and spliced the tune with another, added a call and response pattern to the verse, and created one of the great sea chanteys of our literature (see "Sacramento").

[1] "The Miner's Lament—No. 2," from *Johnson's New Comic Songs*.

HO! FOR CALIFORNIA

Bright and strong

1. We've formed our band and we're all well-manned To jour-ney a-far to the prom-ised land, Where the gold-en ore is rich in store, On the banks of the Sac-ra-men-to shore. Then, ho! Boys ho! To Cal-i-for-nia__ go. There's plen-ty of gold in the world we're told On the banks of the Sac-ra-men-to.

Heigh ho! and a-way we go, Dig-ging up the gold on the Fran-cis-co.

We've formed our band, and we're all well manned
To journey afar to the promised land,
Where the golden ore is rich in store,
On the banks of the Sacramento shore.

Chorus:

Then, ho! Boys ho!
To California go.
There's plenty of gold in the world we're told
On the banks of the Sacramento.
Heigh ho! and away we go,
Digging up the gold on the Francisco.
Heigh ho! and away we go,
Digging up the gold on the Francisco.

As off we roam through the dark sea foam,
We'll ne'er forget kind friends at home.
But memory kind shall bring to mind
The love of those we left behind.

(Chorus)

O! don't you cry, nor heave a sigh,
For we'll all come back again by and by;
Don't breathe a fear, nor shed a tear,
But patiently wait for about two year.

(Chorus)

We expect our share of the coarsest fare,
And sometimes sleep in the open air.

10

On the cold damp ground we'll all sleep sound
Except when the wolves come howling 'round.

(Chorus)

As the gold is *thar* most any *whar*,
And they dig it out with an iron bar,
And where 'tis thick, with a spade or pick,
They can take out lumps as big as a brick.

(Chorus)

As we explore that distant shore,
We'll fill our pockets with the shining ore;
And how 'twill sound as the wind goes 'round
Of our picking up gold by the dozen pound.

(Chorus)

O! the land we'll save for the bold and brave
Have determined there never shall breathe a slave
Let foes recoil, for the sons of toil
Shall make California *God's Free Soil.*

Final Chorus:

Then, ho! Boys ho!
To California go.
No slave shall toil on God's Free Soil
On the banks of the Sacramento.
Heigh ho! and away we go,
Chanting our songs of Freedom O.
Heigh ho! and away we go,
Chanting our songs of Freedom O.

11

Sacramento

TRADITIONAL

From a variety of sources, but primarily from *Shanties From the Seven Seas*, Stan Hugill.

> Some say we're bound for Liverpool,
> Some say we're bound for France,
> Heave away, my Johnny, heave away, away!
> I think we're bound for 'Frisco, boys,
> To give the girls a chance,
> And away, my Johnny boy, we're all bound to go! [1]

THE lure of the gold fields created a clamorous demand for passage to California. From New York, Boston, Philadelphia, Baltimore, and all the ports of the Atlantic seaboard, a wave of vessels set sail for the waiting "banks of the Sacramento shore"— and the American clipper ship came into its own. In dry docks all along the coast a mighty surge of ship construction got under way. During 1848, it is estimated that less than half-a-dozen vessels dropped anchor in San Francisco Bay. In 1849, more than 700 ships of every shape and description sailed through the Golden Gate, unloading tens of thousands of adventurous fortune hunters on the California shore. Many a craft sailed west around Cape Horn only to lay abandoned in the San Francisco harbor, as seamen deserted their berths and set out for the gold country with a pick in one hand and a wash-bowl in the other, the dream of sudden wealth gleaming in their eyes.

On vessels flying the Stars and Stripes, and on ships of every nation, the voyage around the rugged Cape with the pot of gold at journey's end found its way into the songs the sailors sang.

The best of these gold rush chanteys was "Sacramento," an exuberant free-singing roarer which the seamen had put together from the Hutchinsons' California song (see above) and Stephen Foster's "Camptown Races," with verses from a score of other chanteys thrown in for good measure. And long after the gold was gone, the song lived on, a

melodic memory of the great days of sail and the fearsome voyage around Cape Horn.

[1] "Heave Away," from *Songs of American Sailormen*, Joanna C. Colcord.

SACRAMENTO

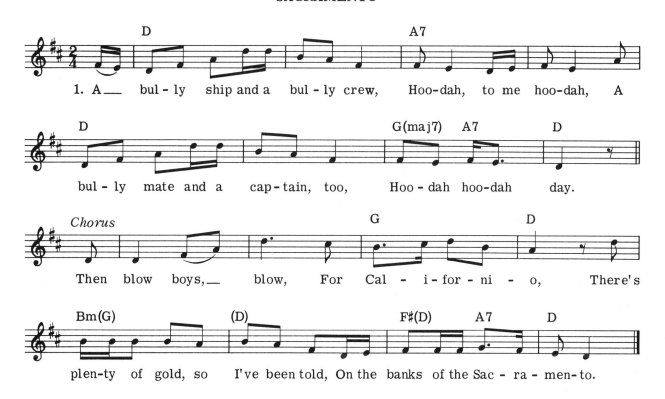

A bully ship and a bully crew,
Hoo-dah, to me hoo-dah,
A bully mate and a captain, too,
Hoo-dah, hoo-dah day.

Chorus:

Then blow, boys, blow,
For Californi-o,
There's plenty of gold
So I've been told
On the banks of the Sacramento.

Round Cape Horn in the months of snows,
Hoo-dah, to me hoo-dah,
If we get there nobody knows,
Hoo-dah, hoo-dah day.

(Chorus)

Oh, around the Horn with a mainsail set,
Around Cape Horn and we're all wringing wet.

Oh, around Cape Horn in the month of May,
Oh, around Cape Horn is a very long way.

To the Sacramento we're bound away,
To the Sacramento's a hell of a way.

Oh, a bully ship with a bully crew,
But the mate is a bastard through and through.

Ninety days to 'Frisco Bay,
Ninety days is damn good pay.

Sing and heave and heave and sing,
Heave and make them handspikes ring.

I wish to God I'd never been born,
To go a-rambling around Cape Horn.

Sweet Betsy from Pike

WORDS: John A. Stone ("Old Put")
MUSIC: "Villikins and His Dinah"

From *Put's Golden Songster.*

When I left old New York to go hunting after gold,
Chunks bigger than my head I could pick up, I was told;
I stopped at Sacramento on a devil of expense,
And they sent me to the mountains where I've not been sober since.[1]

THE California miner of the 1850's had two main amusements for the hours when he was not occupied seeking his fortune with pick and pan: gambling and music. And while the '49er was a gambler at heart (who else would travel 3,000 miles in quest of an elusive "color" in the ground?), his money never lasted long enough to make the tables of chance more than an occasional stopping-off place.

But music was everywhere; in the saloons, in the music halls, in the ramshackle, overcrowded hotels and inns.

"Some of the establishments have small companies of Ethiopian melodists who nightly call upon 'Susanna' and entreat to be carried back to old Virginny. These songs are universally popular, and the crowd of listeners is often so great as to embarrass the player at the monte tables and injure the business of the gamblers. I confess to a strong liking for the Ethiopian airs, and used to spend half an hour every night in listening to them and watching the curious expressions of satisfaction and delight in the faces of the overland emigrants, who always attended in a body."[2]

At first, the songs were those the miners had brought with them; but in time a new kind of song grew up, a product distinctly Californian, singing of miners for miners. A small band of professional minstrels and song writers began to ply their trade on the improvised stages of the Barbary Coast.

The best of these writer–entertainers was a colorful character by the name of John A. Stone, a one-time prospector himself, who had made the overland trip in 1850 and spent some fruitless years in the mines. Assuming the pseudonym of "Old Put," Stone became San Francisco's foremost minstrel composer and the singing voice of the Gold Rush. His songs caught the spirit and flavor and tempo of the miners, who roared at his broad self-satires and topical verses. Between the years 1853 and 1858 he penned more than fifty different miners' songs.

The songs were written for Stone's own traveling minstrel company known as *The Sierra Nevada Rangers,* a singing group that traveled from camp to camp entertaining the miners and earning their pay in gold dust. In 1855, Stone put some two dozen of his songs into a collection which he called *Put's Original California Songster.* Writing about his songs in the third person, Stone says in the preface:

"Many of his songs show some hard edges, and he is free to confess that they may fail to please the more aristocratic portion of the community who have but little sympathy with the details, hopes, trials or joys of the toiling miner's life; but he is confident that the class he addresses will not find them exaggerated, nothing extenuated, nor aught set down 'in malice.'"[3]

[1] "Hunting After Gold," from *Put's Original.*
[2] From "Eldorado: California and Forty-Niners" by Bayard Taylor (1850).

[3] From the Preface to *Put's Original.*

14

The little volume enjoyed a phenomenal sale. In a few years' time, some 15,000 copies had been sold, and new editions were printed with regularity. In 1858, *Put's Golden Songster* appeared with another good-sized batch of original pieces. In this new collection was the song which gave California its first folk heroine: "Sweet Betsy from Pike."

Probably composed around 1856 or 1857, "Sweet Betsy" was a typical Old Put production. Written as a narrative ballad to an old English music hall tune, "Villikins and His Dinah," the song followed a pattern which Stone was to use successfully time and again. Betsy, Ike, and the members of the wagon train were characters with whom the miners could identify. The specific references in the verses were all in the realm of the listeners' experiences—Pike County, the Platte River, crossing the desert. A verse about Brigham Young and Mormon polygamy was always good for a laugh, and a slight venture into the risqué plus an occasional honest-to-damn cuss word all gave the song the Old Put stamp.

Stone died in 1864 and is buried in the little town of Greenwood on the Nevada border. But Sweet Betsy is still alive and kicking, a testament to the vitality of our folk song legacy and to that creative genius of the San Francisco music hall stage, Old Put.

SWEET BETSY FROM PIKE

Oh, don't you remember sweet Betsy from Pike,
Who crossed the big mountains with her lover Ike,
With two yoke of cattle, a large yellow dog,
A tall shanghai rooster and a one-spotted hog.

Chorus:

(Singin') Tooral lal looral lal looral lal la,
Tooral lal looral lal looral lal la.

One evening quite early they camped on the Platte,
'Twas near by the road on a green shady flat,
Where Betsy, sore-footed, lay down to repose,
With wonder Ike gazed on that Pike County rose.

(Chorus)

Their wagons broke down with a terrible crash,
And out on the prairie rolled all kinds of trash;
A few little baby clothes done up with care,
'Twas rather suspicious, though all on the *square*.

(Chorus)

The shanghai ran off and their cattle all died,
That morning the last piece of bacon was fried;
Poor Ike was discouraged and Betsy got mad,
The dog drooped his tail and looked wondrously sad.

(Chorus)

They stopped at Salt Lake to inquire the way,
When Brigham declared that sweet Betsy should stay;
But Betsy got frightened and ran like a deer,
While Brigham stood pawing the ground like a steer.

(Chorus)

They soon reached the desert, where Betsy gave out,
And down in the sand she lay rolling about;
While Ike, half distracted, looked on with surprise,
Saying, "Betsy, get up, you'll get sand in your eyes."

(Chorus)

Sweet Betsy got up in a great deal of pain,
Declared she'd go back to Pike County again;
But Ike gave a sigh, and they fondly embraced,
And they traveled along with his arm 'round her waist.

(Chorus)

They suddenly stopped on a very high hill,
With wonder looked down upon old Placerville;
Ike sighed when he said, and he cast his eyes down,
"Sweet Betsy, my darling, we've got to Hangtown."

(Chorus)

Long Ike and sweet Betsy attended a dance;
Ike wore a pair of his Pike County pants;
Sweet Betsy was covered with ribbons and rings;
Says Ike, "You're an angel, but where are your wings?"

(Chorus)

A miner said, "Betsy, will you dance with me?"
"I will that, old hoss, if you don't make too free;
But don't dance me hard, do you want to know why?
Dog on you; I'm chock full of strong alkali!"

(Chorus)

This Pike County couple got married of course,
But Ike became jealous, obtained a divorce;
Sweet Betsy, well satisfied, said with a great shout,
"Good-by, you big lummox, I'm glad you've backed out!"

(Chorus)

17

Joe Bowers

Author unknown

Lyrics from *Johnson's Comic Songs;* tune from sheet music (circa 1866) for a Confederate song, "I'm A Good Old Rebel," bearing the notation: "To the tune of 'Joe Bowers.'"

I thought when I first started from Pike,
And drove an ox-team o'er the plains,
That when I got here I should make a big strike,
And get some pay for my pains.[1]

OUT of the long trek across the plains and the search for gold in the California hills, folk symbols emerged. "I've seen the elephant," one '49er would say to another, and they would both laugh with the long, sad laughter of the frontier, the laughter of men who have been through hell and forty miles beyond.

The symbol for the miner himself was a man named Joe Bowers. The product of a song writer's imagination, Joe Bowers, like many another pioneer, set out from Pike County, Missouri, in search of his fortune for the girl he left behind.

"There was among the emigrants a considerable number of persons from Pike County, Missouri. Some of these had the sign, 'From Pike County, Mo.' painted on their wagon covers. Others, when asked whence they came, promptly answered, 'From Pike County, Missouri, by gosh, sir!' . . . soon abbreviated to 'Piker.'"[2]

So typical a symbol was he, that many a pioneer believed Joe Bowers to be a real person. One writer claims that Joe was an ox-driver, really had a brother named Ike and a sweetheart named Sally, that he crossed the plains in 1849, and that he was born on Salt River, Pike County, in 1829. But the burden of historical evidence lies the other way, and there seems little question now but that Joe

Bowers is a creature of invention. His song, however, has made him a figure of overwhelming immediacy and a lasting symbol of the great rush for gold.

As Joe Bowers became an American folk legend, so the mystery of his origin deepened. Conceding that Joe Bowers lived only in song, the question became: Who wrote the song? A host of claimants has been advanced for authorship, ranging from a '49er named Frank Smith (Bret Harte's candidate) to Mark Twain. Careful analysis of the available evidence, however, has boiled the leading possibilities for authorship down to two. One is a man named John Woodward, an itinerant member of a San Francisco minstrel troupe known as *Johnson's Pennsylvanians* (first publication of the song is in an 1858 songster called *Johnson's Comic Songs*). The other leading candidate is "Old Put" himself.[3]

The song subsequently passed into folk tradition, although many a singer must have had some old broadside or songster copy of the text to refresh his recollection, since collected versions of the song have remained surprisingly close to the original. During the Civil War it was a favorite among the troops on both sides who sang it with an unrestrained relish, particularly savoring the slightly daring implications of "Sally had a baby, and the baby had red hair."

Echoes of the ballad found their way into many

[1] "The Pike County Miner," from *The Gold Digger's Song Book.*
[2] From *Crossing the Plains (Days of '57)*, a narrative of early emigrant travel to California by the Ox-Team method by William Audley Maxwell.

[3] Louise Pound's full and fascinating account of the various authorship claims appears in *Western Folklore*, Vol. XVI, No. 2 (April, 1957), under the title, "Yet Another Joe Bowers."

other folk songs, a generation of cowboys singing years later:

Come all you reckless and rambling boys
Who have listened to this song,
It hasn't done you any good,
It hasn't done you any wrong;
But when you court a pretty girl,
Just marry her while you can,
For if you go across the plains,
She'll marry another man.[4]

This song was undoubtedly sung with no accompaniment whatsoever and may still be handled that way. If sung at a good clip with guitar, the starred (*) chords may be all you will need. If the key is too high for your voice, try A minor. Even with piano, certain verses should be sung faster with the accompaniment simplified to a single arpeggiated chord every bar or two.

[4] "The Rambling Cowboy," from *Songs of the Cowboys* by N. Howard Thorp.

JOE BOWERS

Not too slow—more lusty than sad

name it is Joe Bow - ers, I've got a broth-er Ike; I

come from old Mis - sou - ri, yes, all the way from Pike; I'll

tell you why I left there and how I came to roam, And

poco rit.

20

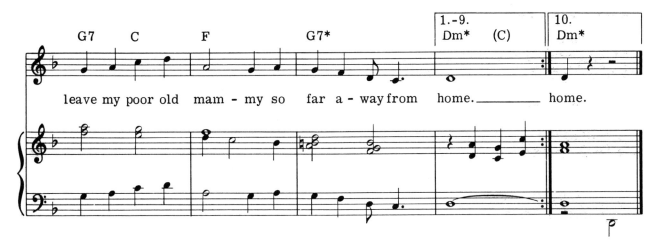

leave my poor old mam - my so far a - way from home._____ home.

My name it is Joe Bowers, I've got a brother Ike;
I come from old Missouri, yes, all the way from Pike;
I'll tell you why I left there and how I came to roam,
And leave my poor old mammy so far away from home.

I used to love a gal there, they called her Sally Black,
I axed her for to marry me, she said it was a whack;
Says she to me, "Joe Bowers, before we hitch for life,
You'd orter have a little home to keep your little wife."

Says I, "My dearest Sally, oh Sally, for your sake,
I'll go to Californy, and try to raise a stake."
Says she to me, "Joe Bowers, oh you're the chap to win.
Give me a buss to seal the bargain," and she threw a dozen in.

I shall ne'er forgit my feelin's when I bid adieu to all;
Sally cotched me round the neck, then I began to bawl;
When I sot in, they all commenced—you ne'er did hear the like,
How they all took on and cried, the day I left old Pike.

When I got to this 'ere country, I hadn't nary (a) red,
I had such wolfish feelin's I wished myself most dead;
But the thoughts of my dear Sally soon made them feelin's git,
And whispered hopes to Bowers—Lord, I wish I had 'em yit!

At length I went to mining, put in my biggest licks,
Come down upon the boulders just like a thousand bricks;
I worked both late and early, in rain and sun and snow,
But I was working for my Sally, so 'twas all the same to Joe.

I made a very lucky strike, as the gold itself did tell,
And saved it for Sally, the gal I loved so well;
I saved it for my Sally, that I might pour it at her feet,
That she might kiss and hug me, and call me something sweet.

But one day I got a letter from my dear, kind brother, Ike,
It came from old Missouri, sent all the way from Pike;
It brought me the gol-darn'dest news as ever you did hear—
My heart is almost bustin' so pray, excuse this tear.

It said my Sal was fickle, that her love for me had fled;
That she'd married with a butcher whose hair was awful red!
It told me more than that—oh! it's enough to make one swear,
It said Sally had a baby, and the baby had red hair!

Now, I've told you all I could tell, about this sad affair,
'Bout Sally marryin' the butcher, and the butcher had red hair.
Whether 'twas a boy or gal child, the letter never said,
It only said its cussed hair was inclined to be red!

Crossing the Plains

Words: John A. Stone ("Old Put")
Music: "Caroline of Edinboro"

Lyrics from *Put's Original California Songster;* music adapted from the singing of Mrs. Dan Bishop (Clay County, Kentucky), 1917, in *English Folk Songs from the Southern Appalachians,* Cecil J. Sharp.

When first I heard the people tell
Of finding gold in veins,
I bade my friends a long farewell,
And started o'er the plains.[1]

THERE were no easy routes to California in 1849. The long voyage around Cape Horn was tedious, time-consuming and expensive. Over the isthmus at Panama was only slightly less expensive, but the tropical journey was filled with unforeseen hardships. Overland across the plains entailed dangers of thirst, sickness, climate, and unfriendly Indians.

The fastest way to the gold fields (and the least expensive) was the overland route—across the Great Plains, through the desert, over the mountains. A good trip could be made in as little as sixty days. But there were no good trips across the plains. Disease and death rode the California trail, and thousands who left Missouri never lived to see Sacramento.

With every mile, the forty-niner encountered a new threat. Cholera, alkali, lack of water, hostile Indians, the much celebrated "diaree," plus all the unforeseen contingencies and the natural antagonisms between human beings made the overland journey a fearsome enterprise.

[1] From "That Is Even So," in *Put's Golden Songster.*

But most of them did get through, and a hundred carefully kept diaries and journals have come down to us through history, awesome first-hand accounts of an epic drama played on an epic stage.

"Passed the camp next to ours. Saw them digging a grave. A man died there last night of measles. Crossed the Big Sandy today. Evening: Crossed the Little Sandy this afternoon. I had an idea that in crossing the prairie, it would be perfectly level, but it is far different, just one hill after another. Not high, but very steep; in the ravines there are many sloughs which are mirey and difficult to cross, particularly just after rain. . . . The road so far as the eye can see is lined with wagons drawn by oxen. They can travel much faster than expected. We came twenty miles today. . . . Saw four graves today, all children. The thought of those crude little graves has haunted me all day." [2]

Hammer-ons, useful throughout this song, are indicated by (H) in the piano part.

[2] From the *Journal of Esther Belle McMillan Hanna,* on the trail to Oregon (1852). (See Allen, *Canvas Caravans.*)

CROSSING THE PLAINS

1. Come all you Cal - i - for - ni-ans, I pray o - pen wide your

ears, If you are go - ing 'cross the plains, with snot - ty mules or

steers; Re - mem - ber beans be - fore you start, like-wise dried beef and

ham, Be - ware of ven-i - son, damn the stuff, it's of - ten-times a

Come all you Californians, I pray ope wide your ears,
If you are going 'cross the Plains, with snotty mules or steers;
Remember beans before you start, likewise dried beef and ham,
Beware of venison, damn the stuff, it's oftentimes a ram.

You must buy two revolvers, a bowie knife and belt,
Says you, "Old feller, now stand off, or I will have your pelt";
The greenhorn looks around about, but not a soul can see,
Says he, "There's not a man in town, but what's afraid of me."

You shouldn't shave, but cultivate your down, and let it grow,
So when you do return, 'Twill be as soft and white as snow;
Your lovely Jane will be surprised, your ma'll begin to cook;
The greenhorn to his mother'll say, "How savage I must look!"

"How do you like it overland?" his mother she will say,
"All right, excepting cooking, then the devil is to pay;
For some won't cook, and others can't, and then it's curse and damn,
The coffeepot's begun to leak, so has the frying pan."

It's always jaw about the teams, and how we ought to do,
All hands get mad, and each one says, "I own as much as you."
One of them says, "I'll buy or sell, I'm damned if I care which,"
Another says, "Let's buy him out, the lousy son of a bitch."

You calculate on sixty days to take you over the Plains,
But there you lack for bread and meat, for coffee and for brains;
Your sixty days are a hundred or more, your grub you've got to divide,
Your steers and mules are alkalied, so foot it—you cannot ride.

You have to stand a watch at night, to keep the Indians off,
About sundown some heads will ache, and some begin to cough;
To be deprived of health we know is always very hard,
Though every night some one is sick, to get rid of standing guard.

Your canteens, they should be well filled, with poison alkali,
So when you get tired of traveling, you can cramp all up and die;
The best thing in the world to keep your bowels loose and free,
Is fight and quarrel among yourselves, and seldom if ever agree.

There's not a log to make a seat, along the river Platte,
So when you eat, you've got to stand, or sit down square and flat;
It's fun to cook with buffalo wood, take some that's newly born,
If I knew once what I know now, I'd a gone around the Horn!

The desert's nearly death on corns, while walking in the sand,
And drive a jackass by the tail, it's damn this overland;
I'd rather ride a raft at sea, and then at once be lost,
Says Bill, "Let's leave this poor old mule, we can't get him across."

The ladies have the hardest time, that emigrate by land,
For when they cook with buffalo wood, they often burn a hand;
And then they jaw their husbands round, get mad and spill the tea,
Wish to the Lord they'd be taken down with a turn of the di-a-ree.

When you arrive at Placerville, or Sacramento City,
You've nothing in the world to eat, no money, what a pity!
Your striped pants are all worn out, which causes people to laugh,
When they see you gaping round the town like a great big brindle calf.

You're lazy, poor, and all broke down, such hardships you endure,
The post office at Sacramento all such men will cure;
You'll find a line from ma and pa, and one from lovely Sal,
If that don't physic you every mail, you never will get well.

Coming Around the Horn

WORDS: John A. Stone ("Old Put")
MUSIC: "Dearest Mae" by Francis Lynch and L. V. H. Crosby

Lyrics from *Put's Original California Songster;* music from *Minstrel Songs Old and New* (1882).

> Such a going round the Horn and catching of a cold,
> And a sitting on the bench with the white folks;
> Such a going to Californy and digging out the gold,
> Where the niggers get as much as the white folks.[1]

In 1849, the trip to San Francisco via the rugged Cape might take as long as 240 days, the Brig *Pauline* sailing from Boston harbor on January 13 and dropping anchor inside the Golden Gate on September third. Two years later, with the great clipper ships dominating the seas, *The Flying Cloud* would sail from New York to San Francisco in the record time of 89 days.

In the first months after the discovery of gold in California, scores of ships set sail for the distant San Francisco docks. The newspapers of the Eastern cities were filled with reports of voyages to the Pacific:

"The schooner-smack *Mary Taylor*, of nearly 90 tons burthen, goes out, excellently well commanded . . . and will be manned by a joint stock company of first rate men, who will not fail of finding gold either by digging, or otherwise, before they come back.
The schooner *Velasco*, another first rate vessel, will sail soon with a joint stock company of the 'right sort' from Groton, who will come home, 'high hook' in the gold line, or we are very much mistaken in the men." [2]

It was the age of the great sailing ship—and also of the blackface minstrel.

Sired by Thomas Dartmouth ("Daddy") Rice, who originated a new theatrical style with his "Jump Jim Crow" in the late 1820's, "Negro" minstrelsy had become the foremost medium for popular song by the time of the Gold Rush. America's most gifted writers and performers—Dan Emmett, Stephen Foster, E. P. Christie, and others—made the burnt-cork makeup of the blackface minstrel the standard theatrical convention of the day.

At its best, "Negro" minstrelsy was ingenious, inventive, and distinctively American—a musical revolt against old world standards and idiom. It was also, of course, demeaning of the Negro, a product of the inbred racist prejudice of the age of slavery. The stereotypes which it fostered and perpetuated have lasted more than a century as an offensive scar on our national culture.

But in the 1840's and 1850's, the "Ethiopian Serenaders," the blackface minstrels of mirth and melody ruled the American musical stage. From New York to California their songs were sung—songs like "Camptown Races," "Boatmen Dance," "Lucy Neal," "Jim Crack Corn," and "Dandy Jim of Caroline." None of these was more popular than a silly little ditty called "Dearest Mae":

> Oh! dearest Mae, you're lubly as de day,
> Your eyes so bright dey shine at night,
> When de moon am gwan away.[3]

In San Francisco, "Old Put" used the minstrel tune for the classic song about the trip around Cape Horn.

---

[1] From "Going Round the Horn," in *Hooley's Opera House Songster* (1863).
[2] The New London *Chronicle*, December 29, 1848 (in *Greyhounds of the Sea,* Cutler).

[3] From *The Christy Minstrel's Songbook,* vol. 1 (circa 1860).

COMING AROUND THE HORN

1. Now min-ers if you'll lis-ten,___ I'll tell you quite a tale, A-

bout the voy-age 'round Cape Horn, they call a pleas-ant sail; We

bought a ship and had her stowed with hous-es tools and grub, But

curse be the day we ev-er sailed in the poor old rot-ten tub.

Chorus

O, I re-mem-ber well the lies they used to tell, Of

gold so bright it hurt the sight And made the min-ers yell.

Now, miners, if you'll listen, I'll tell you quite a tale,
About the voyage 'round Cape Horn, they call a pleasant sail;
We bought a ship and had her stowed with houses, tools and grub,
But cursed the day we ever sailed in the poor old rotten tub.
Chorus:

Oh, I remember well the lies they used to tell,
Of gold so bright it hurt the sight
And made the miners yell.

We left old New York City with the weather very thick,
The second day we puked up boots, oh wasn't we all seasick?
I swallowed pork tied to a string, which made a dreadful shout,
I felt it strike the bottom, but I could not pull it out.
(Chorus)

We all were owners in the ship, and soon began to growl,
Because we hadn't ham and eggs, and now and then a fowl;
We told the captain what to do, as him we had to pay,
The captain swore that he was boss, and we should him obey.
(Chorus)

We lived like hogs, penned up to fat, our vessel was so small,
We had a "duff" but once a month, and twice a day a squall;
A meeting now and then was held, which kicked up quite a stink,
The captain damned us fore and aft, and wished the box would sink.
(Chorus)

Off Cape Horn, where we lay becalmed, kind Providence seemed to frown,
We had to stand up night and day, none of us dared sit down;
For some had half a dozen boils, 'twas awful, sure's you're born,
But some would try it on the sly, and got pricked by the Horn.

(Chorus)

We stopped at Valparaiso, where the women are so loose,
And all got drunk as usual, got shoved in the calaboose;
Our ragged, rotten sails were patched, the ship made ready for sea,
But every man, except the cook, was uptown on a spree.
(Chorus)

We sobered off, set sail again, on short allowance, of course,
With water thick as castor oil, and stinking beef much worse;
We had the scurvy and the itch, and any amount of lice,
The medicine chest went overboard, with bluemass, cards and dice.
(Chorus)

We arrived at San Francisco, and all went to the mines,
We left an agent back to sell our goods of various kinds;
A friend wrote up to let us know our agent, Mr. Gates,
Had sold the ship and cargo, sent the money to the States.

(Chorus)

We'll Give 'Em Jessie

WORDS: Unknown
MUSIC: "Wait for the Wagon" attributed to R. Bishop Buckley

From *The Freemen's Glee Book* (1856).

Old Benton had a daughter,
Fair Jessie was her name,
The Rocky Mountain Ranger
A-courting her he came.[1]

IF there was one man who, in the early days, could be considered the "Voice of the West," that man was John Charles Frémont. One of the most controversial figures to walk across the stage of American history, Frémont's expeditions to the Pacific in the early 1840's won him the nickname, "The Pathfinder." The paths which Frémont charted led the Mormons to Salt Lake, the '49ers to Sacramento, and the pioneers of the northwest to the Oregon Territory. His chief scout and closest companion in his westward adventures was the fabulous Kit Carson.

John C. Frémont was the stepchild of American destiny. Courageous explorer, able soldier, astute politician, he cast a shadow on his times which history has inadequately reflected. Frémont was born in Savannah, Georgia, 1813, the illegitimate son of an adulterous romance between a royalist French émigré and an upper-class Virginia lady of FFV rank. (She was married to a veteran of the American Revolution.)

Frémont grew up to become a brilliant student with a pronounced scientific bent. He enlisted in government service where he performed a variety of tasks. In Washington he met Jessie Benton, eleven years his junior, the daughter of Missouri Senator Thomas Hart Benton, and the toast of the capitol. The young lieutenant won the heart of sixteen-year-old Jessie Benton, and they married in 1841 without the benefit of her parents' consent. It didn't take the stormy Senator long, however, to accept his fiery new son-in-law, and between the two of them, westward expansion took long strides aimed at unifying the continent under American hegemony.

In time, Frémont would become California's first United States Senator, a noted general (who anticipated Lincoln's emancipation policy too early for his own good), and the Republican Party's first Presidential candidate in the election of 1856. This song, celebrating Frémont's role in the opening of the West, is from that election campaign. Jessie, of course, was Frémont's wife, and the title and theme of the song was a play on words, with the phrase "We'll give 'em Jessie" the equivalent of "We'll give 'em the business," as well as the good old-fashioned political device of advancing the distaff side of the candidate's appeal.

Um-pah suggested for verses; then sharp strums following the rhythm of the notes in the chorus.

[1] From "The Campaign of 1856," in *Ballads and Songs Collected by the Missouri Folklore Society* by H. M. Belden.

WE'LL GIVE 'EM JESSIE

Ye friends of Freedom, rally now,
And push the cause along;
We have a glorious candidate,
A platform broad and strong;
"Free Speech, Free Press, Free Soil, Free Men,
Frémont," We have no fears
With such a battle cry, but that
We'll beat the Buchaniers.

Chorus:

We'll give 'em Jessie,
We'll give 'em Jessie,
We'll give 'em Jessie,
When we rally at the polls.

31

Our leader scaled the mighty hills,
'Twixt East and West the bars,
And from the very topmost peak
Flung out the stripes and stars;
Nor cold, nor heat, thirst, hunger, naught
Of horror moved his fears,
With such a captain can we fail
To beat the Buchaniers.

(Chorus)

In after time his dauntless arm
Unlocked the Golden Gate,
His eloquence to Freedom gave
The El Dorado State.
In every word, in every deed,
Such manliness appears,
Frémont's the man to lead us on
To beat the Buchaniers.

(Chorus)

Then rally, rally, every man
Who values Liberty,
Who would not see our fair land given
To blighting Slavery.
Our cause, "Free Speech, Free Press, Free Soil,
Free Men"—So now three cheers
For the people's candidate, Frémont,
Who frights the Buchaniers.

(Chorus)

32

Sioux Indians

TRADITIONAL

Adapted from the singing of Pete Seeger (Folkways Records—*Frontier Ballads*) by Earl Robinson.

> We saw the Indians coming,
> We heard them give their yell;
> My feelings at that moment
> No mortal tongue could tell.[1]

THE bronzed men of the plains watched in fascinated awe as the wagon trains rolled westward. Driven by hunger or fear or dreams of conquest, an occasional Indian tribe would send a war party out against the whites. More often than not, the Indians watched calmly and in resplendent silence as the mighty trek unfolded before their eyes.

Many a white man had boasted back home about the Indians he would slay when he went out West. Some of these self-appointed shotgun heroes sought out their victims on the plains. Perhaps the Sioux of this traditional song were provoked by some incident such as this one, described by a pioneer of 1852:

". . . The next night we camped on the river, and to our left, about 500 yards, was a little grove of ash trees, where, about two weeks before, the Indians had tied a young man about seventeen years of age to one of the trees and skinned him alive. He belonged to a family that came from Illinois and was going to California. The boy had sworn that he would kill the first Indian he saw, and just before they camped for the night he saw an old squaw sitting by the side of the road, and took his gun out of the wagon and shot her dead. They had not been camped more than half an hour when about 200 Sioux warriors came riding up the river toward the camp, and seeing the old squaw lying beside the road, they stopped four or five minutes and then galloped up to the camp. There were eight wagons in the train. As soon as the Indians came up they asked who had killed the squaw, but no one would tell. At last the Indians told them if they did not tell who had shot her, they would massacre the whole train. Then the captain pointed out the boy who had shot the squaw. As soon as he was pointed out the chief ordered two of the warriors to take the boy. The boy ran and jumped into the wagon where his mother and sister were sitting, and calling for his father to save him, crawled under the blankets. The Indians jumped into the wagon and pulled him out by the heels, while his mother and sister cried as if their hearts were breaking. They took him to that little grove and treated him as already described in sight of the whole camp. The wild screams of the boy as they tore the skin from his body was more than his mother could stand and she fainted. . . . It lasted about half an hour, then all was still and his friends went to the spot and cut him loose from the tree and buried him at the end of the little grove." [2]

This song may be sung unaccompanied and very freely, holding on to certain words for special emphasis, extra poignancy, or pure cussedness. The birdseyes (fermate) indicate some of the places where Pete Seeger holds the note.

[1] From "The Texas Cowboy," in *Folksongs of Mississippi* by Arthur Palmer Hudson.

[2] From *The Life and Adventures of E. S. Carter*, 1852.

SIOUX INDIANS

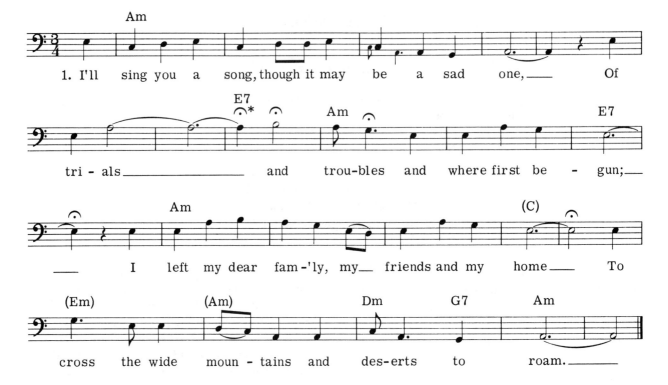

1. I'll sing you a song, though it may be a sad one,___ Of tri - als_____ and trou-bles and where first be - gun;___ I left my dear fam-'ly, my___ friends and my home___ To cross the wide moun - tains and des-erts to roam._____

I'll sing you a song, though it may be a sad one,
Of trials and troubles and where first begun;
I left my dear fam'ly, my friends and my home
To cross the wide mountains and deserts to roam.

I crossed the Missouri and joined a large train,
Which bore us over mountains, through valley and plain;
And often of an evening a-hunting we'd go
To shoot the fleet antelope and wild buffalo.

We heard of Sioux Indians all out on the plains,
A-killing poor drivers and burning their trains,
A-killing poor drivers with arrows and bows;
When captured by Indians no mercy they'd show.

We traveled three weeks till we come to the Platte,
A-pitching our tents at the head of the flat;
We spread down our blankets on the green shady ground
Where the mules and the horses were grazing around.

While taking refreshment, we heard a loud yell,
The whoop of Sioux Indians come up from the dell.
We sprang to our rifles with a flash in each eye,
And says our brave leader, "We'll fight till we die."

They made a bold dash and they come near our train;
The arrows fell around us like showers of rain,
But with our long rifles we fed them hot lead,
Till many a brave warrior around us lay dead.

34

We shot their bold chief at the head of their band,
He died like a warrior with his bow in his hand.
When they saw their brave chief lie dead in his gore,
They whooped and they yelled and we saw them no more.

In our little band there were just twenty-four,
And of the Sioux Indians five hundred or more;
We fought them with courage, we spoke not a word,
The whoop of Sioux Indians was all could be heard.

We hooked up our horses and started our train;
Three more bloody battles this trip on the plain.
And in our last battle three of our brave boys fell,
And we left them to rest in the green shady dell.

A La Ru

(SPANISH CRADLE SONG)

From *Los Pastores*, as performed at Los Griegos, Albuquerque, New Mexico; collected and transcribed by J. D. Robb. From *Hispanic Folk Songs of New Mexico*, J. D. Robb.

¿Quién les da posada
a estos peregrinos
que vienen cansados
de andar los caminos?

Es José y María
su esposa amada,
que a tus puertas viene
a pedir posada.

Who, to these poor pilgrims,
Shelter will be grudging,
As they come exhausted
O'er the highways trudging?

Joseph, I, and Mary,
Come to you tonight,
Begging you for lodging
In our sorry plight.[1]

LONG before the wagons had moved west across the plains, the Spanish had come to the California territory. Searching for gold and exploring the mysteries of the New World, the Spanish *conquistadores* looted the treasures of ancient Indian civilizations. In the wake of the paid soldiers came the mercenaries of God, the Spanish missionaries bringing the light of Christianity to the heathen lands. As early as 1542, the Spanish were in San Diego, and over the course of three centuries the territory of New Spain was carved out in the furthest reaches of the western hemisphere.

Spanish development of Mexico and California was inseparably bound up with the Catholic Church and its missionaries. Among the devices employed by the missionaries for the spreading of the gospel were simple plays and folk operas telling the story of Christ. Perhaps the most famous of these is the nativity play, *Los Pastores*, still performed annually at Christmas time in the Spanish southwest. *Los Pastores* may actually be a New World creation, although its style, its music, and its tradition is based in Spanish heritage.

The lullaby, "A La Ru," is one of the most beautiful songs from *Los Pastores*. It has survived, and even conquered, the centuries of massive change in the West, and still is sung today by Mexican-Americans in Arizona, New Mexico, Colorado and California, a living monument to the continuity of the folk process.

Suggest fast three-beat um-*pah-*pah, *occasionally skipping the first or second* pah *for variety and emphasis, plus bass runs (B.R.) as indicated.*

[1] From "Pedimento de las Posadas" (The Search for Lodgings), from *Los Pastores* as performed at Los Griegos, Albuqerque, New Mexico. From *Hispanic Folk Songs of New Mexico*, J. D. Robb.

A LA RU

Duérmete, Niño lindo,
en los brazos del amor
mientras que duerme y descansa
la pena de mi dolor.

Chorus:

A la ru, a la me,
a la ru, a la me,
a la ru, a la me,
a la ru, a la ru, a la me.

No temas al rey Herodes
que nada te ha de hacer;
en los brazos de tu madre
y ahí nadie te ha de ofender.

(Chorus)

Oh sleep, Thou Holy Baby,
With Thy head against my breast;
Meanwhile the pangs of my sorrow
Are soothed and put to rest.

Chorus:

A la ru, a la me,
A la ru, a la me,
A la ru, a la me,
A la ru, a la ru, a la me.

Thou need'st not fear King Herod,
He will bring no harm to you;
So rest in the arms of Your Mother
Who sings You a la ru.

(Chorus)

Song of Happiness

(NAVAJO INDIAN SONG)

Recorded by Willard Rhodes from the singing of a group of Junior High School Children at Fort Wingate Indian School; *Music of the Sioux and Navajo* (Folkways Records FE4401).

When I die, do not cry
Unless you really loved me;
But if you love me, you will cry,
But if you love me, you will cry,
And you will not remarry soon after I die.[1]

THE first man to claim the western land was the Indian, with a history on the North American continent dating back thousands of years. As with most primitive peoples, music, song and dance played a central role in all aspects of Indian life. In ceremonials connected with worship, hunting, farming, spinning, war, and relaxation, the Indian utilized a song tradition which had developed over the ages to express the full range of emotions and to beseech the gods for favors.

History has no soul, and perhaps the West could only be won and settled at the expense of Indian lands and heritage. Certainly, no government in Washington ever made more than a token effort to provide security for the red man or to seek justice for him. In most cases, the Federal Government became the very instrument for betrayal of treaties,

promises, and sacred pledges made to the Indian by his more "civilized" white brother.

With the advent of the white man, new songs and chants dealing with this cruel and amazing phenomenon found their way into Indian music. The Navajo "Song of Happiness," reproduced here, is an example of one such expression. The song dates from the confinement of the Navajo warriors at Fort Sumner after the capitulation to Kit Carson in 1864. While the braves were kept in the fort, the Indian women gathered outside the walls and sang this song to sustain the morale and the hopes of their loved ones.

This song is best sung unaccompanied. However, if the guitar strings (and the wood) are hit with the hand, producing a percussive, drumlike chord, then the indicated chord symbols may prove useful. I recommend the C-chord be played without third, as follows:

[1] "Farewell Song of a Pawnee Warrior," from *Songs of the Pawnee and Northern Ute* (Archive of American Folksong recording), recorded by Frances Densmore.

The Pacific Railroad

Words and music by George F. Root

From *The Pacific Glee Book* (1869).

The great Pacific railway
For California hail!
Bring on the locomotive,
Lay down the iron rail;
Across the rolling prairies
By steam we're bound to go,
The railroad cars are coming, humming
Through New Mexico.[1]

In the 1860's, from New York to San Francisco via Cape Horn was 19,000 miles and a minimum of three months. Short-cutting through the steaming jungles of Panama reduced the crossing time to four weeks. From Missouri to San Francisco by overland stage took seventeen days, but only a small amount of freight could be transported in that fashion. The fastest trip of all was made by the daring riders of the Pony Express who made the crossing in eight days, carrying two saddlebags of mail.

Meanwhile, the country was being settled. San Francisco, Denver, Salt Lake City, and a hundred mining centers and prairie towns needed food, supplies, clothing, merchandise. The dream of a railroad to span the continent became a national necessity.

In 1863, construction of the first trans-continental railroad began. The Union Pacific Railroad undertook to lay track from Nebraska west; the Central Pacific from California east. Six years later, on May 10, 1869, the two lines joined at Promontory, Utah. The link had been forged.

As the golden spike was driven into the ground, one could almost see in the shadows 1,500 miles of track, the sweat and blood and mangled bodies of thousands of Irish and Chinese laborers, the incredible feats of engineering skill which had surmounted obstacles of sleet and stone, peak and precipice, and hundreds of millions of dollars in profits, land grants, and graft in the bank accounts of a handful of powerful capitalists. But the nation was one—physically, practically, inseparably one— a geographical and political unit with a combined wealth and strength the world had never known before.

In Chicago, George Frederick Root celebrated the event in song. Root, to whose songs the Union had marched to victory in the Civil War ("Battle Cry of Freedom," "Tramp, Tramp, Tramp," "Just Before the Battle, Mother") caught the national mood in a paean of exultation and joy.

[1] From *A San Francisco Songster* (1849-1939) published by the Works Progress Administration; History of Music in San Francisco Series, Vol. 2.

THE PACIFIC RAILROAD

1. Ring out, oh bells! Let can-nons roar In loud-est tones of thun-der. The

i - ron bars, From shore to shore, Are

laid, and na - tions won-der. Thro' des-erts vast and for-ests deep, Thro'

moun-tains grand and hoar-y, A path is o - pen'd for all time, And

we be-hold the glo - ry. Ring out, oh bells! Let can-nons roar, In

loud - est tones of thun-der, The i - ron bars from shore to shore Are

laid, Are laid, are laid, are laid, are laid, are laid, are laid—And—na-tions won-der.

Ring out, oh bells! Let cannons roar
In loudest tones of thunder,
The iron bars, from shore to shore,
Are laid, and nations wonder.
Thro' deserts vast and forests deep,
Thro' mountains grand and hoary,
A path is open'd for all time,
And we behold the glory.

Chorus:

Ring out, oh bells! Let cannons roar
In loudest tones of thunder,
The iron bars from shore to shore
Are laid, are laid, are laid, are laid.
And nations wonder.

(Chorus)

We who but yesterday appeared
As settlers of the border,
Where only savages were reared
'Mid chaos and disorder;
We wake to find ourselves midway
In continental station,
And send our greetings either way
Across the mighty nation.

(Chorus)

We reach out towards the Golden Gate,
And eastward to the oceans;
The tea will come at lightning rate,
And likewise Yankee notions.
From spicy islands of the West,
The breezes now are blowing,
And all the world will do its best
To keep the cars a-going.

(Chorus)

41

PART 2

"On the Plains of Mexico"

I'll take my knapsack on my back,
My rifle on my shoulder.
I'm going away to the Mexican War,
I'm going to be a soldier.[1]

[1] From "Going To The Mexican War," in *Folksongs of Mississippi* by Arthur Palmer Hudson.

THE WAR between the United States and Mexico (1846–1848) was this country's most highly profitable military conflict. By the terms of the peace treaty signed at Guadalupe Hidalgo early in 1848, Mexico ceded to the United States an area comprising the present states of California, Nevada and Utah, most of Arizona and New Mexico, and parts of Wyoming and Colorado. The war also confirmed the annexation of Texas, comprising a total addition to the U. S. national domain of 1,193,061 square miles.

It was a war forged in that self-serving ideological maelstrom known to history as "manifest destiny," that theory of national aggrandizement which enlists God and/or fate on the side of the American dollar. It was a war which helped to shape the image and set the pattern for America's role in the Western Hemisphere for a hundred years—and more.

In actual fact, there were *two* Mexican Wars. The first was the War for Texas Independence (1836), highlighted by the massacre at the Alamo and the overwhelming defeat administered to Santa Anna at the Battle of San Jacinto. The second war (1846) was triggered by America's annexation of Texas and was deliberately engineered by a group of influential political leaders (including President Polk) who had decided that the logical western border of the United States lay along the Pacific Ocean from San Diego to the northern portion of the Oregon Territory. These leaders were highly successful in developing public enthusiasm for the conflict which resulted in an overwhelming outburst of national jingoism. On the wings of a patriotic martial spirit thus unleashed, American military forces won a smashing triumph and made possible the westward movement which followed.

The songs of the Mexican War reflected the mood of the times. Outrageously nationalistic, the songs made no secret of American war aims:

> Dey're kicking up gunpowderation,
> About de Texas annexation.
> Since Mexico makes sich ado,
> We'll flog her and annex her too.[2]

If the American war aim was a sizable grab of Mexican land, the American soldier in Mexico also had an immediate aim of primary accumulation which he expressed in verse:

> The Mexicans are doomed to fall,
> God has in wrath forsook 'em,
> And all their goods and chattels call
> On us to go and hook 'em.
>
> We're the boys for Mexico,
> Sing Yankee Doodle Dandy,
> Gold and silver images,
> Plentiful and handy.[3]

---

[2] From "Uncle Sam and Mexico," in *Rough and Ready Songster* (circa 1848).
[3] From "We're the Boys for Mexico," in *Rough and Ready Songster* (circa 1848).

In the spirit of the age, the United States also had ambitions for territorial expansion to the Northwest. In the early months of the conflict with Mexico, the issue of the Oregon border ("54°40′ or fight") was usually joined with the war in the Southwest:

> Hark! Freedom's eagle loudly calls,
> His cry rings through our hills and halls,
> He calls to arms each freedom's son,
> For Texas and for Oregon.[4]

While politicians and penny-songster poets proclaimed their ardor for war, a handful of Americans kept the national conscience alive. A young Congressman from Illinois by the name of Abraham Lincoln declared in the House of Representatives, "I will not bathe my hands in the blood of

[4] From *National Songs, Ballads & Other Patriotic Poetry chiefly relating to the War of 1846* by William M'Carty.

the people of Mexico." Ralph Waldo Emerson, John Greenleaf Whittier, James Russell Lowell and Henry Wadsworth Longfellow all spoke out against the conflict, while the Abolitionist Hutchinson family put their protest into song.

But it remained for that great New England philosopher, Henry David Thoreau, to create a genuine piece of folklore out of his opposition to the war. Refusing to pay his taxes as a protest against the war, Thoreau was arrested and put in jail. Emerson came to visit him in prison, so the story goes, and on seeing his old friend behind bars, exclaimed: "Henry, what are *you* doing *in there?*" To which Thoreau replied: "Ralph! What are *you* doing *out there?*"

But the spirit and tempo of the times was war and national expansion. And the songs of the age were brewed in the same caldron over the same flames.

Battle of Buena Vista.

Remember the Alamo!

WORDS: T. A. Durriage
MUSIC: "Bruce's Address"

Text from *The Rough and Ready Songster,* compiled "by an American Officer"
(circa 1848); music from *The Boston Melodeon* (1852).

For Texas now is free,
Young Texas now is free,
And when I shine among the stars
How happy I shall be.[1]

IN the year 1821, a man by the name of Moses Austin secured a charter from the government of New Spain (soon to become Mexico) for the settlement of American colonists in Texas. Shortly thereafter, some 200 American families began the process of colonization and Texas was officially proclaimed a state in the Mexican Republic.

Fifteen years later, Americans wrenched Texas away from Mexico in a violent outburst of anger, defying a government which had become increasingly despotic and arbitrary in the treatment of its populace, and of its English-speaking citizenry in particular.

A series of armed clashes between Texans of American background and the Mexican authorities had erupted in 1835. Various local conventions proclaimed their independence of the central government and asserted the right of Texas to secede. In response to these rebellious acts, Mexican President Santa Anna organized an army of several thousand men late in 1835 to march on the Texans and restore the authority of his regime.

On February 23, 1836, Santa Anna's army reached the city of San Antonio. Charged with the mission of delaying Santa Anna's advance in order to give Sam Houston time to build up a revolutionary army, the Texas garrison there decided to make a stand against the Mexicans. Under the command of Lt. Col. William Travis, the Texans moved into an old Spanish mission known as "The Alamo," so-called for the cottonwood (in Spanish,

"alamo") trees which grew along the banks of a ditch outside the east wall.

An assaulting Mexican force of more than 3,000 troops lay siege to the 187 Texans who had converted the Alamo into a fortress. It took the attacking soldiers almost two weeks to breach the walls of the mission, and when the final successful offensive was launched, the Mexicans had orders to kill every man in the fort. On March 6, 1836, the Alamo fell and its defenders (among them a pair of the frontier's greatest legendary heroes, Davy Crockett and Jim Bowie) were killed.

Meanwhile, Texas had been proclaimed a republic. Six weeks later, as Sam Houston addressed his troops before the fateful battle of San Jacinto, he spoke the words which have become a part of the folklore of our history:

"The army will cross and we will meet the enemy. Some of us may be killed, must be killed; but, soldiers, remember the Alamo! The Alamo! The Alamo!" [2]

And from the 783 men who comprised the entire Texan army came an echo which has resounded through history:

Remember the Alamo!

A few minutes later, the Texans went into battle, completely routed Santa Anna's forces in a foray of vengeful bloodshed, and redeemed the pledge of the Alamo with the Lone Star of the Texan flag.

[1] From "Song of Texas," in *Rough and Ready Songster* (circa 1848).

[2] Quoted in Wellman, *Glory, God and Gold.*

REMEMBER THE ALAMO!

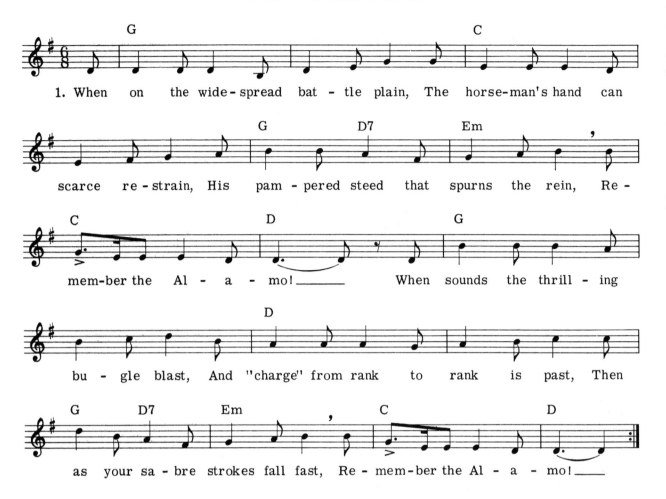

1. When on the wide-spread bat - tle plain, The horse-man's hand can scarce re-strain, His pam-pered steed that spurns the rein, Re-mem-ber the Al - a - mo! ___ When sounds the thrill - ing bu - gle blast, And "charge" from rank to rank is past, Then as your sa - bre strokes fall fast, Re - mem-ber the Al - a - mo! ___

When on the wide-spread battle plain,
The horseman's hand can scarce restrain,
His pampered steed that spurns the rein,
　Remember the Alamo!

When sounds the thrilling bugle blast,
And "charge" from rank to rank is past,
Then as your sabre-strokes fall fast,
　Remember the Alamo!

Heed not the Spanish battle yell,
Let every stroke we give them *tell,*
And let them fall as Crockett fell,
　Remember the Alamo!

For every wound and every thrust,
On prisoners dealt by hands accurst,
A Mexican shall bite the dust,
　Remember the Alamo!

The cannon's peal shall ring their knell,
Each volley sound a passing bell,
Each cheer, Columbia's vengeance tell,
　Remember the Alamo!

For if, disdaining flight, they stand,
And try the issue hand to hand,
Woe to each Mexican brigand!
　Remember the Alamo!

Then boot and saddle! draw the sword;
Unfurl your banner bright and broad,
And as ye smite the murderous horde,
　Remember the Alamo!

Play two chords each bar on the accented words (at the beginning and the middle of each measure).

Green Grow the Lilacs

Traditional, from the singing of Tony Kraber

O, boys, we're goin' for to fight,
Yo-ho, yo-ho!
We'll take the greasers now in hand
And drive 'em in the Rio Grande,
Way down in Mexico.[1]

For a fighting man to kill, he must personalize and despise his enemy. On the human level, where the blood drenched the Texas soil, the war against Mexico was a war between "greasers" and "gringos."

The term "greaser" was supposedly first applied by the Spaniards to American and English traders in California who bought hides and tallow. The traders soon transferred the sobriquet to the Spaniards who sold these products and the "Norte Americanos" used it as a derogatory appellative for all Spaniards, and particularly Mexicans.[2]

The word "gringo" has a more romantic story attached to it. The favorite song among Irish-American troops serving in the Mexican campaign, so the story goes, was an old lilting melody called "Green Grow the Laurels." It was such a favorite, and sung so often, that Mexican troops, hearing the constant repetition of the words "Green Grow" began to call all Americans "Gringos." It's a good story, and many a folklorist has delighted in perpetuating it through the retelling. Unfortunately, there doesn't seem to be a word of truth in it. As several excellent authorities have amply demonstrated, *gringo* is a derivation from the Spanish *griego*, or Greek, and was used for a considerable length of time as a word meaning *foreigner* or *alien*. In the context and wake of Mexican-American relations from 1846 on, *gringo* has come to signify a "North American," specifically a citizen of the United States, and is not intended as a compliment.

But if the story concerning "gringo" and "Green Grow the Laurels" is not good history, it is certainly good folklore, and is by now a part of the heritage of the Mexican War.

It is also a good song, and has quite a history of its own, dating back at least to the wars of the Scottish restoration when loyal followers of Prince Charlie sang:

"We'll change the green laurel to the bonnet so blue."

In various Irish versions, the refrain concerned the "orange and blue," with the present "red, white and blue"—an American variation. Somewhere along the line an Oklahoma poet by the name of Lynn Riggs changed the flower from laurels to lilacs and wrote a play using the song's title. Years later, this play was adapted into a classic work of the American musical stage, *Oklahoma!*, the songs of which, in turn, are becoming a part of the American song heritage.

If you play guitar and the chord F7 is too difficult, try this song in D and use a capo.

[1] From "Way Down in Mexico," in *Cowboy Songs* by John A. and Alan Lomax.
[2] Bancroft, Hubert Howe, *California Pastoral.*

GREEN GROW THE LILACS

Chorus

Green grow the li - lacs, all
spark-ling with dew, I'm lone - ly, my dar - ling, since part-ing with
you._____ But by our next meet-ing I'll hope to prove
true, And change the green li - lacs to the Red, White and Blue._____

Chorus:

Green grow the lilacs, all sparkling with dew,
I'm lonely, my darling, since parting with you.
But by our next meeting I'll hope to prove true,
And change the green lilacs to the Red, White and Blue.

I once had a sweetheart, but now I have none,
Since she's gone and left me, I care not for one.
Since she's gone and left me, contented I'll be,
For she loves another one better than me.

(Chorus)

I passed my love's window, both early and late,
The look that she gave me, it made my heart ache.
Oh, the look that she gave me was painful to see,
For she loves another one better than me.

(Chorus)

I wrote my love letters in rosy red lines,
She sent me an answer all twisted and twined,
Saying, "Keep your love letters and I will keep mine,
Just you write to your love and I'll write to mine."

(Chorus)

Santy Anno

Traditional, from the singing of J. M. Hunt ("Sailor Dad"), of Marion, Virginia (1935). Collected, adapted, and arranged by John A. and Alan Lomax, copyright 1957, Ludlow Music Inc., used by permission. (From *Our Singing Country*, John A. and Alan Lomax.)

Oh, Santiana's dead and gone,
Away, Santiana!
And all the fighting has been done,
All across the plains of Mexico.[1]

Of all the folk heroes to emerge from the Mexican War, the least likely and the longest-lived was the Mexican general himself, Antonio López de Santa Anna. Mexico's strongest political leader in the early years of the republic, Santa Anna was a peculiar mixture of political and military talent and ineptitude. No better and no worse than a hundred other petty rulers of his time, Santa Anna had the misfortune to be on the stage of history in the wrong place at the wrong time. Three centuries of despotic Spanish rule had not prepared Mexico for the responsibilities of independence, and she had no leaders who were capable of defending her immense territory. Mexico in the 1830's and 1840's was up for grabs, and an expansionist America was not slow to sense its moment of destiny.

At San Jacinto, Monterey, Buena Vista, Cerro Gordo, Chapultepec, Mexico City, Santa Anna was always the defeated commander of Mexican forces who outnumbered their American opponents. Few men in history have had the misfortune to be directly responsible for such a swift series of military reverses.

In the years following the Mexican War, verses concerning the Mexican commandant began to make their way into the chanteys which American and British sailors sang aboard their ships. And with an inexplicable perversity, these shipboard songs turned history on its head, made Santa Anna the victor and Zachary Taylor the loser "on the plains of Mexico."

Oh, Santa Anna gained the day,
Heave away, Santy Anna,
He gained the day at Monterey,
All on the plains of Mexico.

Zachary Taylor ran away,
Heave away, Santy Anna,
He ran away at Monterey,
All on the plains of Mexico.[2]

Perhaps it was the British seaman who first mocked history and his constant rival, the American sailing man, with this taunt. The few versions in which history has been righted (including the one appearing here) come from Amercian sources. But many an American seaman also sang of Santy Anna who

. . . gained the day,
All on the plains of Mexico.

[1] From "Santianna," in *Shanties from the Seven Seas*, Stan Hugill.

[2] *Ibid.*

SANTY ANNO

1. We're

sail-ing down the riv-er from Liv-er-pool, Heave a-way, San-ty An-no;___ A-

round Cape Horn to Fris-co Bay, All___ on the plains of Mex-i-co._____

Chorus

So heave her up and a-way we'll go, Heave a-way,___ San-ty An-no;___

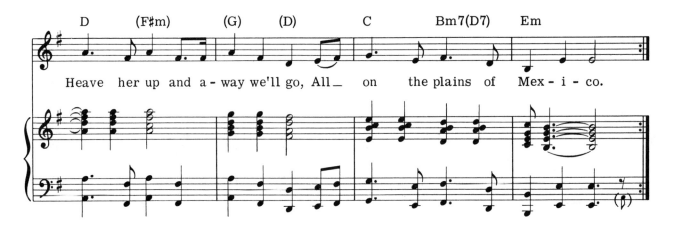

Heave her up and a-way we'll go, All_ on the plains of Mex - i - co.

We're sailing down the river from Liverpool,
Heave away, Santy Anno,
Around Cape Horn to Frisco Bay,
All on the plains of Mexico.

Chorus:

So heave her up and away we'll go,
Heave away, Santy Anno;
Heave her up and away we'll go,
All on the plains of Mexico.

She's a fast clipper ship and a bully good crew,
Heave away, Santy Anno,
A down-East Yankee for her captain, too,
All on the plains of Mexico.

(Chorus)

There's plenty of gold so I've been told,
Heave away, Santy Anno,
There's plenty of gold so I've been told
Way out West to Californi-o.

(Chorus)

Back in the days of Forty-nine,
Heave away, Santy Anno,
Those are the days of the good old times,
All on the plains of Mexico.

(Chorus)

When Zachary Taylor gained the day,
Heave away, Santy Anno,
He made poor Santy run away,
All on the plains of Mexico.

(Chorus)

General Scott and Taylor, too,
Heave away, Santy Anno,
Made poor Santy meet his Waterloo,
All on the plains of Mexico.

(Chorus)

When I leave the ship, I will settle down,
Heave away, Santy Anno,
And marry a girl named Sally Brown,
All on the plains of Mexico.

(Chorus)

Santy Anno was a good old man,
Heave away, Santy Anno,
Till he got into war with your Uncle Sam,
All on the plains of Mexico.

(Chorus)

The Maid of Monterey

Words and music by John Hill Hewitt

From the original sheet music published by F. D. Benteen, Baltimore, Maryland (1851). See also Dobie, *Follow de Drinkin' Gou'd.*

A bugle horn is chanting now a chorus far and free,
And everything rejoices for the glorious victory.
The American flag is waving high, the troops have gained the day,
And everything rejoices on the field of Monterey.[1]

A DECISIVE battle in the Mexican–American War was General Zachary Taylor's capture of the strategic Mexican city of Monterey. Judged by the standards and statistics of the mighty holocaust which would redden the continent a few years later, the Battle of Monterey was a relatively minor skirmish. American casualties numbered close to 500, including 120 killed in action. Mexican killed and wounded numbered 367.

The relatively high casualty list at Monterey inspired a number of songs which emphasized the tragedy of the battle. "The Field of Monterey," quoted above, mourns "the loved and lost now sleeping on the field of Monterey," while "The Storming of Monterey" recalls

> The living, wounded, and the dead,
> The beasts and birds of prey;

Great God! That was a night of dread
That night of Monterey.[2]

In the years immediately following the war, a song literature concerning the conflict was created. The music was, by and large, of a piece with the popular patriotic and/or sentimental music of the day. One of the most popular of these was John Hill Hewitt's "The Maid of Monterey," composed in 1851. In time, the song drifted into Texas folk heritage and has been kept alive solely by oral tradition, in a form substantially unchanged from the original. "Mustang Gray," a song which follows later in this section, was probably derived from "The Maid of Monterey."

I suggest a slow um-pah *accompaniment here with one* um-pah *per bar. In the last three bars but one, guitar chord diagrams are indicated simply.*

[1] "The Field of Monterey," from *Ozark Folksongs*, Vol. 4, by Vance Randolph.

[2] "The Storming of Monterey," from *Rough and Ready Songster*, (circa 1848).

THE MAID OF MONTEREY

1. The moon was shin-ing bright-ly Up - on the bat-tle plain; The

gen - tle breeze fanned light-ly the fea-tures of the slain. The guns had hushed their

thun - der, The drum in si-lence lay; When came the Se - ño - ri - ta, The

Maid of Mon-te - rey. The guns had hushed their thun-der, The drum in si-lence

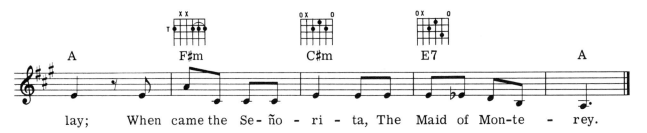

lay; When came the Se - ño - ri - ta, The Maid of Mon-te - rey.

The moon was shining brightly
Upon the battle plain;
The gentle breeze fanned lightly
The features of the slain.

The guns had hushed their thunder,
The drum in silence lay;
When came the *señorita,*
The Maid of Monterey. } Repeat

She cast a look of anguish
On dying and on dead;
Her lap she made the pillow
Of those who groaned and bled.

And when the dying soldier
For one bright gleam did pray,
He blessed the *señorita,*
The Maid of Monterey. } Repeat

She gave the thirsty water,
And dressed the bleeding wound;
And gentle prayers she uttered,
For those who sighed around.

And when the bugle sounded,
Just at the break of day,
We blessed the *señorita,*
The Maid of Monterey. } Repeat

For, though she loved her nation,
And prayed that it might live;
Yet for the dying foemen
She had a tear to give.

Then, here's to that bright beauty,
Who drove death's pang away,
The meek-eyed *señorita,*
The Maid of Monterey, } Repeat

Buena Vista

Author and composer unknown

From *Songs for the People*, Albert G. Emerick (1852).

> Then strike by noble Taylor's side,
> Till freedom's stars, in triumph wide,
> Shall float from the Pacific's tide,
> Unto the Rio Grande.[1]

THE Battle of Buena Vista was the last of General Zachary Taylor's great military triumphs in the Mexican War. The victory brought the war in northern Mexico to a close, leaving to General Winfield Scott the distinction of winning the decisive military engagements at Vera Cruz and Mexico City.

The battle at Buena Vista (in Spanish, "beautiful view") had all the elements of melodrama. Once again, American troops were vastly outnumbered by their foe. General Taylor, "Old Rough and Ready," had defied the orders of his military superiors, abandoning the strategy of a defensive war in his area. Not a particularly able general, Zachary Taylor was a model of courage under fire and an inspiration to his outmanned forces. Despite his military shortcomings, Taylor had sense enough to make the decisive move of the conflict, a strategic retreat to a particularly strong defensive position where the battle took place—about the only

position in the area where the American forces had a chance against the enemy.

Adding to the melodrama of the scene was Santa Anna's demand for "unconditional surrender" and Taylor's immediate refusal. Despite repeated assaults, the Mexicans could not dislodge the Americans from their entrenched positions. In the deadly hail of fire which rained on the Buena Vista plains, many an American officer gained the military experience which he would bring to the Civil War. Finally, the Mexican troops retreated, their casualties numbering some 1,500 as against an estimated United States loss of half that number.

On the wings of this victory, Zachary Taylor became a national hero. In a typical outburst of patriotic sentiment (since repeated in our history), highlighted by a flurry of popular songs of the day, Taylor was swept into the Presidency in 1848.

> Then hail to Zach, the first of men,
> With sword or word, or with the pen,
> To the people ever true and steady,
> We'll find him still "Old Rough and Ready." [2]

[1] "Strike for Our Rights, Avenge Your Wrongs," from *Rough and Ready Songster*.

[2] "Hurrah for 'Rough and Ready,'" *ibid.*

BUENA VISTA

1. Near Bue-na Vi-sta's moun-tain chain, Hur-rah! Hur-rah! Hur-rah! Brave

Tay-lor met his foes a-gain, Hur-rah! Hur-rah!_ Hur - rah! Though

thou-sands to our tens ap-pear, Our boys have hearts that know no fear, Hur-

rah! Hur-rah! Hur - rah! Hur-rah! Hur - rah! Hur-rah! Hur - rah! Hur-

Chorus

rah! Hur-rah! Hur - rah! Hur - rah! Hur - rah! Hur-rah! Hur - rah!

Near Buena Vista's mountain chain,
Hurrah! Hurrah! Hurrah!
Brave Taylor met his foes again,
Hurrah! Hurrah! Hurrah!
Though thousands to our tens appear,
Our boys have hearts that know no fear,
Hurrah! Hurrah! Hurrah! Hurrah!
Hurrah! Hurrah! Hurrah!

Chorus:

Hurrah! Hurrah! Hurrah! Hurrah!
Hurrah! Hurrah! Hurrah!

That day heard Santa Anna boast,
Hurrah! Hurrah! Hurrah!
Ere night he'd vanquish all our host!
Hurrah! Hurrah! Hurrah!
But then the braggart did not know
That Taylor never yields to foe!
Hurrah!, etc.

58

Kentucky, by brave Marshall led,
Hurrah! Hurrah! Hurrah!
Seeks vengeance for her gallant dead;
Hurrah! Hurrah! Hurrah!
And while for Vaughan, McKee and Clay
The teardrop flows, they win the day!
Hurrah!, etc.

There's Hardin brings up Illinois,
Hurrah! Hurrah! Hurrah!
With Bissell's line of gallant boys!
Hurrah! Hurrah! Hurrah!
And Indiana, led by Lane,
All bravely struggle on the plain!
Hurrah!, etc.

O'Brien, Sherman, Washington!
Hurrah! Hurrah! Hurrah!
Their batteries pour the foes upon;
Hurrah! Hurrah! Hurrah!
While Captain Bragg, at "Zach's" command,
"More grape" bestows on every hand,
Hurrah!, etc.

Young Arkansas, whose gallant yell,
Hurrah! Hurrah! Hurrah!
Amidst the din of battle fell,
Hurrah! Hurrah! Hurrah!
Still claims brave Pike her sons to lead,
Soon to revenge the bloody deed!
Hurrah!, etc.

No page in history e'er can show,
Hurrah! Hurrah! Hurrah!
So bright a victory o'er a foe,
Hurrah! Hurrah! Hurrah!
As we this day did proudly gain
On Buena Vista's bloody plain!
Hurrah!, etc.

Mustang Gray

Authorship ascribed to James T. Lytle
Music transcribed from the singing of James Hatch

From "Mustang Gray: Fact, Tradition and Song," by J. Frank Dobie, in *Tone The Bell Easy*, Number 10 in Publications of the Texas Folklore Society. Reprinted by permission of the Texas Folklore Society.

Then mount and away, give the fleet steed the rein,
The Ranger's at home on the prairies again;
Spur, spur in the chase, dash on to the fight.
Cry vengeance for Texas and God speed the right! [1]

THERE were no fiercer fighters in Zachary Taylor's army than the band of Texas volunteer cavalrymen who called themselves the Texas Rangers. And of all the Texas Rangers who fought at Monterey and Vera Cruz, none was fiercer, braver or more bloodthirsty than the man called "Mustang Gray."

Born Maberry B. Gray in South Carolina, he came to Texas in 1835 at the age of twenty-one. Within the year he had fought in the battle of San Jacinto. After Texas independence had been won, Gray became notorious as a cattle raider preying upon the Mexican civilian population along the Rio Grande. Undoubtedly influenced by the ethos of the slave system, Mustang Gray soon became known throughout Texas for unprovoked violence directed against all Mexicans. A folklore concerning the atrocities he committed has become a part of the Texas legend.

Gray served as a lieutenant in the Texas Mounted Volunteers, called "Rangers," during the Mexican War, eventually commanding a company of his own known as the "Mustang Grays." The company soon took on the character of its leader.

"Some of the so-called Texas Rangers . . . were mostly made up of adventurers and vagabonds.

. . . The gang of miscreants under the leadership of *Mustang Gray* were of this description. This party, in cold blood, murdered almost the entire male population of the rancho of Guadalupe, where not a single weapon, offensive or defensive, could be found! Their only object was plunder!" [2]

Mustang Gray died a few years after the Mexican War, presumably of cholera or yellow fever. His end, appropriately enough, came in a small Mexican town, and, according to legend and ballad, his body was carried across the Rio Grande and interred in American soil.

Frank Dobie believes that the ballad of "Mustang Gray" was composed by James T. Lytle, a Texas Ranger during the Mexican War, and the author of the popular "Song of the Texas Ranger," quoted above.

The ballad itself seems to have been strongly influenced by "The Maid of Monterey," and the story it tells can undoubtedly be better ascribed to folklore than to history. But fact or fiction, the song lives—preserving in melody "a noble ranger . . . the bravest of the brave." Thus does folklore select from history only that which preserves an image preconceived.

[1] "Song of the Texas Ranger," from *Sound Off!* by Edwin Dolph.

[2] From *Chile Con Carne* by S. Compton Smith (1857) quoted in "Mustang Gray: Fact, Tradition and Song" by J. Frank Dobie, from *Tone The Bell Easy.*

MUSTANG GRAY

Slow, sad, drunken, brave, maudlin, lonesome, loud—take your choice. A slow two count bar; guitar chords on 1st and 3rd beats.

There was a brave old Tex-an,___ They called him Mus-tang Gray;___ He left his home when but a youth, Went rang-ing far a-way.

Chorus

But he'll go no more a-rang-ing, The sav-age to af-fright;___ He's heard his last war whoop,_ And fought his last fight.___

There was a brave old Texan,
They called him Mustang Gray;
He left his home when but a youth,
Went ranging far away.

Chorus:

But he'll go no more a-ranging,
The savage to affright;
He has heard his last war whoop,
And fought his last fight.

He ne'er would sleep within a tent,
No comforts would he know;
But like a brave old Tex-i-can,
A-ranging he would go.

When Texas was invaded
By a mighty tyrant foe,
He mounted his noble warhorse
And a-ranging he did go.

(Chorus)

Once he was taken prisoner,
Bound in chains upon the way;
He wore the yoke of bondage
Through the streets of Monterey.

A *señorita* loved him
And followed by his side;
She opened the gates and gave to him
Her father's steed to ride.

(Chorus)

God bless the *señorita*,
The belle of Monterey;
She opened wide the prison door
And let him ride away.

And when this veteran's life was spent,
It was his last command,
To bury him on Texas soil
On the banks of the Rio Grande.

(Chorus)

And there the lonely traveler,
When passing by his grave,
Will shed a farewell tear
O'er the bravest of the brave.

Now he'll go no more a-ranging,
The savage to affright;
He's heard his last war whoop
And fought his last fight.

61

Clarín de Campaña

(THE TRUMPETS OF BATTLE)

English text: Arthur Kevess

Collected during the War of the American Intervention, 1847. Present text communicated by Angel Salas, the music collected and transcribed by Graciela Amador. Learned from Jenny Wells Vincent. English text © 1966 by Arthur Kevess.

Madre mía Guadaluparam
échame tu benedición,
yo ya me voy a la guerra,
ya viene la Intervención!

Little Mother of Guadalupe,
Give me your blessing,
I'm going to the wars,
Here comes the Intervention.[1]

THE history books are written in the national image. American accounts of the war with Mexico refer to the "Mexican–American War," a calm, dispassionate mask for the naked aggression which characterized United States foreign policy of the era. In Mexico, the historians call it "La Guerra de la Intervención Americana, 1847" (The War of the American Intervention, 1847).

This one is a real soldier song. The songs of "honor," "empire," and "freedom" are written by the professional songwriters at home. Real soldier songs concern love or wine or death—and this Mexican song has all three.

[1] "El Corrido Mexicano," from *Canciones Mexicanas,* Mendoza.

62

CLARÍN DE CAMPAÑA

Mientras tengan licor las botellas,
hagamos con ellas más dulce el vivir, *(repeat)*
recordando que tal vez mañana
clarín de campaña nos llame a morir. *(repeat)*

Mientras tengan perfume las flores,
olviden dolores y vengan a amar, *(repeat)*
recordando que tal vez mañana
clarín de campaña nos llame a pelear. *(repeat)*

Mira Muerte, no seas inhumana
no vengas mañana, déjame vivir; *(repeat)*
recordando que tal vez mañana
clarín de campaña nos llame a pelear. *(repeat)*

Vengan, vengan, muchachas hermosas,
venid presurosas, que vengan a amar; *(repeat)*
recordando que tal vez mañana
clarín de campaña nos llame a pelear. *(repeat)*

While there's wine in our glass let's be merry,
Forget pain and worry, forget how we sigh. *(repeat)*
For tomorrow the cannon may thunder,
Tomorrow the trumpets may call us to die. *(repeat)*

Lovely girls in mantillas and laces,
Come share our embraces and love us tonight, *(repeat)*
For tomorrow the cannon may thunder,
Tomorrow the trumpets may call us to fight. *(repeat)*

Listen, Death, I have heard all about you,
I can do without you, so pass me right by, *(repeat)*
For tomorrow the cannon may thunder,
Tomorrow the trumpets may call us to die. *(repeat)*

People say, though the body is mortal,
The soul through its portal to heaven takes flight, *(repeat)*
Oh, tomorrow the cannon may thunder,
Tomorrow the trumpets may call us to fight. *(repeat)*

El Tecolote

(THE OWL)

Mexican folk song

From the collection of J. D. Robb, who transcribed it from the singing of Adolfo Maes in Canjilou, New Mexico, 1949. Used by permission.

ANOTHER song that was popular among Santa Anna's legions; again love, whiskey, and the life of the soldier is the theme.

EL TECOLOTE

1. ¿Te - co - lo - te de dón - de vie - nes? ¿Te - co-
1. Lit - tle owl where do you come from, Lit - tle

lo - te de dón - de vie - nes? Del pue - blo de Co - lo - ra - do, del pue -
owl where do you come from? Col - o - ra - do is__ the place, sir, Col - o -

blo de Co - lo - ra - do. ¡Ay! Ven - go a traer - te u - na no -
ra - do is__ the place, sir, Ay! And I come to bring you

ti - cia, Ven-go a traer-te u-na no - ti - cia, que tu a - mor e - stá per-
tid - ings, Yes_ I come to bring you tid - ings, That your love is in_ dis-

Estribillo
Refrain

di - do, que tu a - mor e - stá per - di - do. ¡Ay! Pá - ja - ro,
grace, sir, That your love is in_ dis - grace, sir, Ay! Sing lit - tle

cu cu cu. Pá - ja - ro, cu cu cu. Po-bre - ci - to a-ni-ma-
bird, cur-ru cur - ru! Sing lit-tle bird, cur-ru cur-ru! Ah, the life of an an-i-mal's

li - to tie - ne ham - bre el te-co-lo-ti - to, Ay.
try - ing. Poor lit-tle owl, For hun-ger it's cry-ing. Ay.

D.C.

66

1

¿Tecolote de dónde vienes?
¿Tecolote de dónde vienes?
Del pueblo de Colorido,
del pueblo de Colorido. Ay!
Vengo a traerte una noticia,
Vengo a traerte una noticia,
que tu amor está perdido
que tu amor está perdido. Ay!

Estribillo

Pájaro, cu cu cu.
Pájaro, cu cu cu.
Pobrecito animalito
tiene hambre el tecolotito. Ay!

2

¿Tecolote de dónde vienes?
¿Tecolote de dónde vienes?
Tan fresco y tan de mañana
tan fresco y tan de mañana. Ay!
Vengo de hacer ejercicio,
Vengo de hacer ejercicio
en las tropas de Santa Ana,
en las tropas de Santa Ana. Ay!

Estribillo

3

¿Tecolote de dónde vienes?
¿Tecolote de dónde vienes?
De arriba de una zotea.°
de arriba de una zotea.° Ay!
Vengo de ver un borracho
Vengo de ver un borracho
Empinarse la botella
Empinarse la botella. Ay!

Estribillo

° Azotea.

1

Little owl where do you come from,
Little owl where do you come from?
Colorado is the place, sir,
Colorado is the place, sir, Ay!
And I come to bring you tidings,
And I come to bring you tidings,
That your love is in disgrace, sir,
That your love is in disgrace, sir. Ay!

Refrain

Sing little bird curru curru!
Sing little bird curru curru!
Ah, the life of an animal's trying.
Poor little owl. For hunger it's crying. Ay!

2

Little owl, where do you come from,
Little owl, where do you come from?
For the dawn hardly is breaking
For the dawn hardly is breaking, Ay!
With the troops of Santa Anna
With the troops of Santa Anna
Exercise I have been taking
Exercise I have been taking, Ay!

Refrain

3

Little owl, where do you come from,
Little owl, where do you come from?
I've been up there on the roof, sir,
I've been up there on the roof, sir. Ay!
I've been watching while a drunkard
I've been watching while a drunkard
Guzzles down seventy proof, sir,
Guzzles down seventy proof, sir. Ay!

Refrain

PART 3

"Come, Come, Ye Saints!"

Come join the army, the army of our Lord,
Brigham is our leader, we'll rally at his word.
Sharp will be the conflict with the powers of sin,
But with such a leader we are sure to win.[1]

[1] From *Saints of Sage and Saddle* by Austin and Alter Fife.

FOUNDED BY THE VICTIMS of religious persecution, America has always officially encouraged freedom of religious persuasion while making deviation from "accepted" religious forms increasingly difficult. Quakers, Shakers, Catholics, Jews, atheists—all have, at one time or another, suffered from the tyranny of majority faith.

The Established Church of seventeenth-century England drove the Puritans from their native land to the New World in the West. Two centuries later, descendants of these first American settlers would join with other white Protestant Americans of Anglo–Saxon heritage to drive the members of another religious minority from their homes to a New World in the West.

Members of the Church of Jesus Christ of Latter-Day Saints, more popularly known as Mormons, followed their faith from upper New York State to the Great Basin of the Salt Lake Valley in Utah. In travels covering more than 2,000 miles and sixteen years, the Mormons wrote a dramatic chapter in the history of western America.

The Mormon story actually begins in the little town of Palmyra in upper New York State in 1823. It was there, according to the *Book of Mormon,* that Joseph Smith, the founder of the Mormon Church, had the first divine vision which led to the revelation of the faith's holy scriptures.

Inspired by a belief in the "one true faith," disdaining all other theologies as "gentile," and preaching their gospel with a fervor matched only by their zeal in farming and the mechanical arts, the Mormons quickly won adherents to their Church. In 1831, the Saints moved westward to Ohio, and then on to Jackson County, Missouri.

After a few years, the Mormons were forced to leave their Missouri homes, settling finally in the town of Carthage, Illinois, which they renamed Nauvoo. Here Mormonism flourished and both the faith and a frontier civilization grew. Converts to Mormonism from the Eastern states (and from England) flocked to the wilderness Zion. The appeal of Mormonism was to the poor and disenfranchised who could work with their fellows-in-faith for a better life in this world as well as in the next.

By 1844, some 15,000 of the faithful had made Nauvoo Illinois' largest and most prosperous city. But as the Saints grew in numbers, so the suspicion and hostility of their frontier neighbors likewise grew. Bound together by a common belief and a strong-willed prophet, inspired, they believed, by divine revelation, the Mormons worshipped together, worked together, and voted together. They became a force to be reckoned with in any community where they settled, while, because of their industry and sense of cooperation, their enterprises flourished.

A series of clashes between Mormons and Illinois civil authorities finally culminated in the arrest of Joseph Smith. On June 27, 1844, a mob broke into the jail where Smith was held, and murdered the prophet and his brother. This lynching became the signal for a mass outbreak of violence and terror against the Mormons in Illinois.

With the death of Smith, Brigham Young became the guiding force of the Mormon Church. Under Young's leadership, the Mormons reached an uneasy truce with the authorities. In return for protection from further persecution, the Mormons agreed to evacuate Nauvoo by the spring of 1845.

Once again, the Saints looked West. When spring came, the Mormons began the long trek which would end some 1,500 miles to the west on the shores of the Great Salt Lake.

According to Mormon legend, advance scouts reached the Great Basin on July 21, 1847. Three days later, the main body of Saints came to the valley, at which point Brigham Young said: "It is enough. This is the place."

The long Mormon hegira was over.

On the shores of the Great Salt Lake, separated by distance and desert from their persecutors, the Saints began to build a new civilization. They called their state, "Deseret." At its heart was the Mormon Church, exercising complete control over the economy, the culture, the social and spiritual life of the community.

In the process of travail and triumph, a cultural expression uniquely Mormon developed. Important to that expression were the Mormon songs, a body of musical literature which has great significance as both history and folklore.

The tunes for these songs came from the secular and religious music of nineteenth-century America. Standard hymns, minstrel and music hall melodies, popular semi-art songs of the day, provided the musical framework. The heart and the texts came from Mormon faith and Mormon experience.

Come, Come, Ye Saints

Words: William Clayton
Music: "All Is Well"

From the singing of L. M. Hilton, *Mormon Folk Songs* (Folkways Records FA2036).

Early this spring we'll leave Nauvoo,
And on our journey we'll pursue,
We'll go and bid the mob farewell,
And let them go to heaven or hell.

So on the way to California,
In the spring we'll take our journey,
Far above Arkansas fountains,
Pass between the Rocky Mountains.

The mobocrats have done their best,
Old Sharp and Williams with the rest,
They've burnt our houses and our goods
And left our sick folks in the woods.

Now since it's so we have to go
And leave the City of Nauvoo,
I hope you'll all be strong and stout,
And then no mob can back you out.[1]

In the spring of 1845, the Saints left Nauvoo, Illinois, leaving behind homes, farms, possessions, the fruits of six years of labor, to seek a new home in the desert. They left behind their martyred dead and, with faith in Brigham Young, marched westward.

The first leg of the journey from Nauvoo terminated at Council Bluffs, Iowa, where the Mormons established their Winter Quarters. It was a hard journey, and a long one. Even Mormon spirits, usually borne high on the wings of faith, had reached a low ebb. At one point on the trip, when an atmosphere of gloom and discouragement seemed to be permeating the ranks of the faithful, Brigham Young asked his secretary, a talented musician by the name of William Clayton, to write a hymn which would help to inspire the Saints once again.

According to Mormon legend, Clayton then retired to his wagon, emerging two hours later with the words to this most popular of all Mormon hymns. For his melody, he chose an old hymn tune, "All Is Well," popular among sacred harp groups of the 1840's.

The song helped renew the spirit of the weary travelers and has been kept alive in Mormon tradition until today as a memory of that arduous journey and as a constant renewal of the faith.

[1] "Early This Spring We'll Leave Nauvoo," from *Saints of Sage and Saddle*, Austin and Alta Fife.

73

COME, COME, YE SAINTS

1. Come, come ye Saints, no toil nor la-bor fear, But with joy wend your way,

Though hard to you, this jour-ney must ap-pear, Grace shall be as your day. 'Tis

bet-ter far____ for us to strive,__ Our use-less cares__ from us to drive. Do

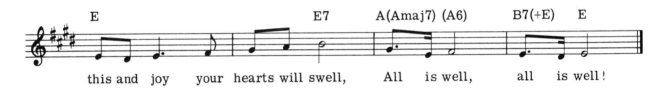

this and joy your hearts will swell, All is well, all is well!

Come, come, ye Saints, no toil nor labor fear,
But with joy wend your way,
Though hard to you, this journey may appear,
Grace shall be as your day.
'Tis better far for us to strive
Our useless cares from us to drive.
Do this and joy your hearts will swell,
All is well, all is well!

Why should we mourn or think our lot is hard?
'Tis not so, all is right.
Why should we think to earn a great reward
If now we shun the fight?
Gird up your loins, fresh courage take,
Your God will never us forsake.
And soon we'll have this tale to tell,
All is well, all is well.

We'll find the place which God for us prepared,
Far away, in the West,
Where none shall come to hurt or make afraid,
There the Saints will be blessed.
We'll make the air with music ring,
Shout praises to our God and King,
Above the rest these words we'll tell,
All is well, all is well!

And should we die before our journey's through,
Happy day, all is well.
We then are free from toil and sorrow, too,
With the just we shall dwell.
But if our lives are spared again,
To see the Saints their rest obtain,
Oh, how we'll make this chorus swell,
All is well, all is well!

Sea Gulls and Crickets

From the singing of L. M. Hilton, *Mormon Folk Songs* (Folkways FA2036).

The grasshoppers, crickets, and mobbers all combined
Were powerless to crush our noble cause.
The more we are hated, the more we are maligned,
The more the Church of Jesus grows.[1]

By the spring of 1848, the Mormons had taken hold of the land, having between three and four thousand acres under cultivation. Late March rains damaged the flimsy structures which the Saints had erected as dwellings, but the crops thrived. But in June came the worst of all the trials which the faithful had faced since settling in Salt Lake.

"Then big black grasshoppers began to come—about as long as your finger, a-hopping and jumping like monsters out of a fairy story, and a-mowing down every green shoot like a herd of sheep. . . . Sometimes when there was a breeze the air was black with them until you couldn't see the sky. And then they called special meetings and we sang hymns and prayed and asked the Lord to deliver us from this plague of crickets so we wouldn't have to live on sego roots and thistle greens for another winter. And we fasted for three days. And then on the afternoon of the third day of fasting we saw like a white cloud rising from the lake and a-coming towards, and when it got closer we saw it was a flock of great big birds. . . . And they came a-cawing and a-flapping their wings and lit right in the grain fields where the hoppers were thickest. And they began to gobble down the hoppers like all fury. And when they were so full they were about to bust why they'd hop upon a ditch bank, or fly down here to the salt flats and heave the stuff right up until their stomachs were empty again, and here they'd come back again as hungry as ever. . . . They kept at it until there wasn't a hopper to be seen."[2]

In Salt Lake City today, a tourist may see the monument to the sea gulls which stands in Temple Square, a memory in stone of Mormon history, a commemoration of one of the great "miracles" of the faith.

[1] From *Saints of Sage and Saddle*, Fife.

[2] From *The Relief Society Magazine* (Salt Lake City), quoted in *Saints of Sage and Saddle*, Fife.

SEA GULLS AND CRICKETS

Rather slowly

1. The win-ter of for - ty - nine had passed, A win-ter of haunt-ing fears, ___ For

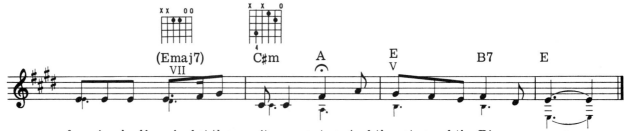

fam-ine had knocked at the cit - y gates And threat-ened the Pi - o - neers. ___

The winter of Forty-nine * had passed,
A winter of haunting fears,
For famine had knocked at the city gates
And threatened the Pioneers.

But spring with its smiling skies lent grace
And cheered the hosts within;
And they tilled their fields with a new-born trust
And the courage to fight and win.

With the thrill of life, the tender shoots
Burst forth from the virgin plain;
And each day added its ray of hope,
The blessing of ripened grain.

But lo, in the east strange clouds appeared,
And dark became the sun;
And down from the mountain sides there swept
A scourge that the boldest shunned.

The crickets by tens of millions came,
Like fog on a British coast;
The finger of devastation marked
Its course on the Mormon host.

With a vigor that desperation fanned,
They battled and smote and flew,
But the clouds still gathered and broke afresh
'Til the fields that waved were few.

With visions of famine and want and woe
They prayed from their hearts sincere,
When lo, from the west came other clouds
To succor the Pioneers.

'Twas sea gulls feathered in angel-white,
And angels they were forsooth.
The sea gulls there by the thousands came
To battle in very truth.

They charged down upon the cricket hordes,
And gorging them day and night,
They routed the devastating foe,
And the crickets were put to flight.

All heads were bowed as they thanked their God,
And they reaped while the Devil raved,
The harvest was garnered to songs of praise
And the Pioneers were saved.

* Most contemporary accounts place the year of the inva-
sion of the crickets as 1848. Nevertheless, with the historical contrariness of folklore, the song has the date of
1850.

The Mountain Meadows Massacre

Author unknown

From *Saints of Sage and Saddle*, Austin and Alta Fife, Indiana University Press.

> Remember the wrongs of Missouri;
> Forget not the fate of Nauvoo;
> When the God-hating foe is before you,
> Stand firm and be faithful and true.[1]

THE Mormons were hardly settled in their desert home, when fate took a hand in breaching the wall of isolation which the faithful had constructed.

A favorite stopping-off place for many California-bound overland gold-seeking expeditions in the 1850's was Salt Lake, where supplies of food and water could be replenished and fresh animals secured. Indeed, the Mormon economy flourished on the highly profitable trading which ensued.

In 1857, a band of emigrants known as the Fancher Party was passing through southern Utah in the vicinity of the Mormon settlement at Cedar City. Included in the party were a number of rowdies from Missouri who took no pains to hide their contempt for the Indians in the area, as well as the Mormons they encountered. Nicknaming their oxen Brigham, Joseph, and Heber, the Missourians raided Mormon chicken coops and had their cattle deliberately trample Mormon fields. Their opinion of Mormon women was summed up by the succinctly, frequently and loudly expressed word, "whore." All the while, these same travelers boasted of the part they or their friends had played in the Missouri massacre of the Mormons two decades earlier.

For the frontier Saints, 200 miles removed from the astute hand of Brigham Young, these provocations reached a breaking point. The result was an insane tragedy of horror and murder which has come to be known as the Mountain Meadows Massacre.

On September 7, 1857, a band of Indians (there is some reason to believe that at least a few Mormons wearing red paint were among them) attacked the Fancher Party. Several of the party were killed before the attack was beaten off. A state of siege at Mountain Meadows between the two forces set in. Meanwhile, a group of Mormons hatched a plot by which a terrible blood vengeance would be achieved.

On September 11, the Mormons approached the Fancher Party camp. They offered the party safe conduct through the Indian lines to Cedar City, on condition that all arms be temporarily surrendered and that Mormon guards accompany each emigrant individually. The terms were accepted and the camp was broken. As the party left the Meadows, the Mormon guards turned on their captives and shot them to death. At the same moment, Indians attacked the women and older children who remained in camp. The entire emigrant train (about 140 people), with the exception of 17 small children under the age of seven, was massacred at Mountain Meadows.

As the years passed, the memory of Mountain Meadows grew in the minds of the Mormons as a cowardly stain which could be eradicated only in blood justice. Twenty years later, one of the leaders of the plot, John Lee, was convicted by a Utah jury for the murders and he was subsequently executed on the site of the Mountain Meadows massacre.

By 1870, this song had been composed. In later years, the ballad has found its way into oral tradition. Interestingly enough, it is known by both Mormons and non-Mormons, although the former have managed to hide the song fairly well over the years, keeping it locked in some secret portion of the folk memory as a grim reminder of the crime known as vengeance.[2]

---

[1] From a song by Charles Penrose, to the tune of "Columbia the Gem of the Ocean," in *Latter Day Saints Hymnal* (1927 edition), quoted in *Music in the Southwest*, Howard Swan.

[2] For additional information and comparative texts, see "A Ballad of the Mountain Meadows Massacre" by Austin Fife in *Western Folklore*, Vol. 12, No. 4.

THE MOUNTAIN MEADOWS MASSACRE

Not slow; accent every chord ♩ = 70

1. Come all you sons of Lib-er-ty, un-to my rhyme give ear, 'Tis of a blood-y mas-sa-cre, you pres-ent-ly shall hear, In splen-dor o'er the moun-tains, some thir-ty wag-ons came, They were 'wait-ed by a

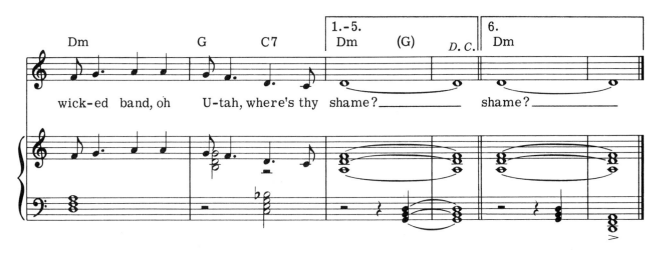

Come all you sons of Liberty, unto my rhyme give ear,
'Tis of a bloody massacre, you presently shall hear,
In splendor o'er the mountains, some thirty wagons came,
They were awaited by a wicked band, oh Utah, where's thy shame?

In Indian colors all wrapped in shame, this bloody crew was seen,
To flock around this little train, all on the meadows green,
They were attacked in the morning, as they were on their way,
They forthwith corralled their wagons, and fought in blood array.

Till came the captain of the band, he surely did deceive,
Saying, "If you will give up your arms, we'll surely let you live."
When once they had given up their arms, thinking their lives to save,
The words were broken among the rest, which sent them to their graves.

When once they had given up their arms, they started for Cedar City,
They rushed on them in Indian style, oh what a human pity,
They melted down with one accord like wax before the flame,
Both men and women, old and young, oh Utah, where's thy shame?

Both men and women, old and young, a-rolling in their gore,
And such an awful sight and scene was ne'er beheld before,
Their property was divided among this bloody crew,
And Uncle Sam is bound to see this bloody matter through.

The soldiers will be stationed, throughout this Utah land,
All for to find those murderers out, and bring them to his hand,
By an order from their president, this bloody deed was done,
He was the leader of the Mormon Church, his name was Brigham Young.

*If played with guitar only and sung by a lower
voice, this may be more happily transposed down to A
minor; then capo up if desired.*

The Handcart Song

From the singing of L. M. Hilton, *Mormon Folk Songs* (Folkways, FA2036).

> Hurrah for the Camp of Israel!
> Hurrah for the handcart scheme!
> Hurrah! Hurrah! 'Tis better far
> Than the wagon and ox-team.[1]

THE Zion in the desert which was slowly and surely rising on the shores of the Great Salt Lake existed as a dream and a promise for many thousands in both the United States and Western Europe. Very early in the history of the Mormon settlement, Brigham Young understood that many strong hearts and willing hands were necessary for the achievement of the Deseret dream. A conscious program of Mormon recruitment was undertaken. Missionaries were dispatched to the Eastern states and to Europe where they told the story of the glorious Utopia which was coming to life in the western desert.

To many an improverished farmer or workingman in England, Scotland, and the Scandinavian states, the promise of a Mormon "heaven on earth" must indeed have seemed like divine revelation. But if these new converts were long on faith, they were short on cash. The need to reduce the expenses for immigrants from abroad became paramount. At this point, Brigham Young devised a plan:

"In regard to foreign immigrants for another year, have them take the northern route through New York and Chicago and land at Iowa City, the western terminus of the Rock Island railroad. . . . There they will be provided with handcarts on which to haul their provisions and clothing. We will send experienced men to that point with instructions to aid them in every way possible; and let the Saints who intend to emigrate to Utah the coming season understand that they are expected to walk and draw their carts across the plains. Sufficient teams will be furnished to haul the aged, infirm, and those

who are unable to walk. A few good cows will furnish milk, and some beef cattle to kill on the road. Now gird up your loins and come while the way is open." [2]

Between the years 1855 and 1860, ten companies of handcart pioneers, a total of 1,600 men, women, and children, undertook the journey. Most of these were European converts to the faith.

"When we (Swiss Mormon emigrants) reached Florence, Nebraska, near present Omaha, we were forced to stop for a while because there were not enough teams to take us across the plains to Salt Lake City. The men set to work making handcarts and my father, being a carpenter, helped to make thirty-three of them. Ours was a small two-wheeled vehicle with two shafts and a cover on top. The carts were very much like those the street sweepers use in the cities today, except that ours were made entirely of wood without even an iron rim. . . . Our company was organized with Oscar O. Stoddard as captain. It contained 126 persons with twenty-two handcarts and three provision wagons drawn by oxen. We set out from Florence on July 6, 1860, for our thousand-mile trip. There were six to our cart. Father and mother pulled it; Rosie (two years old) and Christian (six months old) rode; John (nine) and I (six) walked. Sometimes, when it was down hill, they let me ride, too." [3]

Sometime during those years, some unknown traveler penned the words to this song which has since become a part of the Mormon heritage.

[1] From *Rocky Mountain Saints*, T. B. H. Stenhouse, quoted in *Music in the Southwest*, Howard Swan.

[2] Brigham Young in a letter to Franklin D. Richards, from *The Founding of Utah*, Levi Young, quoted in *Music in the Southwest*, Howard Swan.
[3] From *Recollections of a Handcart Pioneer of 1860*, Mary Ann Hafen, quoted in *A Treasury of Western Folklore*, B. A. Botkin.

THE HANDCART SONG

Happy

1. {Ye Saints who dwell on Eur-ope's shore, Pre-pare your-selves for man-y more   To
{For you must cross the rag-ing main Be-fore the prom-ised land you gain, And

leave be-hind your na-tive land, For sure God's judg-ments are   at hand.
with the faith-ful make   a   start   To   cross the plains with your hand-cart.

Chorus, Lively

For some must push and some must pull, As   we   go march-ing up   the hill   So

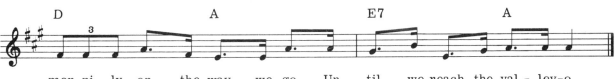

mer-ri-ly   on   the way   we go,   Un-til   we reach the val-ley-o.

Ye Saints who dwell on Europe's shore,
Prepare yourselves for many more
To leave behind your native land,
For sure God's judgments are at hand.
For you must cross the raging main
Before the promised land you gain,
And with the faithful make a start
To cross the plains with your handcart.

Chorus:

For some must push and some must pull,
As we go marching up the hill,
So merrily on our way we go,
Until we reach the valley-o.

The lands that boast of modern light,
We know are all as dark as night,
Where poor men toil and want for bread,
Where peasant hosts are blindly led;
These lands that boast of liberty
You ne'er again would wish to see,
When you from Europe make a start
To cross the plains with your handcart.

(Chorus)

As on the road the carts are pulled,
'Twould very much surprise the world
To see the old and feeble dame
Thus lend a hand to pull the same;
And maidens fair will dance and sing,
Young men more happy than the king,
And children, too, will laugh and play,
Their strength increasing day by day.

(Chorus)

But some will say, "It is too bad,
The Saints upon the foot to pad,
And more than that, to pull a load
As they go marching o'er the road."
And then we say, "It is the plan
To gather up the best of men,
And women, too, for none but they
Will ever travel in this way."

(Chorus)

And long before the valley's gained,
We will be met upon the plains
With music sweet and friends so dear,
And fresh supplies our hearts to cheer;
And then with music and with song,
How cheerfully we'll march along,
And thank the day we made a start
To cross the plains with our handcarts.

(Chorus)

When you get there among the rest,
Obedient be and you'll be blessed,
And in God's chambers be shut in
While judgments cleanse the earth from sin;
For we do know it will be so,
God's servant spoke it long ago,
We say it is high time to start
To cross the plains with our handcarts.

(Chorus)

Brigham Young

After the singing of Rosalie Sorrels, *Folksongs of Idaho and Utah* (Folkways FH5343); the last verse from *Saints of Sage and Saddle*, Austin and Alta Fife.

Now, Brigham Young, the Mormon,
Has got just fifty wives,
And about six-hundred babies
For to make a little noise;
He's forty-nine ahead of me,
For I am content with one;
The old fellow's motto, I believe,
Is: Whole Hog or None! [1]

It is doubtful that Mormonism would have survived without Brigham Young. The dynamic personality, the rare organizing ability, the astute political insight which characterized the Mormon leader was a key factor in the successful migration West and the establishment of the Mormon settlement.

Young, who was born in Vermont in 1801, succeeded to the leadership of the Mormon Church after the murder of Joseph Smith. A man of intense drive and deep conviction, Brigham Young was a symbol for both the faithful and the gentiles. In 1852, five years after the founding of Deseret, Brigham Young publicly announced the doctrine of plural marriage as a basic part of Mormon theology. Joseph Smith had proclaimed polygamy nine years earlier as a divine revelation, but only a handful of the Saints engaged in this practice before Brigham Young's pronouncement.

From that point on, polygamy and Brigham Young became, for the outside world, the crucial symbols of the Mormon faith. The subject became a favorite for topical song writers, and no blackface minstrel of the day could feel that his act was complete unless at least one number contained some pointed reference to the Mormon leader and his overabundance of partners. Sometimes it was hard to tell whether the singer was critical of Brigham Young, sympathetic, or just plain envious.

I'll sing you a song that has often been sung
About an old Mormon they called Brigham Young.
Of wives he had many who were strong in the lungs,
Which Brigham found out by the length of their tongues. [2]

In the Mormon beds out West,
There the concubines do rest,
While husbands visit Emily and Jane!
Oh! how the babies do abound
By the thousands all around
While the husband now slips in to see Elaine. [3]

But Brigham Young, who thrived on controversy, would not bow to the pressures for abandoning the doctrine of polygamy:

"If you tell them a Mormon has two wives they are shocked. . . . If you whisper such a thing into the the ears of a gentile who takes a fresh woman every night, he is thunderstruck with the enormity of the crime. . . . I would rather take my valise in my hand today, and never see a wife or a child again, and preach the gospel until I go into the grave, than to live as I do, unless God commands it. I never entered into the order of plurality of wives to gratify passion. And were I now asked whether I desired and wanted another wife, my

[1] From "Whole Hog or None," as sung by Harry Fox, in a De Marsan broadside of the period. (NYC)

[2] From *Cowboy Songs*, John A. Lomax, who attributes it to *Put's Golden Songster*.
[3] "In The Mormon Beds Out West," from Mrs. Blanche Lambourne of Salt Lake City, quoted in *Ballads and Songs from Utah*, Lester A. Hubbard.

reply would be, It should be one by whom the Spirit will bring forth noble children." [4]

Despite the attacks of the gentile world, Brigham Young was revered by his followers, who sang:

Brigham Young is the lion of the Lord,
The prophet and revealer of His word,
The mouthpiece of God and to all mankind,
And he rules by the power of His word, His word,
And he rules by the power of His word. [5]

Though written up an octave the chorus refrain is usually sung down. But if you have a high voice the effect is great.

For those who play both the guitar and banjo, this is a wonderful "tongue in cheek" song. You may do it

straight, four chords to a bar, changing chords as indicated in the verse, or you may do a fast um-pah and perhaps work in some of the extra changes indicated in the chorus—or, if you are ambitious, a fast arpeggio technique would be effective. Here it is indicated for the fifth and sixth bars of the song proper. Just pick with thumb, index, and middle finger on strings 1, 2, and 3.

By using the bass line of the piano part, all of these, and other styles, can of course be varied from verse to verse, with interludes between.

For piano players, this is a fun accompaniment which may take just a little practice to learn. It is recommended that you alternate the introduction and the interlude between verses rather than playing both at the same time.

[4] Brigham Young, quoted in *Men to Match My Mountains*, Irving Stone.
[5] "Brigham Young, Lion of the Lord," from the singing of Salley A. Hubbard, Salt Lake City (1946), quoted in *Ballads and Songs from Utah*, Lester A. Hubbard.

Strings: 3-2-1-2 3-2-1-2 3-2-1-2 *etc.*

BRIGHAM YOUNG

lived with his five-and-for-ty wives in the cit-y of the Great Salt Lake, Where they

breed and swarm like hens on a farm and cack-le like ducks to a drake.

Chorus

Brig-ham, Brig-ham Young, it's a mir-a-cle he sur-vives, With his

roar-ing rams and his pret-ty lit-tle lambs, and his five-and-for-ty wives.

Fine

86

Interlude

2. Brig-ham

Brigham Young was a Mormon bold, and a leader of the roaring ram,
And the shepherd of a heap of fine tub sheep and a passel of pretty little lambs;
And he lived with his five-and-forty wives in the city of Great Salt Lake,
Where they breed and swarm like hens on a farm and cackle like ducks to a drake.

Chorus:

Brigham, Brigham Young, it's a miracle he survives,
With his roaring rams and his pretty little lambs, and his five-and-forty wives.

Number forty-five's about sixteen, number one is sixty and three,
And among such a riot how he ever keeps 'em quiet is a downright mystery to me,
For they cackle and claw and they jaw, jaw, jaw, each one has a different desire,
It would aid the renown of the best shop in town to supply them with half they require.

(Chorus)

Brigham Young was a stout man once, but now he is thin and old,
And I'm sorry to relate, there's no hair upon his pate, where he once wore a covering of gold.
For his oldest wife won't wear white wool, the young ones won't take red,
And in tearing it out and taking turn about, they have torn all the wool from his head.

(Chorus)

Now his youngest wives they sing psalms all day, the old ones all sing songs,
And among such a crowd he had it pretty loud, they're as noisy as Chinese gongs.
When they advance for a Mormon dance, he is filled with the direst alarms,
For they're sure to spend the night in a tabernacle fight to see who has the fairest charms.

(Chorus)

Well, there never was a house like Brigham Young's, so curious and so queer,
For his wives were double and he had a lot of trouble, and gained on him year by year.
Now he sits in his state and bears his fate in a sanctified sort of way;
He has one wife to bury and one wife to marry and a new kid born every day.

(Chorus)

Now if anybody envies Brigham Young, let them go to Great Salt Lake,
And if they have leisure to examine at their pleasure, they'll find it's a great mistake.
One wife at a time, so says my rhyme, is enough for the proudest don,
So ere you strive to live lord of forty-five, live happy if you can with one.

(Chorus)

88

Echo Canyon

From the singing of L. M. Hilton, *Mormon Folk Songs* (Folkways FA2036).

> Haste, O haste, construct a railway,
> Where the vales of Ephraim bloom;
> Cast ye up—cast up a highway,
> Where "swift messengers" will come;
> Soon we'll see the proud Atlantic,
> With the great Pacific joined—
> Through the skill of swift conveyance
> Leaving distance all behind.[1]

In 1868, a national dream was on the verge of realization. Two snakelines of steel rail and wooden tie were inexorably rushing toward each other to bind the country into a single unit. The Saints had founded their Utopia in isolation from a "gentile" world, erecting a natural barrier of sand and distance between themselves and a hostile world. But the era of industrialism would not be denied, and the transcontinental railroad was destined to be joined in Deseret.

Brigham Young did not share the trepidations of the more pessimistic in his flock. "I wouldn't give much for a religion," he said, "which could not withstand the coming of a railroad." When, in the spring of 1868, Samuel B. Reed, representing the Union Pacific Railroad, approached him with a proferred contract for Mormons to grade ninety miles of railroad westward from Echo Canyon, Brigham Young accepted. An important consideration in Young's decision to cooperate with the railroad was the fact that the Mormon economy that spring was having its troubles. Population in Salt Lake and its environs (swelled by the immigration from abroad) was outstripping Mormon capacity to produce. The Echo Canyon construction job presented an opportunity to infuse the sluggish economy with new wealth.

Mormon labor battalions were organized for the task. Working cooperatively by day, living cooperatively in their work camps, the Mormons proved strong and reliable laborers. One newspaper correspondent visiting a Saints' camp wrote:

"After the day's work was done, the animals turned out to herd and the supper over, a nice blending of voices in sweet singing proved that the materials exist among the men for a capital choir, and there is some talk of organizing one." [2]

In one such camp, some anonymous laborer constructed a song which told the story of Mormons and the Echo Canyon grade. The song struck a spark and took hold, surviving through oral tradition among descendants of these railroad construction men until today.

[1] "In Jehovah's Arm We Trusted," by E. R. Snow, from *The Deseret News* (Feb. 2, 1854), quoted in *Music In the Southwest*, Howard Swan.

[2] Edward Sloan, in *The Deseret News* (July 31, 1868), quoted in *The Great Iron Trail*, Robert West Howard.

ECHO CANYON

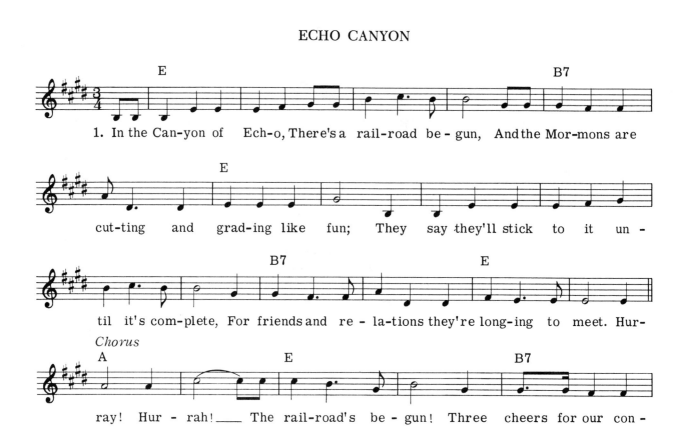

1. In the Can-yon of Ech-o, There's a rail-road be - gun, And the Mor-mons are cutting and grad-ing like fun; They say they'll stick to it un - til it's com-plete, For friends and re - la-tions they're long-ing to meet. Hur-

Chorus

ray! Hur - rah!___ The rail-road's be - gun! Three cheers for our con - trac-tor, his name's Brig-ham Young; Hur - ray! Hur - rah! We're light-

heart-ed and gay, Just the right kind of boys to build a rail - way.

In the Canyon of Echo, there's a railroad begun,
And the Mormons are cutting and grading like fun;
They say they'll stick to it until it's complete,
For friends and relations they're longing to meet.

Chorus:

Hurray! Hurrah! The railroad's begun!
Three cheers for our contractor, his name's Brigham Young;
Hurray! Hurrah! We're lighthearted and gay,
Just the right kind of boys to build a railway.

Now there's Mister Reed, he's a gentleman, too,
He knows very well what we Mormons can do;
He knows in our work we are faithful and true,
And if Mormon boys start it, it's bound to go through.

(Chorus)

Our camp is united, we all labor hard,
And if we are faithful, we'll gain our reward;
Our leader is wise and a great leader, too,
And all things he tells us, we're right glad to do.

(Chorus)

The boys in our camp are lighthearted and gay,
We work on the railroad ten hours a day;
We're thinking of fine times we'll have in the fall,
When we'll be with our ladies and go to the ball.

(Chorus)

We surely must live in a very fast age:
We've traveled by ox team and then took the stage,
But when such conveyance is all done away,
We'll travel in steam cars upon the railway.

(Chorus)

The great locomotive next season will come
To gather the Saints from their far distant home,
And bring them to Utah in peace here to stay,
While the judgments of God sweep the wicked away.

(Chorus)

PART 4

"The Days of '49"

> My heart is filled with the days of yore,
> And oft do I repine,
> For the days of old, the days of gold,
> The days of Forty-nine.[1]

[1] "The Days of '49," from *The Great Emerson New Popular Songster*, San Francisco (1872).

San francisco in the 1850's was a roaring, sprawling community—half city, half mudflat. Newly grown, newly Americanized, newly named (up until 1847 it was known as Yerba Buena), San Francisco was an outpost of easy money and easy virtue.

The tens of thousands of gold seekers who passed through the Golden Gate on their way to the mines brought with them a variety of national backgrounds. As the city grew, its idiom reflected the diversity of its cultures—Spanish, English, Irish, Indian, French, German, Russian.

The miners brought their dreams, their lore, their songs. Most came to make their pile and return back East; but only a handful went home. For the miner, there was always another digging, another chance for the lucky strike. Before he knew it, he was an old settler and a citizen of California.

> The miners came in '49,
> The whores in '51;
> And when they got together
> They produced the native son.[2]

The music of the age was the music of the San Francisco music halls and the mining camp saloons. Among the cultured elite of the Pacific Coast, a patronage of opera and formal European concert music developed. But the popular music of the era had its roots in the minstrel stage of the East. Following quickly on the heels of the first boatloads of gold seekers were the "Philadelphia Minstrels" who opened at the Bella Union Theater October 22, 1849. A year later, "The Virginia Serenaders" were playing in Washington Hall.

[2] Traditional San Francisco rhyme, quoted in *The Barbary Coast*, Herbert Asbury.

The chief form of amusement in the early days was gambling, and many a freewheeling miner squandered the hard-earned gold of a summer in one night at the tables of chance on the Barbary Coast. In order to attract customers, the first gambling halls competed in offering various forms of entertainment. Magicians, tap dancers, scantily clad *señoritas* and professional vaudevillians offered their wares on the stages of the Bella Union, the El Dorado, the Alhambra, and the Verandah. From the gambling halls, troupes of professional entertainers moved on to the mining camp circuit, presenting their acts for the amusement-starved miners throughout the Sacramento Valley.

Many of these entertainers were themselves onetime miners, frustrated fortune hunters who turned to song when the color ran out. From the ranks of these roving singers and itinerant fiddlers emerged the true minstrels of the Gold Rush, men like John Stone ("Old Put"), "Doc" Robinson, John Woodward, Mart Taylor, Ben Cotton and all the other denizens of the San Francisco–Sacramento–Placerville circuit.

The Gold Rush minstrel was a commentator on his times. He had rhymes for politics, women, local personalities, and internationally famous figures. He commented on all subjects, from business practices to temperance, from styles in clothing to Mormon jokes. He was combination town crier, local newspaper, court jester and village idiot. His texts came from a fertile imagination while his tunes came from the music hall stages of the East. At his worst, he was cliché-ridden and a careless versifier; at his best, he had that spark of genius which memorializes an age.

The Days of Forty-nine

Author unknown

From *The Great Emerson New Popular Songster*, San Francisco (1872); another song with the same title, by Samuel C. Upham, to the tune of "Auld Lang Syne." The words here also fit "Auld Lang Syne" and one source suggests that tune for the song.

> I well remember those old times,
> The days of forty-nine, sir,
> When miners gaily singing went
> Into each golden mine, sir.[1]

JOE Bowers, Sweet Betsy and long-suffering Pike County Ike became the musical symbols of the long trek West. Tom Moore, New York Jake, Rackensack Jim and all the other lusty characters of "The Days of '49" became the symbols of the decade that followed, the legendary folk heroes of pick and pan.

Joe Bowers, Betsy and Ike were born in the late fifties on the San Francisco music hall stage. In similar fashion, almost twenty years later, some professional entertainer of the Barbary Coast created the colorful cast of "Days of '49." The author

of the song may have been a local vaudevillian by the name of Charles Rhodes, but no one knows for sure. Only its appeal is certain, for the song has lasted as a popular symbol of the free and easy days when San Francisco was young.

So popular did it become, in fact, that some of the "better" citizens felt the song tended to give a wrong picture of the upright pioneers of those early days. One such citizen tried to set the record straight with a parody about "The Good Old Days of '50, '1, and '2," but old Tom Moore who was able to survive the hard luck of '49, easily outlasted his betters of *'50, '1, and '2.*

[1] "Old Forty-Nine," from *Gold Digger's Song Book* (1856).

THE DAYS OF FORTY-NINE

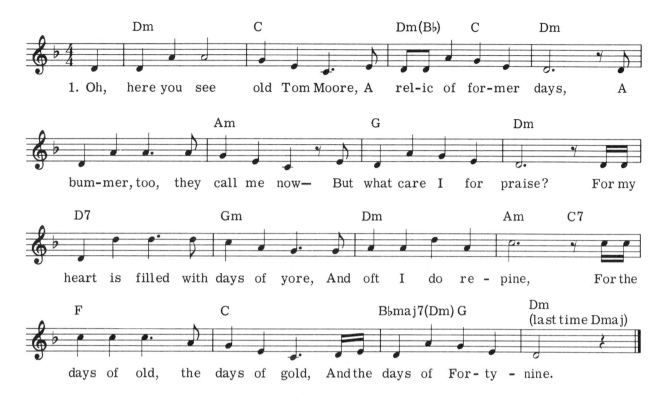

1. Oh, here you see old Tom Moore, A rel-ic of for-mer days, A bum-mer, too, they call me now— But what care I for praise? For my heart is filled with days of yore, And oft I do re-pine, For the days of old, the days of gold, And the days of For-ty - nine.

Oh, here you see old Tom Moore,
A relic of former days,
And a bummer, too, they call me now—
But what care I for praise?
For my heart is filled with the days of yore,
And oft do I repine,
For the days of old, the days of gold,
And the days of Forty-nine.

I'd comrades then who loved me well,
A jovial, saucy crew;
There were some hard cases, I must confess,
But still they were brave and true;
Who'd never flinch, whate'er the pinch,
Would never fret or whine,
But like good old bricks, they stood the kicks,
In the days of Forty-nine.

There was Kentuck' Bill, I knew him well,
A fellow so full of tricks,
At a poker game he was always thar,
And as heavy too, as bricks.
He'd play you draw, he'd ante a slug,
And go a hatful blind,
But in a game with Death, Bill lost his breath,
In the days of Forty-nine.

There was Monte Pete, I'll ne'er forget,
For the luck that he always had,
He'd deal for you both night and day,
Or as long as you had a scad.
One night a pistol laid him out,
'Twas his last lay-out in fine,
It caught Pete sure, right in the door,
In the days of Forty-nine.

There was New York Jake, a butcher boy,
So fond of getting tight;
And whenever Jake got on a spree,
He was sp'iling for a fight.
One day he ran agin' a knife,
In the hands of old Bob Cline,
So over Jake we held a wake,
In the days of Forty-nine.

There was Rackensack Jim who could outroar
A buffalo bull, you bet;
He roared all day, he roared all night,
And I believe he's roaring yet.
One night he fell in a prospect hole,
'Twas a roaring bad design,
For in that hole Jim roared out his soul,
In the days of Forty-nine.

There was poor lame Jess, a hard old case,
Who never would repent;
Jess never missed a single meal,
Nor ever paid a cent.
But poor old Jess like all the rest,
Did to death at last resign,
For in his bloom, he went up the flume,
In the days of Forty-nine.

Of all the comrades I had then,
Not one remains to toast;
They have left me here in my misery,
Like some poor wandering ghost.
And as I go from place to place,
Folks call me a traveling sign:
Saying, "Here's Tom Moore, a bummer sure,
Of the days of Forty-nine."

The Good Old Days of '50, '1, and '2

WORDS: J. Riley Mains
MUSIC: "Days of '49"

From a broadside sheet (circa 1876) in the Bancroft Library at the University of California, Berkeley.

Tom Moore has sung of '49,
And the Pioneers who came
Across the plains and 'round the Horn
In search of gold and fame,
But in his song he tells us not
One word of those we knew,
Those pioneers of the good old days
Of '50, '1, and '2.

There's "Kentuck' Bill" and "Monte Pete,"
He holds them up to fame,
New York Jake and Ransack Jim
And old lame Jess the same;
But men like these were not the boys
So hardy, tough and true,
That flumed the streams and worked the mines
In '50, '1, and '2.

There's Captain Love and gallant Burns,
Dave Buell tall and brave,
Likewise Bob Fall and also Thorn,
Were the dread of the Robber's Cave.
They would trace them o'er the mountain steep,
Ravines and canyons through,
Those men of pluck in the good old days
Of '50, '1, and '2.

There was Joaquin and three-fingered Jack,
To catch them seemed in vain,
Though followed on their bloody track
O'er mountain, hill and plain;
But they at last were forced to yield
To men whom well I knew,
Those gallant souls who knew no fear
Of '50, '1, and '2.

Where are they now, that gallant band,
Those friends that once were mine?
Some sleep beneath the willow's shade,
Some 'neath the lofty pine.
Whilst some have sank beneath the wave,
Deep in the ocean's blue,
Those cherished friends of bygone years
Of '50, '1, and '2.

I once had wealth, it brought new friends,
I thought them true, I'll own,
But when kind fortune ceased to smile
Those summer friends had flown,
And now I wander on alone
Life's thorny pathway through,
But I'll ne'er forget those dear old friends
Of '50, '1, and '2.

'Tis true there's some old pioneers,
That unto wealth have grown,
But there are many that are poor,
And I am one, I'll own.
But never shun a ragged coat
If the heart beneath is true,
Of a pioneer of the good old days
Of '50, '1, and '2.

And now kind friends I've sung my song,
I've had my little speak,
But when I think of those good old days,
Tears ofttimes wet my cheek,
We opened then the Golden Gate
And its treasures unto you,
We boys who came in '49,
And in '50, '1, and '2.

When I Went Off to Prospect

WORDS: John A. Stone ("Old Put")
MUSIC: "King of the Cannibal Islands"

From *Put's Original California Songster;* music from *The Gold Rush Song Book*, Eleanora Black and Sidney Robertson.

He who comes to the mines to find better times
Had better have tarried in Pike,
For in fifty, I'm told, who are toiling for gold,
There's but one who can count on a strike.[1]

THE dream of every prospector was gold, but the hero of the gold-rush songs was the hard luck miner who moved from hardship to misery with the ease of an experienced practitioner in the art of trouble. No indignity of man or nature was too great or too trivial to descend on the '49er. Lice, hunger, marked cards, outrageous prices, and just plain mud became a way of life.

But the prospector was nothing if not an optimist. As each new claim petered out, he moved on to the next, always hopeful, always sure that fortune rested at the bottom of the next pan. And as he drifted and searched, he defied his destiny with the names he gave to his enterprises. Laughing at misfortune, he called his claim *Poor Man's Creek, Poverty Hill,* and *Barefoot Diggings.* Or he might beard the devil himself and dare Satan to do his worst by calling his mine *Hell's Delight* or *Devil's Basin.* The miner knew himself for a fool

[1] "Poor Diggings," from *Gold Digger's Song Book* (1856).

and called his mines *Jackass Gulch, Greenhorn Canyon, Puke Ravine,* and *Chucklehead Diggings.* He called on the meanest creatures of the animal kingdom to frighten off the evil spirits of misfortune, and he named his mines *Skunk Gulch, Centipede Hollow, Rattlesnake Bar* and *Coyote Hill.* Once in a while he would put his faith in Providence and call his stake *Christian Flat,* or *Piety Hill,* or *Gospel Gulch.* More often he would draw his imagery from the world of violence and sudden death, giving his claims such titles as *Murderer's Bar, Gouge Eye, Blue-Belly Ravine,* and *Dead Man's Bar.* A cooperative of Negro miners hopefully labeled their enterprise *The Rare, Ripe Gold & Silver Mining Company,* while another company of colored prospectors staked out *The Sweet Vengeance Mine.* Bret Harte immortalized *Poker Flat,* and Old Put, with a natural instinct for the folklore of his own times, incorporated a dozen or so in this ballad of a hard-luck miner.

WHEN I WENT OFF TO PROSPECT

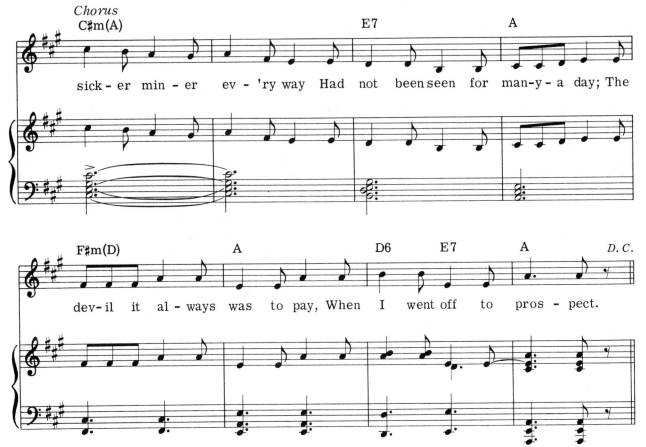

Chorus

sick - er min - er ev - 'ry way Had not been seen for man-y-a day; The dev-il it al - ways was to pay, When I went off to pros - pect.

I heard of gold at Sutter's Mill,
At Michigan Bluff and Iowa Hill,
But never thought it was rich until
  I started off to prospect.
At Yankee Jim's I bought a purse,
Inquired for Iowa Hill, of course,
And traveled on, but what was worse,
  Fetched up in Shirt-tail Canyon.

Chorus:

A sicker miner every way
Had not been seen for many a day;
The devil it always was to pay,
When I went off to prospect.

When I got there, the mining ground
Was staked and claimed for miles around,
And not a bed was to be found,
  When I went off to prospect.
The town was crowded full of folks,
Which made me think 'twas not a hoax;
At my expense they cracked their jokes,
  When I was nearly starving.

(Chorus)

I left my jackass on the road,
Because he wouldn't carry the load;
I'd sooner pack a big horn toad,
  When I went off to prospect.
My fancy shirt, with collar so nice,
I found was covered with body lice;
I used unguentum once or twice,
  But could not kill the grey-backs.

(Chorus)

At Deadwood I got on a tight,
At Groundhog Glory I had a fight;
They drove me away from Hell's Delight,
  When I went off to prospect.
From Bogus-Thunder I ran away,
At Devil's Basin I wouldn't stay;
My lousy shirt crawled off one day,
  Which left me nearly naked.

(Chorus)

Now all I got for running about,
Was two black eyes, and bloody snout;
And that's the way it did turn out,
  When I went off to prospect.
And now I'm loafing around dead broke,
My pistol and tools are all in soak,
And whisky bills at me they poke,
  But I'll make it right in the morning.

(Chorus)

Life in California

Words: Dr. D. G. ("Doc") Robinson
Music: "Used Up Man"

From *Comic Songs; or Hits at San Francisco* by Dr. D. G. Robinson, San Francisco (1853); music from *100 Comic Songs, Music & Words*, by J. W. Turner, Boston (1858).

Oh, ladies and gentlemen, what shall I do?
I'm an object of pity, I'm certain to you,
I'm all out of cash, and I'm out at the knees,
And nothing sticks to me but flour, mud and fleas.[1]

WAS the first '49er a wandering actor, an itinerant player and singer of songs? Dr. "Yankee" Robinson, born in Maine, arrived in San Francisco on January 1, 1849. Blessed with a biting tongue and a sharp wit, "Doc" Robinson became the first of the gold rush minstrels.

Political satire was his forte, and the local guardians of law and order were his prime target. San Francisco's City Council was always fair game:

Soon they got a Council in,
The city's cash to peddle.
Each took four thousand to begin,
Then voted each a medal.[2]

Dandies who couldn't pay their board and laundry bills, self-appointed mediums who heard "spirits rapping," visiting "countesses" from abroad —all these and other assorted humbugs found their way into the songs which "Doc" Robinson poured forth nightly at the San Francisco Theater.

But Robinson's most popular number was this parody to an eastern minstrel stage favorite, a song which had been used in 1840 ("Van, Van, He's a Used-Up Man") to elect one President and defeat another.

[1] "Dr. Robinson's Misfortunes," from *Comic Songs; or Hits at San Francisco* by Dr. D. G. Robinson (1853).
[2] *Ibid.*

LIFE IN CALIFORNIA

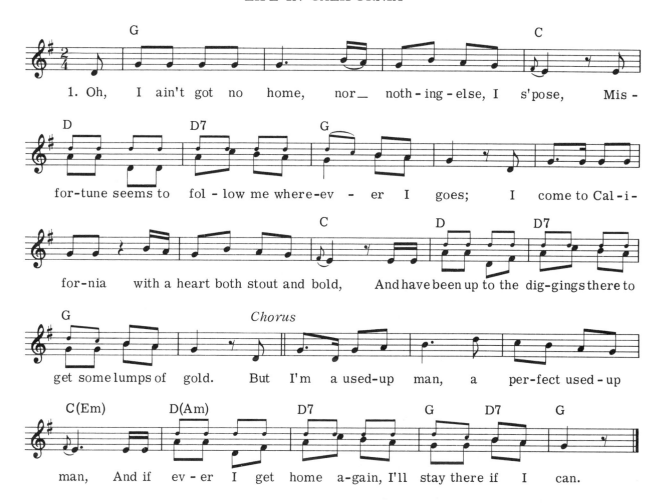

Oh, I ain't got no home, nor nothing else, I s'pose,
Misfortune seems to follow me wherever I goes;
I come to California with a heart both stout and bold,
And have been up to the diggings, there to get some lumps of gold.

Chorus:

But I'm a used-up man, a perfect used-up man,
And if ever I get home again, I'll stay there if I can.

I lives way down in Maine, where I heard about the diggings,
So I shipped aboard a darned old barque, commanded by Joe Higgins;
I sold my little farm and from wife and children parted,
And off to California sailed, and left 'em broken hearted.

But here's a used-up man, etc.

When I got to San Francisco, I saw such heaps of money,
And the way the folks at Monte played, I thought the game quite funny;
So I took my little pile, and on the table tossed it,
And the chap who dealt me out the cards says, "My friend, you have lost it!"

So you're a used-up man, etc.

I got into a steamboat and started up the river,
Where I thought the darned mosquitos would ha' taken out my liver;
When I got to Sacramento, I buckled on this rigging,
And soon I found a decent place, and so I went to digging.

But I'm a used-up man, etc.

I got into the water where the "fever-n-ager" took me,
And after I was froze to death, it turned about and shook me;
But still I kept to work, a-hopin' 'twould be better,
But the water wouldn't fall a bit, but kept a-getting wetter.

But I'm a used-up man, etc.

I 'spose if I should die, they'd take me to the Mission,
Or else Jim Riddle'd sell me off to pay up my physician;
I've tried to keep up courage, and swore I wouldn't spree it,
And here's my pile for five months' work, I'd lief as not you'd see it.

For I'm a used-up man, etc.

I don't know what to do, for all the time I'm dodging
To hunt up grub enough to eat, and find a decent lodging;
I can't get any liquor and no one seems to meet me,
Who'll take me by the collar now, and kindly ask to treat me!

For I'm a used-up man, etc.

I'll go up to the "Woodcock," and see if Tom won't trust me,
For Tom has got too good a heart, I'm sure, to try to bust me;
But if they shouldn't know me there, or say I can't be trusted,
Why then, kind friends, without your help, the poor old miner's busted.

For I'm a used-up man, etc.

I don't know how it is, but I've a dreadful feeling,
If I don't get some business soon, I'll have to take to stealing;
I'd like some city office here, and the tax law wants correcting,
I'd make a first-rate Mayor, too, and only want electing.

For I'm a used-up man, etc.

But to my friends I see tonight, my thanks, I can't express 'em,
And for their generosity, can only say, God bless 'em!
For what of kindness they don't know, I'm sure ain't worth the knowing,
So with my warmest thanks, kind friends, I think I'll be a-going.

For I'm a used-up man, etc.

Seeing the Elephant

WORDS: John A. Stone ("Old Put")
MUSIC: "De Boatman Dance" (by Daniel Emmett)

From *Put's Original California Songster;* music from *Minstrel Songs Old and New,* Oliver Ditson & Co. (1882).

> He mourned his lot and often wept
> To think he ever took the *jaunt,*
> And then he'd rave and swear he b'lieved
> He's soon to see the *Elephant.*[1]

AN elephant cannot be ignored. The size, the mass, the bulk, the overwhelmng presence of an elephant commands attention. And even in the midst of pipe dreams and illusory hopes, there are some hard facts of life which cannot be ignored. The size, the mass, the bulk, the overwhelming presence of certain realities command attention.

Hardly a fortune seeker who bravely set out in the days of '49 to find freedom and wealth in the magic of gold did not, sooner or later, "see the elephant" in the form of cold, thirst, hunger, poverty, disease, and sheer bone weariness—overwhelming realities of life in the gold mines of California.

Of course, one did not have to wait to reach California in order to see the elephant. One pioneer told his diary shortly after departure:

Some of the boys thought that they saw a *small portion of the 'Eliphant.'* [2]

Songs and stories celebrated the mighty beast of the mines and plains. In Mexico, Zachary Taylor met Santa Anna's Army and "showed them the Elephant just about right."

One prospective gold miner contemplated the visage of the beast:

> I'll take a ship some pleasant day,
> And sail across the sea,
> To find the monster Elephant,
> Wherever he may be.
>
> I wonder how the critter looks,
> And if he doesn't stand
> With hind feet on the waters
> And fore feet on the land.
>
> Eph says I'll see him, tusks and all
> Before I reach the diggin's,
> With the long tom lashed upon his back
> And all a miner's riggin's.[3]

In San Francisco, the gold rush was little more than a year old when the first of the great professional entertainers, "Doc" Robinson, staged his own musical show which he called "Seeing the Elephant." And a few years later, the miners' poet laureate; Old Put, permanently enshrined the powerful tusked beast in this song.

With guitar, um-pah through verse and first half of chorus. On "Oh no," strum hard on first and third beat of each bar mainly.

---

[1] "The Miner's Ten Commandments," from *The Golden Era* (1853) quoted in "The Localized Vocabulary of California Verse," Rena V. Grant, *California Folklore Quarterly,* Vol. 1, no. 3.
[2] *The Journal of Madison Berryman Moorman (1850-51).*

[3] "I Am Going To California," from *A San Francisco Songster (1849-1939)* WPA series.

SEEING THE ELEPHANT

1. When I left the States for gold, Ev-'ry-thing I had_ I _ sold: A

stove and bed, a fat old sow, Six-teen chick-ens and a cow. So

Chorus

leave, you min-ers, leave, Oh, leave, you min-ers, leave. Take_

my ad-vice, kill_ off your lice, Or else go up in the moun-tains;

Oh no, lots of dust, I'm go-ing to the cit-y to get on a bust.

When I left the States for gold,
Everything I had I sold:
A stove and bed, a fat old sow,
Sixteen chickens and a cow.

Chorus:

So leave, you miners, leave,
Oh, leave you miners, leave,
Take my advice, kill off your lice,
Or else go up in the mountains;
Oh no, lots of dust,
I'm going to the city to get on a bust,
Oh no, lots of dust,
I'm going to the city to get on a bust.

Off I started, Yankee-like,
I soon fell in with a lot from Pike;
The next was, "Damn you, back, wohaw,"
A right smart chance from Arkansas.

(Chorus)

On the Platte we couldn't agree,
Because I had the di-a-ree,
We there split up, I made a break,
With one old mule for the Great Salt Lake.

(Chorus)

The Mormon girls were fat as hogs,
The chief production, cats and dogs;
Some had ten wives, others none,
Thirty-six had Brigham Young.

(Chorus)

The damned fool, like all the rest,
Supposed the thirty-six the best;
He soon found out his virgin dears
Had all been Mormons thirteen years.

(Chorus)

Being brave, I cut and carved,
On the desert nearly starved;
My old mule laid down and died,
I had no blanket, took his hide.

(Chorus)

The poor coyotes stole my meat,
Then I had nought but bread to eat;
It was not long till that gave out,
Then how I cursed the Truckee route!

(Chorus)

On I traveled through the pines,
At last I found the northern mines;
I stole a dog, got whipped like hell,
Then away I went to Marysville.

(Chorus)

Then I filled the town with lice,
And robbed the Chinese of their rice;
The people say, "You've got the itch,
Leave here, you lousy son of a bitch."

(Chorus)

Because I would not pay my bill,
They kicked me out of Downieville;
I stole a mule and lost the trail,
And then fetched up in Hangtown Jail.

(Chorus)

Canvas roof and paper walls,
Twenty horse thieves in the stalls;
I did as I had done before,
Coyoted out from 'neath the floor.

(Chorus)

I robbed a nigger of a dollar,
And bought unguent to grease my collar;
I tried a pint, not one had gone,
Then it beat the devil how I daubed it on.

(Chorus)

The people threatened hard my life,
Because I stole a miner's wife;
They showed me a rope, to give me signs,
Then off I went to the southern mines.

(Chorus)

I mined a while, got lean and lank,
And lastly stole a monte bank;
Went to the city, got a gambler's name,
And lost my bank at the thimble game.

(Chorus)

I fell in love with a California girl;
Her eyes were gray, her hair did curl;
Her nose turned up to get rid of her chin,
Says she, "You're a miner, you can't come in."

(Chorus)

When the elephant I had seen,
I'm damned if I thought I was green;
And others say, both night and morn,
They saw him coming round the Horn.

(Chorus)

If I should make another raise,
In New York sure I'll spend my days;
I'll be a merchant, buy a saw,
So goodbye mines and Panama.

(Chorus)

I Often Think of Writing Home

WORDS: John A. Stone ("Old Put")
MUSIC: "Irish Molly, O"

From *Put's Golden Songster;* music from the singing of Logan English, *The Days of '49* (Folkways Record FH5255).

The mail has arrived—but no letter,
Why shouldn't he give up the ghost? [1]

THE mails were the lifeline to home and family and friends. Many a homesick miner turned up hopefully every day at the post office. Receiving letters was one thing, however. Writing them was another. Unless there was news of a lucky strike or a sudden bonanza to send back home, what was the point? Besides, philosophized Old Put for his miner audiences,

Writing don't amount to much unless you have the dimes.

[1] "The Vocal Miner," from *Put's Golden Songster* (1858).

This arrangement is for guitar. As the tablature at the top indicates, it is a semi-arpeggio um-pah-pah (pah) which continues almost without change through the song.

(Left hand play notes on 1st and 6th beats of each bar, right hand play 3rd and 4th beats.)

If performed with piano, both hands should share the bass line and the singer should take the tune alone. For an explanation of tablature see my Young Folk Song Book, *Simon & Schuster, N.Y., 1963, p. 14f.*

I OFTEN THINK OF WRITING HOME

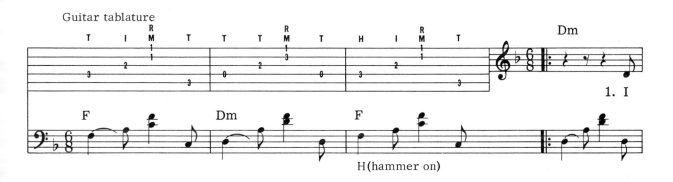

of - ten think of writ - ing home, but ver - y sel - dom write;_____ A

let - ter now and then I get, which fills me with de - light._____ But

while I'm here with Ro - mans I'll do as Ro - mans do,_____ And

let it rip, till I re - turn, and tell them all I know._____ For it

Chorus

keeps a man a hump - ing round to keep up with the times,_____ And

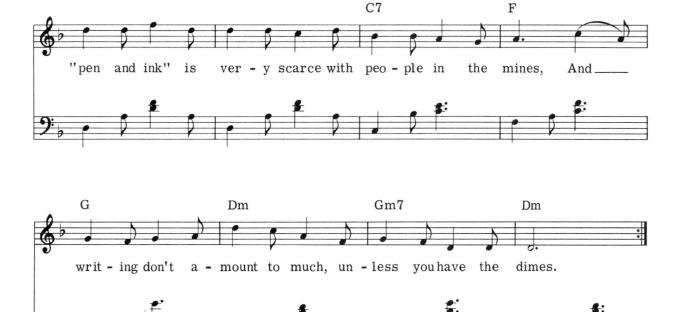

"pen and ink" is ver-y scarce with peo-ple in the mines, And_____

writ-ing don't a-mount to much, un-less you have the dimes.

I often think of writing home, but very seldom write;
A letter now and then I get, which fills me with delight.
But while I'm here with Romans, I'll do as Romans do,
And let it rip, till I return, and tell them all I know.

Chorus:

For it keeps a man a-humping round to keep up with the times,
And "pen and ink" is very scarce with people in the mines,
And writing don't amount to much, unless you have the dimes.

If I would write them every mail, I know it would them please;
But neighbors would then flock around them, like a swarm of bees,
And great would be the cry abroad that such a man's a fool,
And if he was a friend of mine, I'd have him sent to school.

(Chorus)

I've half a mind to drop a line and tell them I'm alive,
And watch the California boats whenever they arrive,
For I intend to home return, whene'er I feel inclined,
Then drop a line informing them I've lately changed my mind.

(Chorus)

I like to live among the hills, and pleasant mountain towns,
And like the cities better since they drove away the hounds;
But were they fifty times as fair, for all I would not fail
To be a man forevermore, and write them every mail.

(Chorus)

113

California As It Is

Words: Thaddeus W. Meighan
Music: "Jeanette and Jeannot" by Charles W. Glover

From the original sheet music (second edition) as "sung to over fifty thousand persons at the American Museum and elsewhere by Pete Morris, the inimitable comic vocalist," published by William Hall & Son, New York, N. Y. (1849).

In old forty-nine, this claim where I mine
Was counted the best in the land,
But expecting good pay, you may work it all day,
And find nothing but gravel and sand.[1]

THE miner lived on dreams. When water was low and the larder was empty, when credit was used up at the nearest commissary, his spirit was nourished by tales and myths of lucky strikes and paupers turned princes overnight.

The stories were outrageous and the miner laughed, but half-believed, because even the outrageous was almost possible in California. They repeated the tales to each other; of the miner who dug out a single lump of pure gold assayed at eight hundred thousand dollars; of the "dumb" Swede who was told by a group of pranksters to cut down a live oak tree and he would find gold under the stump, whereupon the Swede did so hitting a five thousand dollar pocket; of the lazy miner who hung his underwear in a stream overnight rather than wash it out, only to discover in the morning that he was the owner of a pair of gold-plated drawers; of the strike so rich, the miners had to wear green spectacles while digging out the gold in order to avoid being blinded by the glare of the ore.

Like any utopia, California was a sad reality for many an eager gold hunter. By the end of 1849, letters had already reached the east describing the disappointment of those who thought that the muddy streets of Sacramento were paved with gold. The second wave of ships to reach San Francisco began carrying the disillusioned back to eastern ports. From some letter or some first-hand report, a New York songwriter fashioned this ballad of California as it *really* was. Its effect on future westward migration was apparently negligible.

[1] "Poor Diggings," from *The Gold Digger's Song Book* (1856).

CALIFORNIA AS IT IS

Lively

I've__ been to Cal - i - for - nia and I__ have-n't got a dime, I've
on - ly got a spade and pick and__ if I felt quite brave, I'd

1.
lost my health, my strength, my hope, and I have lost my time. I've__

2.
use the two of them 'ere things to scoop me out a grave. This__

dig - ging hard for gold may be pol - i - tic and bold, But you

could not make *me* think so; but you may if you are told, Oh! I've

been to Cal - i - for - nia and I'm mi - nus all my gold, For in-

stead of rich - es plen - ty I have on - ly got a cold, And I

think - in' go - ing min - ing I was reg - u - lar - ly sold.

I've been to California and I haven't got a dime,
I've lost my health, my strength, my hope, and I have lost my time.
I've only got a spade and pick and if I felt quite brave,
I'd use the two of them 'ere things to scoop me out a grave.
This digging hard for gold may be politic and bold,
But you could not make *me* think so; but you may if you are told,
Oh! I've been to California and I'm minus all the gold,
For instead of riches plenty I have only got a cold,
And I think in going mining I was regularly sold.

I left this precious city with two suits of gallus rig,
My boots, though India-rubber, were sufficiently big
For to keep the water out, as well as alligators,
And I tell you now my other traps were very small potatoes;
I had a great machine, the greatest ever seen,
To wash the sands of value and to get the gold out clean,
And I had a fancy knapsack filled with sausages and ham,
And of California diggers I went out the great I Am,
But I found the expedition was a most confounded flam.

Now only listen to me and I'll tell you in a trice
That poking in the dirt for gold ain't more than very nice;
You're starved, stewed, and frozen and the strongest man he says
He's bound to have your money or he'll wallop you like blazes;
I was shot and stabbed and kicked, and remarkably well licked,
And compelled to eat poll parrots which were roasted but not picked,
And I slept beneath a tent which hadn't got a top,
With a ragged blanket round me and the ground all of a sop,
And for all this horrid suffering I haven't got a *cop.*

So here I am without a home, without a cent to spend,
No toggery, no wittles, and not a single friend;
With lizards, parrots, spiders, snakes, and other things unclean,
All crowded in my stomach and I'm very weak and lean.
But I ain't the only one that's got tired of this 'ere fun,
For about a thousand chaps are ready now to run
As hard as they can possibly, from there to kingdom come,
For there ain't nobody, sir, but here they might be *some,*
And enjoy their cakes and coffee and now and then some *rum.*

Moral:
If you've enough to eat and drink and buy your Sunday clothes,
Don't listen to the gammon that from California blows,
But stay at home and thank your stars, for every hard-earned cent,
And if the greenhorns go and dig, why coolly let them went;
If you go, why you will see, the *elephant,* yes sirree,
And some little grains of gold that are no bigger than a flea;
I've just come from California and if any here there be
Who is got that yellow fever they need only look at me,
And I think New York will suit 'em, yes exactly to a T.

The Lousy Miner

WORDS: John A. Stone ("Old Put")
MUSIC: Adapted by Earl Robinson from a traditional melody

From *Put's Original California Songster*.

My happy days are past,
The mines have failed at last,
The canyons and gulches no longer will pay,
There's nothing left for me,
I'll never, never see
My happy, happy home far away.[1]

DIRT was the gold miner's middle name. Not only did he dig in rock and mud in search of shining gold, but his clothes, his shack, his food, reflected the abominable living conditions which he endured in his quest for fortune. Even when he left his primitive camp and headed for San Francisco, he knew no respite. The mud-filled streets and filthy rooming houses of the bursting city only provided more of the same.

At times, it must have seemed that half of life was spent battling assorted rodents, flies, and contaminated food. But the miner's most celebrated torment was provided by the lice "as big as Chili beans" who attached themselves to their unlucky victims with a tenacity which had all the trappings of eternal damnation. The "lousy" miner became the symbol of a generation.

[1] "Unhappy Miner," from *Put's Golden Songster* (1858).

THE LOUSY MINER

1. It's__ four long years since I reached this land, In__ search of gold 'neath the rocks and sand; And yet I'm poor when the truth is told, I'm a lous-y min-er, a lous-y min-er, In search of shin-ing gold.

*The last verse and one or two of the others may be extended as follows:

In search of shin-ing gold, In search of shin-ing gold.

118

It's four long years since I reached this land,
In search of gold among the rocks and sand;
And yet I'm poor when the truth is told,
I'm a lousy miner, I'm a lousy miner,
In search of shining gold.

I've lived on swine till I grunt and squeal,
No one can tell how my bowels feel,
With slapjacks swimming round in bacon grease.
I'm a lousy miner, I'm a lousy miner;
When will my trouble cease?

I was covered with lice coming on the boat,
I threw away my fancy swallow-tailed coat,
And now they crawl up and down my back;
I'm a lousy miner, I'm a lousy miner,
A pile is all I lack.

My sweetheart vowed she'd wait for me
Till I returned; but don't you see
She's married now, sure, so I am told,
Left her lousy miner, left her lousy miner,
In search of shining gold.

Oh, land of gold, you did me deceive,
And I intend in thee my bones to leave;
So farewell, home, now my friends grow cold,
I'm a lousy miner, I'm a lousy miner
In search of shining gold.

Poker Jim

WORDS: Anonymous
MUSIC: "The Raging Canal," ascribed to Pete Morris

From *Johnson's New Comic Songs* #2, San Francisco (1863); music from the sheet music published by C. G. Christman, New York City, reproduced in *Low Bridge! Folklore and the Erie Canal*, Lionel D. Wyld.

A gambler's life I do admire,
The best of rum they do require,
The poker sharp begins to pout,
I played all night and cleaned them out.[1]

MANY a memorable character entered our folklore from the Barbary Coast stage. Sweet Betsy, Ike, Joe Bowers, and the lousy miner were all figures with whom the miners could identify. But what good is a hero without a villain? And so here is the "heavy" of California song—the double-dealing, smooth-talking deceiver and seducer known as "Poker Jim."

"Poker Jim" showed that the miner could expect only hard luck. Even good fortune proved a disaster for the hero of this song, who used his new wealth to bring his wife to California only to have Poker Jim (an ideal symbol in a town where the gam-

[1] "The Gambler," from *Put's Original California Songster* (1855).

blers pocketed the miners' gold as fast as it was panned) "sweet talk" his faithful spouse away.

There is no song more representative of the California Gold Rush than this one. Here is the topical songwriter in typical form, carefully constructing verses on every subject designed to appeal to his audience.

I am sure that the man who wrote "Poker Jim" is also the author of "Joe Bowers." Both appeared in Johnson song books, and the internal similarities are truly remarkable. And dare anyone say that the last two lines of "Poker Jim" were not created by the author of Joe Bowers' final sad cry that "the baby had red hair?"

POKER JIM

1. I'll tell you of my his-to-ry since eight-een for-ty-sev-en, When I
lived in old Mis-sou-ri, and my home was like a heav-en, I
had a bux-om lit-tle wife, as pret-ty as could be— She
said as how she loved me well, and I'm cer-tain I loved she.____

121

Now I'll tell you of my history since eighteen forty-seven,
When I lived in old Missouri, and my home was like a heaven,
I had a buxom little wife, as pretty as could be—
She said as how she loved me well, and I'm certain I loved she.

But there came a lot of news along, I shall ne'er forget the day,
About there being lots of gold in Californi-a;
I said "Goodbye" unto my wife, though my heart felt many pains,
But thought the road to fortune sure lay straight across the Plains.

The first place that I got into now is called Placerville,
In them days it was Hangtown, but they thought that ungenteel;
I went to work right willingly, with shovel, pick and pan,
And every chunk of gold I saved for my own Mary Ann.

In about two years I made a pile, though things were awful dear,
And then I started home again, to fetch my wife out here;
I took passage by the steamer, just because it went so quick,
But I'll never travel so no more, for the darned thing made me sick.

I stayed at home for half a year, and then we left for good,
My wife and children all were well, I was in a merry mood;
I bought a right good ox team, and a wagon for the trip,
And when we started, Mary Ann said, "Joshua, let 'em rip!"

We had a very pleasant time, and all got safely through,
I went to work right willingly, and so did my wife, too;
To make my home a happy one, my Mary Ann did try,
But very shortly after that began my mis-e-ry.

There was a noted gam-ba-ler a-living in our camp,
They called him Poker Jim and, oh, he was an awful scamp!
He used to come and talk to her while I tried to make a strike,
And said she was a fool to love such an ugly damned old Pike.

One night I felt almighty tired, I'd been at work all day,
When I got home the neighbors said my wife had run away;
My heart was nearly bursting, and my head began to swim,
She'd left a letter saying as how she'd eloped with Poker Jim.

I tried to keep my dander up, but felt awful bad, of course,
For the damned old critter she commenced an action for divorce;
She got it, and with Poker Jim she went off and got wed,
And the only ground she got it on, was because I snored in bed!

Hangtown Gals

WORDS: John A. Stone ("Old Put")
MUSIC: "New York Gals"

From *Put's Golden Songster;* music adapted by Earl Robinson.

First came the miners to work in the mine,
Then came the ladies who lived on the line.[1]

As the gold-hungry prospector flocked to California, so a whole army of entrepreneurs followed in his wake. Merchants, land speculators, saloon keepers, entertainers, and a wide assortment of professional con-men came seeking their fortunes, prepared to mine their gold from the easily-picked pockets of pleasure-hungry miners. In the van of this army were those indispensable adjuncts of civilization, the "ladies of pleasure." Some were "imported" by enterprising hotel keepers; others were private operators who came on their own. All were seeking their fortunes at a trade where no man could offer competition, and few women cared to.

Nine miles from Coloma, where James Marshall first discovered gold, the little mining community of Dry Diggings sprouted almost overnight. It was the first mining community, a sprawling conglomeration of tents and shacks without benefit of law or moral code.

[1] Traditional miner's couplet, quoted in *Copper Camp,* WPA Writer's Project of Montana.

In January of 1849, so the legend goes, a band of five armed men attempted to rob a Mexican gambler by the name of Lopez. Apprehended by the miners, a hastily improvised mass tribunal quickly found the culprits guilty of the crime, and then decided that the quintet was likewise guilty of several other misdeeds. After brief deliberation, the assembled miners decided to hang the thieves, a sentence which was carried out with dispatch.

As the story of this hasty dispensation of frontier justice spread to other mining areas, the little town of Dry Diggings was dubbed Hangtown. In later years the "ladies of the line" settled in various California mining communities; but the myth of Hangtown was strong, and popular belief was that the Hangtown whore was an outstanding symbol of a time-honored profession.

In time, Hangtown became Placerville, but the folklore of Hangtown and the fabulous "gals" who walked its streets has been indelibly inscribed on the pages of California history.

123

HANGTOWN GALS

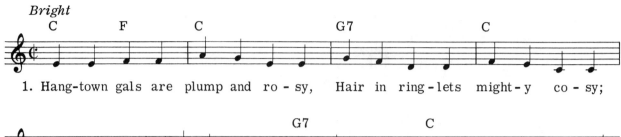

1. Hang-town gals are plump and ro-sy, Hair in ring-lets might-y co-sy;

Paint-ed cheeks and gas-sy bon-nets; Touch them and they'll sting like hor-nets. Oh,

Chorus

Hang-town gals are love-ly crea-tures, Think they'll mar-ry Mor-mon preach-ers;

Heads thrown back to show their fea-tures— Ha, ha, ha!___ Hang-town gals.

Hangtown gals are plump and rosy,
Hair in ringlets mighty cosy;
Painted cheeks and gassy bonnets;
Touch them and they'll sting like hornets.

Chorus:

Oh, Hangtown gals are lovely creatures,
Think they'll marry Mormon preachers;
Heads thrown back to show their features—
Ha, ha, ha! Hangtown gals.

They're dreadful shy of forty-niners,
Turn their noses up at miners;
Shocked to hear them say, "gol durn it!"
Try to blush, but cannot come it.

(Chorus)

They'll catch a neighbor's cat and beat it,
Cut a bean in halves to eat it;
Promenade in silk and satin,
Cannot talk, but murder Latin.

(Chorus)

On the streets they're always grinning,
Modestly they lift their linen;
Petticoats all trimmed with laces,
Matching well their painted faces.

(Chorus)

To church they very seldom venture,
Hoops so large they cannot enter;
Go it, gals, you're young and tender,
Shun the pick-and-shovel gender.

Humbug Steamship Companies

WORDS: John A. Stone ("Old Put")
MUSIC: "Uncle Sam's Farm" (Hutchinson Family)

From *Put's Original California Songster;* music from a folk song version of "Uncle Sam's Farm," "Bounding the U. S.," sung by Ellen Stekert, *Songs of a New York Lumberjack* (Folkways FA2354).

The only legal swindle which the people cannot sever
Is the steamboat imposition on the Sacramento River,
It would surely be a blessing if the company would fail;
Then should any other organize, ride them on a rail.[1]

OF all the '49ers who went to the mines seeking gold, only a few made the lucky "strike" which added up to sudden wealth. And for every miner who made his pile, California had a hundred others ready to steal it away from him. Card sharps, bunco artists, confidence men, shills and grifters of every description plied their trade in the saloons and rooming houses of San Francisco.

But the professional "sharpers" were just Johnny-come-lately amateurs compared to the "legitimate" businessmen who hijacked the local citizenry at every turn. The steamship companies so ably celebrated by "Old Put" were among the prime offenders. Some of their practices were outrageous chicanery; others produced terror and death, like the tragedy of the sinking of the steamship *Central America*. In a rare outburst of damning accusation,

"Old Put" memorialized the murderers for history.

The "Central America," painted so fine,
Went down like a thousand of brick,
And all the old tubs that are now on the line
Will follow her two at a lick.
'Twould be very fine were the owners aboard,
And sink where they never would rise;
'Twould any amount of amusement afford,
And cancel a million of lies.

These murdering villains will ne'er be forgot,
As long as America stands;
Their bones should be left in the ocean to rot,
And their souls be at Satan's commands.
They've murdered and swindled the people for
     years
And never will be satisfied
Till death puts an end to their earthly careers,
Then may they with demons reside.[2]

[1] "Steam Navigation Thieves, from *Put's Golden Songster.*

[2] "Loss of the 'Central America,'" *ibid.*

HUMBUG STEAMSHIP COMPANIES

Rhythmic, perky all the way

1. The —

greatest im - po - si - tion that the pub - lic ev - er saw Are the

Cal - i - for - nia steam - ships that run to Pa - na - ma;

— They're a per - fect set of rob - bers, and ac - com - plish their de-

signs By a gen-er-al in - vi - ta - tion of the peo - ple to the

mines. Then come a-long,_____

come a-long,_____ you that want to go,_____ The

best ac-com-mo - da - tions and the pas-sage ver - y low;_____ Our

127

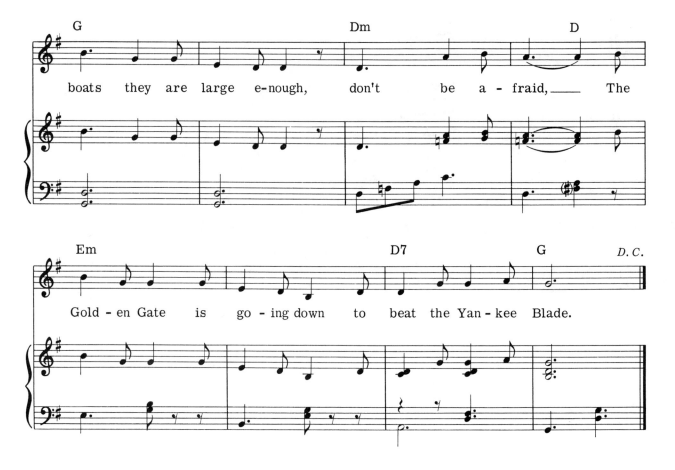

The greatest imposition that the public ever saw
Are the California steamships that run to Panama;
They're a perfect set of robbers, and accomplish their designs
By a general invitation of the people to the mines.

Chorus:

Then come along, come along, you that want to go,
The best accommodations and the passage very low;
Our boats they are large enough, don't be afraid,
The Golden Gate is going down to beat the Yankee Blade.
Then come along, don't be afraid,
The Golden Gate is going down to beat the Yankee Blade.

They have opposition on the route, with cabins very nice,
And advertise to take you for half the usual price;
They get thousands from the mountains, and then deny their bills,
So you have to pay the prices, or go back into the hills.

(Chorus)

When you start from San Francisco, they treat you like a dog,
The victuals you're compelled to eat ain't fit to feed a hog;
And a drunken mate a-cursing and damning you around,
And wishing that the boat would sink and every one be drowned.

128

(Chorus)

The captain goes to dinner and begins to curse the waiter,
Knocks him out of hearing with a thundering big potato;
The cabin maid, half crazy, breaks the meat dish all to smash,
And the steward comes a-running with a plate of mouldy hash.

(Chorus)

You are driven round the steerage like a drove of hungry swine,
And kicked ashore at Panama by the Independent Line;
Your baggage is thrown overboard, the like you never saw,
A trip or two will sicken you of going to Panama.

(Chorus)

California Stage Company

WORDS: John A. Stone ("Old Put")
MUSIC: "Dandy Jim of Caroline"

From *Put's Golden Songster;* music from *Songs for the People*, A. G. Emerick (1852).

You take a California stage,
You'll wear your *soles* out, I'll engage,
The driver's never known to fail,
To show you Foot and Walker's trail.[1]

In the first few decades of the Gold Rush, California's main means of public transportation was the stagecoach. Dozens of stagecoach lines plied their trade in and around San Francisco, providing a rugged frontier service for West Coast and overland travelers. The rules for stage travel were simple and direct:

"Onboard the stage a lady never speaks unless spoken to—properly. The best seat inside a stage is the one next to the driver. Don't let any sly elph (*sic*) trade you his midseat. Don't keep the stage waiting. Don't smoke a strong pipe inside the coach. Spit on the leeward side. If you have anything to drink in a bottle, pass it around."[2]

[1] "Few Days," from *The Gold Digger's Song Book* (1856).

In time, the smaller companies were all absorbed by the California Stage Company which exercised a monopoly over stagecoach travel for many years. Horace Greeley is supposed to have ridden the California Stage into Placerville on a wild and bumpy course which has since been celebrated in folklore. Presumably Old Put was a passenger, also, and his song has become history's epitaph for one of early California's most colorful and notorious enterprises.

I suggest an um-pah accompaniment through verse followed by a marching strum on every beat of the chorus.

[2] From the San Juan Batista Historical Monument, No. 180, quoted in *The Golden Road*, Felix Riesenberg, Jr.

CALIFORNIA STAGE COMPANY

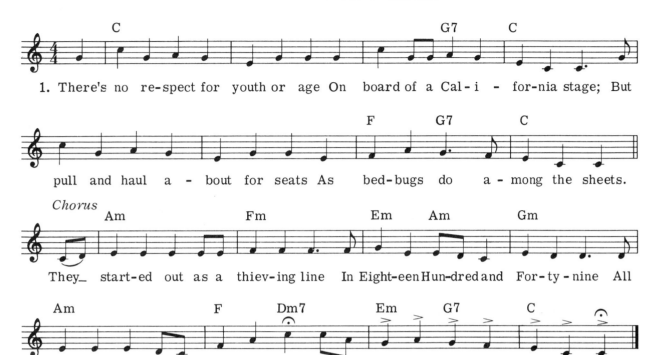

1. There's no re-spect for youth or age On board of a Cal-i - for-nia stage; But pull and haul a - bout for seats As bed-bugs do a - mong the sheets.

Chorus

They_ start-ed out as a thiev-ing line In Eight-een Hun-dred and For-ty - nine All "op - po - si - tion"_ they de - fy, So peo - ple must "root hog or die."

There's no respect for youth or age
On board of a California stage;
But pull and haul about for seats
As bed-bugs do among the sheets.

Chorus:

They started as a thieving line
In Eighteen Hundred and Forty Nine;
All "opposition" they defy,
So the people must "root hog or die."

You're crowded in with Chinamen,
As fattening hogs are in a pen;
And what will more a man provoke,
Is musty plug tobacco smoke.

(Chorus)

The ladies are compelled to sit
With dresses in tobacco spit;
The gentlemen don't seem to care,
But talk on politics and swear.

(Chorus)

The dust is deep in summer time,
The mountains very hard to climb;
And drivers often stop and yell,
"Get out all hands, and push—*up hill!*"

(Chorus)

The drivers, when they feel inclined,
Will have you walking on behind,
And on your shoulders lug a pole,
To help them through some muddy hole.

(Chorus)

They promise, when your fare you pay,
"You'll have to walk but *half* the way";
Then add *aside*, with cunning laugh,
"You'll push and pull the other half!"

(Chorus)

They have and will monopolize
The business, 'till the *people rise,*
And send them "kiteing" down below,
To start a line with Bates and Rowe!

(Chorus)

We Are All A-Panning

WORDS: Mart Taylor
MUSIC: "The Dodger Song"

From *The Gold Digger's Songbook;* music freely adapted by Earl Robinson from "The Dodger Song" *(The People's Songbook),* learned by The Almanac Singers from the singing of Mrs. Emma Dusenberry.

> Noo' we're a' noddin',
> Nid, nid noddin',
> And we're a' noddin',
> At our hoose at hame.[1]

AN old Scottish song celebrating the fact that "Jamie he's cam' hame" ("We're A' Noddin'") found its way to the gold fields of California where a local minstrel by the name of Mart Taylor adapted it to the vicissitudes of the mining life. Taylor was a popular singer of his day and had enough of a following to issue two songsters. The "Gold Digger's Song Book" contained his best work, including this one, and an interesting preface which helps to shed some light on the song-making rivalries of the gold rush era:

"By the earnest request of many of my mining friends in California, who have liberally patronized the entertainments given by my 'Original Company,' I have published in this little volume such of my songs as have been met with marked favor by the respectable audiences before which they have been sung.

I trust that those who may deem them worthy of possessing, will appreciate *one quality* they have above the only Song Book heretofore dedicated to the Miners of California. I refer to the indiscreet use of vulgar phrases, which characterize the said Song Book; which, I am happy to believe, is not suited to the tastes of my friends, the miners—to whom I would respectfully inscribe this little volume." [2]

Decades later, folklorists would come across still another descendant of the old Scottish song. This one, collected in the Ozark Hills, satirized the doctor, the lawyer, the preacher, and the farmer with the refrain:

> Oh, we're all dodgin',
> Dodge, dodge, dodgin',
> Oh, we're all dodgin'
> On our way through the world.[3]

For this song, pick the following rhythm:

Bass note suggestions for the first- and third-beat down picks are given in a few instances. Suggested picking for the last five bars follows:

Suggested picking for last 5 bars:

[1] "We're A' Noddin'," traditional Scottish song, quoted in *Our Familiar Songs,* Johnson.

[2] Preface, *The Gold Digger's Song Book* (1856).
[3] From the singing of Mrs. Emma Dusenberry, quoted in *The People's Songbook.*

WE ARE ALL A-PANNING

Chorus:

We are all a-panning, pan, pan, panning,
We are all a-panning just to get a little gold.

Those who come to California, come to make a little raise,
And they all go to panning in a hundred different ways.
   And they *still* keep panning, pan, pan, panning,
   And they still keep panning just to make a little gold.

(Chorus)

The merchant shows his articles and urges you to buy,
And he says they cost him dearly but "it's all in your eye."
   This is *his* way of panning, pan, pan, panning,
   This is his way of panning just to get a little gold.

(Chorus)

The preacher keeps a-preaching, going everywhere it pays,
He bestows the greatest blessing where he makes the biggest raise.
   'Tis a *pious* way of panning, pan, pan, panning,
   'Tis a pious way of panning just to get a little gold.

(Chorus)

And the crazy politicians all his enemies will curse,
While he seeks to get his fingers in the heavy public purse.
   'Tis a *tricky* way of panning, pan, pan, panning,
   'Tis a tricky way of panning just to get a little gold.

(Chorus)

The attorney all his knowledge of the statutes will reveal,
And you'd think him talking truly when he's lying like the de'il.
   'Tis a *wicked* way of panning, pan, pan, panning,
   'Tis a wicked way of panning just to get a little gold.

(Chorus)

There's the gambler has his cappers who are looking all about,
And when they can find a sucker they are sure to pan him out.
   'Tis a *thieving* way of panning, pan, pan, panning,
   'Tis a thieving way of panning just to get a little gold.

(Chorus)

And the robber comes upon you with a pistol or a knife,
And declares he'll have your money or he's bound to take your life.
   'Tis a *horrid* way of panning, pan, pan, panning,
   'Tis a horrid way of panning just to get a little gold.

(Chorus)

But the miner in his diggings keeps a-panning all the while,
And he's ever well contented when he's adding to his pile.
   'Tis an *honest* way of panning, pan, pan, panning,
   'Tis an honest way of panning just to make a little rise.

(Chorus)

Corrido de Joaquín Murieta

MEXICAN FOLK SONG

WORDS: From Alma Norteña
MUSIC: From the singing of Cleofes Vigil, San Cristóbal, New Mexico

Courtesy Jenny Vincent

I suppose you have heard all the talkin'
Of the very noted horse-thief Joaquín;
He was caught in Calaveras, but he couldn't stand the joke,
So the rangers cut his head off, and have got it now in soak.[1]

DOES folklore have a class point of view? Take the case of California's most notorious bandit, Joaquín Murieta. To the American settler and prospector, Joaquín was a ruthless, cold-blooded murderer, a horse-thief, a human scourge who spread terror through the countryside, counting his accomplishments in the trail of corpses left behind him. To the Mexican, displaced by the "gringo" gold hunters, Joaquín was a nineteenth-century Robin Hood, a daring raider, a folk symbol of resistance to the injustice of tyrannical marauders who had wrested the land from its rightful owners.

Joaquín was a Mexican-born miner who came to the Gold Rush country in 1849. After a series of tragic encounters with American miners in which he was flogged, his brother hanged, his wife raped, and his land stolen from him, Joaquín turned outlaw.

He organized a band which, for three years, terrorized the countryside, stealing and killing with an impunity matched only by their daring and skill. And then came the legends. According to some, every member of the band that had originally raped his wife, as well as all those who had lynched his brother, was hunted down and summarily executed by Joaquín's men. His feats as a horseman, a raider, a gunslinger, were recounted in hushed voices throughout the gold fields. "No matter who was robbed or killed," says Old Put in one of his songs, "'twas all laid to Joaquín."

Tales of sudden death on the highways, of summary roadside justice, of midnight acts of vengeance and daylight raids on armed outposts, of countless women who yearned for only the touch of his fingers, of open-handed fairness with those who dealt with him in friendship, all added to the myth. Joaquín became a figure of mystery, a super-outlaw capable of appearing without warning and covering impossible distances in the briefest of times. And despite all of the exaggeration, there was still enough truth to keep the legend alive.

Eventually, Joaquín was brought to "justice" by a hired gunman, Captain Harry Love. Led to Joaquín's hiding place by a traitorous friend, Love and his men surprised the outlaw and his chief comrade, "Three-Fingered Jack." In a running battle, both outlaws were killed, and as proof of their triumph, Love and his men brought Three-Fingered Jack's mutilated hand and Joaquín's head back to San Francisco. There, these grisly mementoes were placed on display, a San Francisco newspaper in 1853 announcing:

JOAQUÍN'S HEAD is to be seen at King's Corner of Halleck and Sansome Streets. Admission One Dollar.[2]

Twenty-one years old at the time of his death, Joaquín remains alive in folklore, a dimly remembered symbol of terror among descendants of the miners, a flaming symbol of resistance and vengeance in Mexican traditions, nowhere better exemplified than in this still-sung *corrido*.

[1] "Joaquín, The Horse-Thief," from *Put's Original California Songster.*

[2] Quoted in *The Barbary Coast,* Asbury.

135

CORRIDO DE JOAQUÍN MURIETA

Yo no soy americano,
pero comprendo el inglés;
yo lo aprendí de mi hermano
al derecho y al revés,
y a cualquier americano,
lo hago temblar a mis pies.

Cuando apenas era niño,
huérfano a mí me dejaron
sin quien me hiciera un cariño;
a mi hermano lo mataron,
ya mi esposa Carmelita
¡cuanto la martirizaron!

I am not American
But I understand English;
I learned it from my brother
Right-side-up and up-side-down,
And I can make any American
Tremble at my feet.

When I was just a little boy
I was left an orphan
Without anybody to love me;
My brother was killed
And my wife, Carmelita,
How she was tortured!

Yo me vine de Hermosillo,
en busca de oro y riqueza;
al indio bueno y sencillo
lo defendí con fiereza,
a buen precio los Sherifes
pagaban por mi cabeza.

Por cantinas he venido,
castigando americanos;
tú serás el capitán
el que mataste a mi hermano,
lo agarraste indefenso,
orgulloso americano.

Me he paseado en California
por el año del cincuenta;
con mi pistola fajada,
y mi canana repleta,
yo soy aquel mexicano,
de nombre Joaquín Murieta.

Ya nos vamos de estampida,
todos vamos a tropel,
con bastante caballada,
y cien mil pesos en papel,
también les traigo a Tres Dedos;
que ha sido un amigo fiel.

I came from Hermosillo
In search of gold and riches.
The good and simple Indian
I defended fiercely;
The sheriffs had put
A good price on my head.

I have been in every café
Fighting with the Americans;
"You then are the captain
Who killed my brother;
You caught him unarmed,
Proud American."

I was traveling in California
In the year (Eighteen hundred and) fifty
With my pistol in my belt
And the cartridge belt was full;
I'm *that* Mexican
Whose name is Joaquín Murieta.

We're going to make a raid,
It will be wild and fast,
With plenty of horses
And a hundred thousand pesos in bills;
I'm also bringing with me "Three Fingers"
Who has been a faithful friend.

*Use a pick if you like, and capo up if the key is
low for your voice.*

137

Twelve Hundred More

WORDS: Anonymous
MUSIC: "Wearing of the Green"

From a broadside sheet (circa 1870's) in the Library of the Society of California Pioneers.

We all are lovers of our home
And dread its future fate,
If Chinamen are still to come
To this our Golden State.[1]

FOR every event in history, the folk have a legend. Sometimes fact and folklore agree with each other; more often they do not. But historical truth seems to have little effect on the persistency with which the tales of the folk live on.

According to the legends of the folk, the great wave of Chinese immigration to California in the 1850's was a direct result of the gold miner's need for clean laundry. Facilities for laundering were so scarce in early San Francisco, so the story goes, that miners began shipping their dirty wash via Pacific Steamer off to the ports of Shanghai and Hong Kong, patiently waiting six months for the return of their clean garments. Discovering particles of gold dust in the miners' dirty clothes, and also motivated by the natural conclusion that they were better off bringing the laundry to the clothes rather than the other way around, Chinese began swarming to these shores in vast numbers.

Fact or folklore—or both—by 1852, there were an estimated 22,000 Chinese in San Francisco. Driven by starvation and abject poverty, the Chinese found the primitive and difficult conditions of early California a near-Utopia by comparison with their previous lot.

Barriers of language, religion, skin color, and cultural background helped create the conditions for a rigid system of discrimination against the Chinese. They were able to work only the poorest of diggings, and if, by some odd chance, a Chinese miner made a strike, some American prospector would quickly jump his claim. As a result, most of the Chinese became servants, laundrymen, and common laborers.

The Chinese provided a scapegoat on whom all the misfortunes of mining could conveniently be blamed.

Here we're working like a swarm of bees,
Scarcely making enough to live,
And two hundred thousand Chinese
Are taking home the gold we ought to have.[2]

And then, in 1865, as work on the Central Pacific's segment of the transcontinental railroad proceeded, Charles Crocker hit on the idea of employing the Chinese "coolies" on the back-breaking construction jobs of digging roadbeds and laying track. To those who objected that the smaller Chinese were too delicate of frame for the massive work required, Crocker replied with a classic rejoinder: "They built the Great Wall of China, didn't they?"

In the years immediately following the building of the railroad, thousands of now-unemployed Chinese returned to San Francisco. Inevitably, the

[1] "One and All," or "The Chinamen Must Go!" from the original sheet music by Will H. Pierce (1878), in the collection of *The Society of California Pioneers.*

[2] "The National Miner," from *Put's Original California Songster* (1855).

138

appearance of "low-cost" Chinese labor on the market worked as a weapon against the other workingmen. The prejudices of the fifties were revived in more virulent form. Anti-Chinese planks were adopted by the Workingman's Party, and a campaign to end Chinese immigration and to send the rest back to China was initiated.

The song "Twelve Hundred More" dates from that period.

The anti-Chinese political songs of the 1870's are now little more than historical footnotes. But in their wake came the stereotypes, still alive in our lore, living scars on our folk memory.

TWELVE HUNDRED MORE

1. O__ work-man dear, and did you hear the news that's go in' 'round? An-
oth-er Chi-na steam-er has been land-ed in the town. To__
day I read the pa-pers and it grieved my heart full sore, To
see up on the ti-tle page, O just "Twelve Hun-dred More!" O,__
Cal-i-for-nia's com-ing down as plain as you can see; They are
hir-ing all the Chi-na-men and dis-charg-ing you and me, But__
strife will be in ev-'ry town through-out the Pa-cif-ic shore, And the
cry of old and young shall be, "O damn Twelve Hun-dred More!"

O workman dear, and did you hear, the news that's goin' round?
Another China steamer has been landed here in town.
Today I read the papers and it grieved my heart full sore,
To see upon the title page, "O just Twelve Hundred More!"

O California's coming down as you can plainly see;
They are hiring all the Chinamen and discharging you and me,
But strife will be in every town throughout the Pacific shore,
And the cry of old and young shall be, "O damn Twelve Hundred More!"

They run their steamers in at night upon our lovely bay;
If 'twas a free and honest trade, they'd land it in the day.
They come here by the hundreds, the country is o'errun,
And go to work at half the price—by them the labor's done.

If you meet a workman in the street, and look into his face,
You'll see the signs of sorrow there, oh damn this long-tailed race!
And men today are languishing upon a prison floor,
Because they've been supplanted by this vile "Twelve Hundred More!"

Twelve hundred honest laboring men thrown out of work today
By the landing of these Chinamen in San Francisco Bay.
Twelve hundred pure and virtuous girls, in the papers I have read,
Must barter away their virtue to get a crust of bread.

This state of things can never last in this, our golden land,
For soon you'll hear the avenging cry, "Drive out the Chinaman!"
And then we'll have the stirring times we had in days of yore,
And the devil take those dirty words they call "Twelve Hundred More!"

Root Hog, or Die

WORDS: A. O. McGrew
MUSIC: "Root Hog, or Die" (Attributed to G.W.H. Griffin)

From "Songs of the Rocky Mountain Frontier" by Levette Jay Davidson, in *California's Folklore Quarterly*, Vol. II, No. 2 (April, 1943). Mr. Davidson cites the *Omaha Times*, Feb. 17, 1859, as the first printed source for the lyric, music from *Minstrel Songs Old and New*.

> In the summer of sixty as you very well know,
> The excitement at Pike's Peak was then all the go;
> Many went there with fortunes and spent what they had
> And came back flat-busted and looking quite sad.[1]

TEN years after the California Gold Rush, a new wave of gold-fever excitement swept the country with the discovery of "color" in the area around Pike's Peak in Colorado. A great surge of novice fortune seekers set out across the plains in the spring and summer of 1859, a raggle-taggle army of greenhorn prospectors and adventurous speculators, uprooted by the Panic of 1857 and seeking the elusive vision of sudden wealth in the western diggings. In their wake, they left a pockmarked mountainside, miles of abandoned wagons, mining rigs, tools and clothing, the state of Colorado, and a body of lore and song which has become part of the American tradition of hard luck and hoaxes.

The bubble of Pike's Peak was based on a small amount of fact and a great amount of fancy. The fact lay in the rich natural mineral wealth of the Colorado Territory. The fancy was the work of businessmen and land speculators in Kansas, Nebraska, and Colorado whose various enterprises were suffering from a shortage of patrons. With the first discovery of gold outcroppings around Cherry Creek, the rumors of a fantastic gold strike were urgently passed on to the rest of the country via carefully planted newspaper reports and frank advertising.

The anticipated results were not long in coming. Tens of thousands of emigrants hastened to Kansas City, Omaha, Independence, Leavenworth. They bought covered wagons, handcarts, tools, clothing, supplies. They fashioned crude signs and nailed them to the sheets of their prairie schooners. "Pike's Peak or Bust!" they proclaimed to the endless prairies as they followed the Platte or the Arkansas Rivers to Colorado.

But for most of them, Pike's Peak *was* a "bust." The wealth was there, but the mountains would not yield their riches to a man with a pick and pan. It would take machinery to separate the gold from the quartz—and great fortunes would be amassed in the years to come by men with the ingenuity and foresight to reap this harvest with power tools and blasting powder.

Meanwhile, the great trek West became a chaotic retreat East. The caravans about-faced and turned back across the prairie, their hopeful signs now reading "Busted, By Gosh!"

As keepsakes of the hoax, the victims left behind songs of Pike's Peak and the gold they never found. The best of these was set to the melody of a blackface minstrel number, "Root Hog, or Die," a stage favorite of the early 1850's.

[1] "In The Summer of Sixty," from *American Ballads and Songs*, Louise Pound.

ROOT HOG, OR DIE

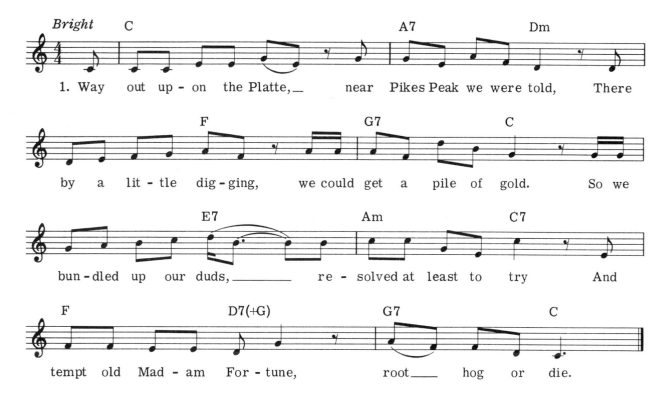

Bright

1. Way out up-on the Platte,__ near Pikes Peak we were told, There
by a lit-tle dig-ging, we could get a pile of gold. So we
bun-dled up our duds,_____ re-solved at least to try And
tempt old Mad-am For-tune, root__ hog or die.

Way out upon the Platte, near Pike's Peak we were told,
There by a little digging, we could get a pile of gold,
So we bundled up our duds, resolved at least to try
And tempt old Madam Fortune, root hog, or die.

So we traveled across the country, and we got upon the ground,
But cold weather was ahead, the first thing we found.
We built our shanties on the ground, resolved in spring to try,
To gather up the dust and slugs, root hog, or die.

Speculation is the fashion even at this early stage,
And corner lots and big hotels appear to be the rage,
The emigration's bound to come, and to greet them we will try,
Big pig, little pig, root hog, or die.

Let shouts resound, the cup pass 'round, we all came for gold,
The politicians are all gas, the speculators sold,
The "scads" are all we want, and to get them we will try,
Big pig, little pig, root hog, or die.

Surveyors now are at their work, laying off the towns,
And some will be of low degree, and some of high renown.
They don't care a jot nor tittle who do buy
The corner lots, or any lots, root hog, or die.

The doctors are among us, you can find them where you will,
They say their trade it is to cure, I say it is to kill;
They'll dose you and they'll physic you, until they make you sigh,
And their powders and their lotions make you root hog, or die.

The next in turn comes lawyers, a precious set are they,
In the public dairy they drink the milk, their clients drink the whey.
A cunning set these fellows are, they'll sap you till you're dry,
And never leave you till they have to root hog, or die.

A preacher now is all we want, to make us all do good;
But at present, there's no lack of *spiritual* food.
The kind I refer to will make you laugh or cry,
And it's real name is Taos, root hog, or die.

I have finished now my song, or if you please, my ditty,
And that it was not shorter is about the only pity.
And now that I have had my say, don't say I've told a lie,
For the subject I've touched will make us root hog, or die.

I'm Off to Boise City

WORDS: Author unknown
MUSIC: Traditional

Collected by J. Barre Toelken from a retired logger in Moscow, Idaho. See "Northwest Traditional Ballads," by Mr. Toelken, in *Northwest Review* (Winter 1962); also *A Garland of American Folksongs* sung by J. Barre Toelken (Prestige Records INT13023).

Oh, Jerusha! Who's gwine to go?
I'm gwine to California, so fotch along de hoe! [1]

BOISE, in the 1860's, was the center for a vast range of mining enterprises in the Northwest. From Owyhee, Ruby, Idaho City, Silver City, and other mining areas, the prospectors came into Boise with their new found wealth (when they had it) or with hopes of raising another stake for one more fling with Lady Luck.

"The chief business of Boise seemed to be drinking whiskey and gambling. The saloons were the handsomest buildings in town, and were thronged at all hours of the day and night. The gamblers occupied corners of these, and drove a brisk trade unmolested by anybody. . . . All the stores, restaurants, and saloons kept a delicate pair of scales, and their customers carried buckskin or leather bags of 'dust,' from which they made payment, and into which they returned their change. Disputes now and then arose, from the 'dust' offered not being up to standard, but these were usually settled amicably, unless the 'dust' proved basely counterfeit, and then the saloons sometimes flashed with bowie-knives, or rung with revolvers." [2]

The Idaho gold rush attracted prospectors from every state of the Union, including veterans of the Sacramento gold fields. It also helped revive some of the gold rush songs of California. Among the songs to grow out of the Idaho mines was this one, "I'm Off to Boise City." Taken literally, and at first glance, this would appear to be a song of Negro miners from those times, and, in fact, some folklorists have accepted it as such. There were, indeed, a considerable number of Negro prospectors in the goldfields but it seems most unlikely that this song was theirs.

For one thing, the song itself is based on an Eastern blackface minstrel ditty of the 1850's entitled "I'm Off For California." The verses parallel each other so directly that one must assume that the "California" song was the first-hand model for the "Boise" song:

Now darkies gather round me—I got a thing to tell;
'Twill make you burst your eyelids, and make your bosom swell;
The white folks all am crazy wid nuffin' in dar mouth,
But de mines ob California—who's a gwan Souff? [3]

[1] "I'm Off For California," H. De Marsan broadside sheet, (circa 1850).
[2] From *The Great West and the Pacific Coast*, James F. Rusling (1874), quoted in *The Frontier Moves West*, Warren S. Tryon.

[3] "I'm Off For California," *op. cit.*

145

I'M OFF TO BOISE CITY

146

147

Come gather 'round me miners, I got something for to tell;
Make you bust your eyelid and cause your bosom to swell:
The white folks must be crazy, the news it just came out,
The news from Boise City, and it's comin' from the South.
Way, hey, Jerusalem.

I have a wooden shovel, and another made of tin,
And the way I scoop that gravel up, it surely is a sin.
If them city white folks ask us who we be,
Just tell 'em it's the California Gold Mining Company.
Way, hey, Jerusalem.

I'm goin' downtown, the telegraph to hire,
And see if they need a colored man to greasen up the wire.
When I get down to Bannock, I'll take a cargo train,
Then on over to Centerville and I'll telegraph again.
Way, hey, Jerusalem.

Old Dan Tucker needn't want for his supper any more,
'Cause Abe's gonna take him down to that old Virginia shore.
I said, "So long and goodbye, my little Mary Blummer,
I'm off to Boise City, but I'll come back to get ya."
Way, hey, Jerusalem.

The elephant ate his pot pie and danced with the crocodile,
Oh, Jerusalem, where I was bound to go.
Was off to Boise City with a shovel and a hoe,
Pack up all your shiny clothes and we'll be on the go.
Way, hey, Jerusalem.

The Dreary Black Hills

Author unknown

Text from a broadside sheet (circa 1876) in the collection of the Society of California Pioneers, bearing the inscription "as sung by Dick Brown," and "published and sold wholesale and retail by Bell & Co., San Francisco"; music from *Singing Cowboy*, Margaret Larkin. Compare this contemporary text with versions collected by Larkin (above) and Lomax. *(Cowboy Songs)* for some fascinating examples of the folk process.

Come all you bold miners and list to my ditty,
I have a few words I wish to relate,
Of a generous company down on Big Rapid,
And most of them hail from the Grasshopper state.[1]

THE great gold rush of 1874 to the Black Hills of Wyoming and South Dakota was one of the grandest swindles ever perpetrated on the American public. It was not a complete hoax, for there certainly was gold in the Black Hills. There was just enough natural wealth, in fact, to make the swindle work.

One of the greatest lessons of the California gold rush was that the real fortunes were not to be made with pick and pan. The money came to those who transported the miners, sold them supplies, fed them, sold them liquor, gambled them for their dust, banked their wealth, entertained them, and bedded them down for a night or a trick.

The business panic of 1873 was a real shocker, one of those brutal economic upsets that almost overnight cause mass unemployment, foreclosures, bank failures, bankruptcies, and all the other woes attendant on the breakdown of the economy. Particularly hard hit were the railroads, and especially the Northern Pacific whose transcontinental line was not yet complete.

It was, apparently, some enterprising Northern Pacific officer who hit upon the idea of a "gold rush" to stimulate business. It had long been known that there was gold in the Black Hills of Wyoming.

Lucky strikes in 1834 and in 1852 (with Indians killing all the prospectors in the early expedition and all but one in the latter) were known to miners all along the Pacific Coast.

In 1873, the area immediately surrounding the Black Hills was Indian Territory, ceded to the Sioux by the treaty of 1868 "so long as the grass shall grow. . . ." But this was only a minor factor in the calculations of the desperate entrepreneurs who had concocted the grand scheme of the 1874 gold rush. Colonel George Custer became part of the plot and led an expedition into the Black Hills country. In a short time his report was spread throughout the nation: there was gold in the Black Hills!

The rush was on. From the soup lines of the eastern cities, from the deserted farms of Kansas and Nebraska (where grasshoppers had added to the trials of the depression with a savage assault on the crops), from the played-out mines of California and the southernmost cattle ranches of Texas, the prospectors came, swarming over the hills with pick and pan in search of fortune.

And in the wake of the miners came the businessmen. The railroad came to life again, transporting the prospectors, bringing goods and supplies to the suddenly booming establishments of Cheyenne. Restaurant operators, saloon keepers, gamblers, hustlers of every sort and description came

[1] "The Opening of the Hills," William Corslet, from "Black Hills Miners' Folklore," Hyman Palais, in *California Folklore Quarterly*, Vol. 4, No. 3.

to the Black Hills and the center for all the mining activity: Cheyenne. Cattlemen began driving their herds to Cheyenne ("... git along little dogies, you know that Wyoming will be your new home") to supply beef to a growing market, and to the stations of the Northern Pacific for delivery to Oregon and Washington.

In the process, the Sioux lost their land when the completely foreseeable conflict between Indian and white was climaxed by the massacre at Little Big Horn.

Now the gold rush of 1874 is only a footnote to history, one page recalled to memory by the song of "The Dreary Black Hills" of Wyoming.

THE DREARY BLACK HILLS

Kind folks, you will pity my horrible tale;
I'm an object that's needy and looking quite stale.
I gave up my trade, selling Wright's Patent Pills,
To go digging for gold in the dreary Black Hills.

Chorus:

Don't go away, stay at home if you can,
Far away from that city, they call it Cheyenne,
Poor old Sitting Bull and Comanche Bill
Will raise up your hair in the dreary Black Hills.

In Cheyenne the Round House is filled up every night
With Pilgrims of every description in sight;
No clothes on their backs, in their pockets no bills,
And yet they are striking out for the Black Hills.

(Chorus)

When I came to the Black Hills, no gold could I find,
I thought of the Free Lunch I left far behind;
Through rain, hail and sleet, nearly froze to the gills,
They call me the orphan boy of the Black Hills.

(Chorus)

Oh, I wish that the man who first started this sell
Was a captive, and Crazy Horse had him in—well,
There is no use in grieving or swearing like pitch,
But the man who would stay here is a son of a —.

(Chorus)

So now to conclude, this advice I'll unfold,
Don't come to the Black Hills a-looking for gold.
For Big Wallapie and Comanche Bill
Are scouting, I'm told, in the dreary Black Hills.

(Chorus)

The Old Settler's Song

(ACRES OF CLAMS)

WORDS: Attributed to Frank Henry
MUSIC: "Old Rosin the Beau"

Composite text from a variety of sources including *The People's Song Book*, Hille, and *Folksongs from the Olympic Peninsula and Puget Sound*, Knox.

> I hope and pray that every man,
> If mineral lands are sold,
> Will drop his shovel, pick and pan,
> And leave the land of gold.[1]

Of all the gold seekers who crossed the plains or sailed around the Horn in the early fifties, only a comparative handful found the wealth of their dreams. Of the seekers who did not find, some went back home (to Boston, New York, Philadelphia, and the farms of the Ohio–Kentucky regions), a short life of adventure over. But most went chasing other rainbows. They followed the rumors and whispers of fabulous strikes in southern California, in Oregon, in the dreary Black Hills of Wyoming. And in the process, these gold hunters settled the far West, finding an undreamed-of gold in the land and the wealth of the riches of nature. All over the West they settled, these hard-luck miners, and in time some of them went as far north as Puget Sound. This is their song, composed by some anonymous frontier poet [2] in the early days before Washington was a state, borrowing the tune of one of the best of the old British music hall songs, "Old Rosin the Beau."

Um-pah-pah is suggested here, occasionally breaking it with bass runs, hammer-ons, and strong strums on some of the F-chords.

[1] "That Is Even So," *Put's Golden Songster.*

[2] J. Barre Toelken credits an Oregon pioneer by the name of Frank Henry with authorship of the original text.

THE OLD SETTLER'S SONG

I've wandered all over this country,
Prospecting and digging for gold,
I've tunneled, hydraulicked and cradled,
And I have been frequently sold.

Chorus:

And I have been frequently sold,
And I have been frequently sold,
I've tunneled, hydraulicked and cradled,
And I have been frequently sold.

For one who gets riches by mining,
Perceiving that hundreds grow poor,
I made up my mind to try farming,
The only pursuit that is sure.

Chorus: The only pursuit that is sure, etc.

So rolling my grub in my blanket,
I left all my tools on the ground,
And started one morning to shank it
For a country they call Puget Sound.

154

Chorus: For a country they call Puget Sound, etc.

Arriving flat broke in mid-winter,
I found it enveloped in fog,
And covered all over with timber,
Thick as hair on the back of a dog.

Chorus: Thick as hair on the back of a dog, etc.

As I looked on the prospect so gloomy,
The tears trickled over my face,
For I felt that my trouble had brought me
To the edge of the jumping-off place.

Chorus: To the edge of the jumping-off place, etc.

I took up a claim in the forest,
And set myself down to hard toil,
For two years I chopped and I loggered,
But I never got down to the soil.

Chorus: But I never got down to the soil, etc.

I tried to get out of the country,
But poverty forced me to stay,
Until I became an old settler,
Then you couldn't drive me away.

Chorus: Then you couldn't drive me away, etc.

But now that I'm used to the climate,
I think that if man ever found
A spot to live easy and happy,
That Eden is on Puget Sound.

Chorus: That Eden is on Puget Sound, etc.

No longer the slave of ambition,
I laugh at the world and its shams,
And I think of my happy condition,
Surrounded by acres of clams.

Chorus: Surrounded by acres of clams, etc.

PART 5

"*Ride Around Little Dogies*"

Come all you jolly cowboys
That follow the bronco steer,
I'll sing to you a verse or two
Your spirits for to cheer.[1]

[1] From "Cowboy Songs and English-Scottish Ballads" by
Louise Pound, in *Nebraska Folklore*, Louise Pound.

THE LONE FIGURE of a man in a saddle astride a horse, riding off in an awesome sunset across the western plains has become a myth and a stereotype of our times. The cowboy has become a romantic legend, the symbol of an uncomplicated age of direct action and elemental justice. But before he became a figure of romance, the cowboy was the working-stiff of the plains, and his trade was an economic fact of American life.

In the period immediately following the Civil War, the raising and marketing of cattle became a major American industry. At first, in the 1860's, cattle roamed the open range and enterprising cowboys roped and branded as many head as they could handle, shipping them off to markets in California and the east.

In the 1870's, the work became more systematized. This was the decade of the great trail herds, of the drives from Texas to Montana and back again, the cowboy in search of grass and water for the longhorn cattle. In the 1870's, the cowboy rode the trail to Abilene and Dodge City and all the other railroad spurs where the beef could be sent on to the slaughterhouses of the east. In later years, the railroads would build right into the heart of the cattle country and the old Chisholm Trail would pass into folklore.

By the middle of the 1880's, cattle raising had become big business, and eastern money began to assume financial control of the massive enterprise. By the turn of the century, railroads and fencing had taken over. The open range and the day of the free-wheeling cowboy were almost gone.

The peak years were from 1870 to 1890; in those two decades, it is estimated that 40,000 cowboys drove more than ten million head of cattle to eastern markets.

The cowboys themselves came from a variety of backgrounds; perhaps the largest number were footloose Confederate veterans. Others had been lumberjacks in the piney woods of Maine and Michigan. Former sailors, miners, and patent medicine men could also be found riding herd on the old Chisholm Trail. Many an emancipated Negro decided to try his luck in the west as well:

> Away out there in Kansas
> So many miles away,
> The colored folks are flocking
> 'Case they are getting better pay.[2]

The particular nature of the cowboy's life helped develop a literature of song which was unique to the hard-riding cattle herders of the western plains. The isolation of life in the cow camp, the lonely society of men, the unique requirements of the

[2] "Goin' From the Cotton Fields," from *Ballads of the Kentucky Highlands*, Harvey H. Fuson. (This may, originally, have been a minstrel song, circa 1870).

job, all helped to contribute to that body of music we now think of as cowboy song.

Most cowboy songs did not originate on the plains. Many were adaptations of popular songs of the 1870's and '80's. Others were reworkings of older sailor and lumberjack pieces. Some were even able to trace their roots back to traditional ballads or half-penny broadsides of English and Irish origin.

A few songs arose directly out of the rigors and needs of the trail and the camp, borrowing freely from many sources but developing a character unique to the cowboy. In time, poets developed who were able to capture the mood and the idiom of the cowboy so well that some of their work became a part of cowboy folklore. But a folk song, which is always derivative, is much more than a sum of its parts. And these songs, the songs of the cowboys of our western plains, are, perhaps, more typical of America than any other aspect of our folk-song heritage.

I Ride an Old Paint

TRADITIONAL COWBOY SONG

This version adapted from Margaret Larkin, *Singing Cowboy*.

Oh, slow up dogies, quit your roving 'round,
You have wandered and tramped all over the ground;
Oh, graze along, dogies, and feed kinda slow,
And don't forever be on the go—
Oh, move slow, dogies, move slow.[1]

Work songs reflect the mood and rhythm of the singer's particular task. Sailors on the old clipper ships fitted their tunes and couplets to the hauling of the bowline or the raising of the sail. Track liners working in unison followed the steady tempo of their leader, swinging their hammers in one rhythm and one beat.

The cowboy's job was to tend his boss's herd, and his work song was designed to keep his charges under control. In a barroom at the end of the trail, or in a bragging session around the campfire, the cowpuncher might cut loose with a fast-paced ballad (like "Zebra Dun" or "Chisholm Trail") or a wild and exuberant musical high jinks. But on the trail, standing watch over several hundred (or several thousand) highly-tensed beasts, the cowboy needed songs which were soft and soothing and steady. For this reason, a great many cowboy songs have a pacifying quality, many of them, like this one, only one step removed from a lullaby.

When the air was charged with the electricity of an imminent thunderstorm, and the possibilities of a sudden violence touching off a stampede were in the wind, the boss would say, "Boys, I reckon you'll have to sing to them tonight."

"Nearly all the old authentic cowboy tunes were slow, as slow as a horse walks around sleeping cattle at night, and the majority of them were mournful."[2]

Keeping watch on his herd at night, the cowboy sang of faithful sweethearts at home and unfaithful sweethearts who could not wait, of wild men and bad men and gunslinging desperadoes, of hard luck and good luck, and the payday waiting at the end of the trail. He sang of places he'd been and places not yet seen. He sang of stampedes and heroes and the hardships of the trail. But most of all he sang of his horse, so frequently that common breed of pinto known as a "paint."

Holding G-chord, change second finger from A string to D string second fret. Pick D string with right thumb on the um *(pah-pah). Immediately after plucking D string pull off second finger, sounding the D string open, continuing with the two pah pahs.*

---

[1] Credited to Harry Stephens, by John A. Lomax, *Adventures of a Ballad Hunter.*

[2] J. Frank Dobie, *The Longhorns.*

I RIDE AN OLD PAINT

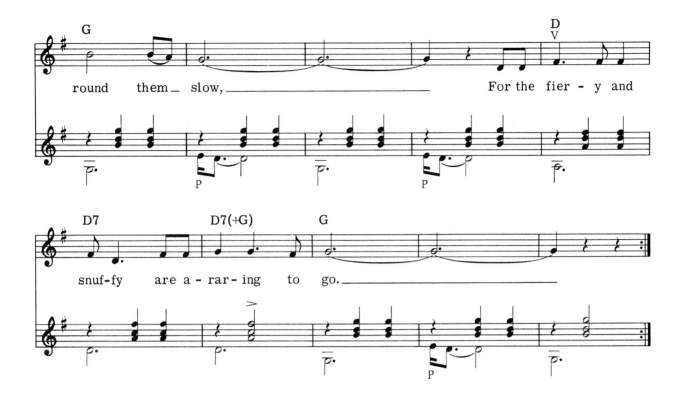

round them slow, _____ For the fier - y and

snuf-fy are a - rar - ing to go. _____

I ride an old paint and I lead an old dan,
I'm goin' to Montana for to throw the houlihan.
They feed in the coulees, they water in the draw,
Their tails are all matted and their backs are all raw.

Chorus:

Ride around little dogies, ride around them slow,
For the fiery and snuffy are a-raring to go.

Old Bill Jones had two daughters and a song,
One went to Denver and the other went wrong.
His wife she died in a poolroom fight,
But still he keeps singing from morning till night.

(Chorus)

Oh when I die, take my saddle from the wall,
Put it on my pony, lead him out of his stall,
Tie my bones to his back, turn our faces to the West,
And we'll ride the prairies that we love the best.

(Chorus)

The Old Chisholm Trail

TRADITIONAL COWBOY SONG

From the singing of Tony Kraber, with additional verses from versions collected by John A. Lomax, Carl Sandburg, N. Howard Thorp, Edith Fowke, Robert W. Gordon.

We left Nueces River in April, '81,
With three-thousand long-horned cattle
And all they knowed was run.
We got them through the brush all right,
Clear up to San Antone,
We got some grub and headed north,
As slick as any bone.[1]

Of all the songs the cowboys sang, none was more popular than the seemingly endless saga of "The Old Chisholm Trail." The tune, such as it is, may have somehow been adapted from Stephen Foster's old minstrel song, "Uncle Ned." Changing the rhythm and the tempo, scores of cowboy rhymesters used the melody to record every complaint, every incident, and every dream of trail life in one ballad. The collected verses number in the hundreds; the couplets which were composed and died around the campfire and on the trail undoubtedly would number in the thousands. But those are gone, along with the millions of longhorns who were driven to market from Southern Texas into Kansas along the Chisholm Trail.

Jesse Chisholm, son of a Scots father and a Cherokee mother, gave the famous trail its name. A rancher in the Indian territory which eventually became part of Oklahoma, Chisholm located a wagon trail from his ranch to a trading post on the north fork of the Canadian River. He later extended it so that he could trade with the Wichita Indians on the Washita River, making his trail a total of two hundred and twenty miles long. This was the original Chisholm Trail.

In time, as the cowboys drove their cattle over the old wagon road, the name became attached to the main pathway from southern Texas all the way to Abilene, Kansas, and the railway cars which would carry the beef to the eastern markets. Hundreds of spurs grew up, leading from ranches throughout Texas to the main trail, and each of these came to be considered part of the Chisholm Trail. At the peak of its use in 1875, the trail ran roughly from San Antonio, Texas, through Austin, Waco, Fort Worth, the Red River Station on to Wichita and Abilene. It crossed the Brazos, the Red, the Canadian, the North Canadian, the Cimarron, and the Arkansas Rivers, among others.

Later, other trails were developed further west. And on all of them, the cowboy brought along his song about the granddaddy of all the trails.

Jesse Chisholm died before he could see the seemingly endless herds of cattle follow the trail which bore his name. Today, the trail itself is but a memory, a legend from the days when the longhorn was king. In Oklahoma, a historical monument marks the spot where Jesse Chisholm found his last resting place:

JESSE CHISHOLM
Born 1805
Died Mar. 4, 1868
No One Left His Home Cold
Or Hungry [2]

[1] "The Ogally Song," from *We Pointed Them North*.

[2] *Red River Valley*, Harry Sinclair Drago.

THE OLD CHISHOLM TRAIL

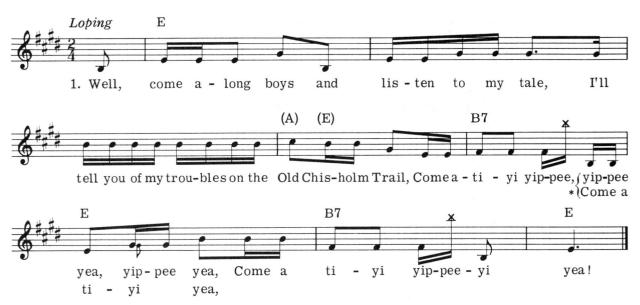

*Tony Kraber's version.

Well, come along boys and listen to my tale,
I'll tell you of my troubles on the **Old Chisholm Trail,**

Chorus:

Come a ti-yi yippee, yippee yeah, yippee yeah,
Come a ti-yi yippee, yippee yeah!

Now, a ten-dollar horse and a forty-dollar saddle,
I'm a-going to punching Texas cattle.

(Chorus)

My horse throwed me off, just like I was a bird,
He throwed me off near the 2-U herd.

(Chorus)

Last time I saw him he was goin' on the level,
A-kickin' up his heels and running like the devil!

(Chorus)

As soon as I recovered from the damned hard jolt,
I got a job a-punchin' for old man Bolt.

(Chorus)

Old Ben Bolt was a fine old man,
And you knowed there was whiskey wherever he'd land.

(Chorus)

Old Ben Bolt was a fine old boss,
But he'd go to see the gals on a sore-backed horse.

(Chorus)

'Twas early in the morning of October twenty-third,
When we started up the trail with the 2-U herd.

(Chorus)

I woke up one morning on the Old Chisholm Trail,
A rope in my hand and a cow by the tail.

(Chorus)

I'm in my saddle before daylight,
And afore I sleeps, the moon shines bright.

(Chorus)

A-roping and a-tying and a-branding all day,
I'm working mighty hard for mighty little pay.

(Chorus)

Well, it's bacon and beans most every day,
I'd as soon be eatin' prairie hay.

(Chorus)

It's cloudy in the west and a-lookin' like rain,
And my damned old slicker's in the wagon again.

(Chorus)

The wind begin to blow and the rain begin to fall,
And it looked, by grab, like we was goin' to lose 'em all.

(Chorus)

Well, I jumped in the saddle and grabbed hold the horn,
Best god-damned cowboy ever was born.

(Chorus)

My feet are in the stirrups and my rope is on the side,
Show me a horse that I can't ride.

(Chorus)

We didn't give a damn if they never did stop,
We'd ride along like an eight-day clock.

(Chorus)

A heifer went loco and the boss said, "Kill it!"
Shot him in the arse with a long-handed skillet.

(Chorus)

166

I'll drive my herd to the top of the hill,
And I'll kiss my gal, by grab, I will.

(Chorus)

I got a gal, prettiest gal you ever saw,
And she lives on the banks of the Deep Cedar Draw.

(Chorus)

Well, I met a little gal and I offered her a quarter,
She says, "Young man, I'm a gentleman's daughter."

(Chorus)

We all hit town, and we hit her on the fly,
We bedded down the cattle on a hill nearby.

(Chorus)

Then we rounded 'em up and we put 'em in the cars,
And that was the end of the Two Old Bars.

(Chorus)

I've herded and I've hollered and I done very well,
Till the boss said, "Boys, just let 'em go to hell!"

(Chorus)

Goin' back to town to draw my money,
Goin' back to town to see my honey.

(Chorus)

I went to the boss to draw my roll,
He figgered me out nine dollars in the hole.

(Chorus)

So I went to the boss and we had a little chat,
I hit him in the face with my big slouch hat.

(Chorus)

The boss says to me, "Why, I'll fire you;
Not only you, but the whole damn crew!"

(Chorus)

I'll sell my horse and I'll sell my saddle;
You can go to hell with your longhorn cattle.

(Chorus)

I'll sell my outfit just as soon as I can,
I won't punch cattle for no damned man.

(Chorus)

I'll sell my saddle and I'll buy me a plow.
And I swear, by God, I'll never rope another cow.

(Chorus)

I'm goin' to Oklahoma to get me a squaw,
And raise papooses for my paw-in-law.

(Chorus)

Now I've punched cattle from Texas to Maine,
And I've known some cowboys by their right name.

(Chorus)

With my feet in the stirrup and my seat in the sky,
I'll quit punchin' cows in the sweet bye-and-bye.

(Chorus)

The Buffalo Skinners

TRADITIONAL COWBOY SONG

From *Cowboy Songs*, John A. and Alan Lomax; a footnote in the Lomax collection quotes J. E. McCauley, of Seymour, Texas, who states: "Song made by Buffalo Jack. I don't know the author or how it come to be wrote, or anything of that kind, but they must have been somebody of that name for a starter." Collected, adapted and arranged by John A. and Alan Lomax. Copyright 1934 and renewed 1962, Ludlow Music Inc., New York, N. Y.

> It's all of the day long as we go tramping round,
> In search of the buffalo that we may shoot him down;
> . . . We rob him of his robe and think it is no harm,
> To buy us food and clothing to keep our bodies warm.[1]

MANY a hard-working, hard-riding man rode the western plains, but none worked harder, rode harder, or fought harder than the buffalo skinner. His was a primitive trade that lasted barely twenty years, from 1870 to 1890. But in that time, the mighty buffalo, once the lord of the prairie, vanished from the face of America.

A handful of enterprising operators made contact with eastern outlets who were primarily interested in buffalo hides. These operators, in turn, hired local bosses who gathered together crews of buffalo skinners from the cowhands and wanderers of the frontier towns. And so the slaughter began. One New York firm bought 177,142 buffalo robes during the years 1876 to 1884 at a total cost of $709,000.

The little Texas town of Jacksboro was a center for this savage trade and, so legend has it, no tougher group of men ever assembled in any one place on earth than were gathered together in this Texas town in the early 1870's.

According to John A. Lomax who first found this old song, the story is a true one. An old-time buffalo hunter who claimed to have been there told Lomax the story:

"It was a hell of a trip down Pease River, lasting several months. We fought sandstorms, flies, bed-bugs, wolves, and Indians. At the end of the season old Crego announced he had lost money and could not pay us off. We argued the question with him.

He didn't see our side of things, so we shot him down and left his damned old bones to bleach where we had left so many stinking buffalo. On the way back to Jacksboro, one of the boys started up a song about the trip and the hard times and old Crego and we all set in to help him. Before we got back to Jacksboro we had shaped it up and the whole crowd could sing it." [2]

The song itself has a history, and perhaps that history will give us some clue as to the ways in which folk songs grow.

A popular English song of the early nineteenth century was "Canada-I-O," a fairly typical romantic piece concerning a sailor and his love. In the early 1850's, a lumberman by the name of Ephraim Braley, returning from a particularly hard trip to Quebec, composed a song he called "Canaday-I-O," based in part on the older English song. It quickly became popular among lumberjacks who adapted it to their own circumstances, singing (in Pennsylvania) of "Colley's Run-I-O," and (further west) of "Michigan-I-O."

In time, the lumberjack song went west, perhaps

---

[1] "The Buffalo Hunters," from *Cowboy Songs*, Lomax.

[2] From *Folk Song U. S. A.*, Lomax.

with some wandering woodsman who decided to take another crack at good luck in a different clime. Out on the buffalo trail, a new and dramatic detail was added to the old story, culminating in an ironic image of old Crego's bones bleached white under the prairie sun. In time the human bones and the buffalo bones would return to the earth together, killer and victim undistinguishable one from the other.

Now the buffalo is gone; the skinners are gone and so are all the Cregos who were hard-bitten skinners of another kind. Even the ballads are all gone—all except this one, perhaps the greatest Western song of them all.

This tune may be played with an um-pah accompaniment as follows, varying it occasionally with a fast, full, six-note strum on the held notes, and also on the first and fourth beats of the last two bars of each verse:

THE BUFFALO SKINNERS

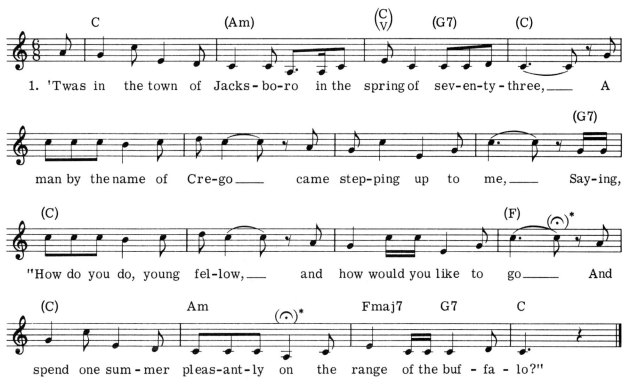

1. 'Twas in the town of Jacks-bo-ro in the spring of sev-en-ty-three,____ A
man by the name of Cre-go____ came step-ping up to me,____ Say-ing,
"How do you do, young fel-low,____ and how would you like to go____ And
spend one sum-mer pleas-ant-ly on the range of the buf-fa-lo?"

*One or the other of these holds (rarely both) is occasionally used to vary the sameness of the rhythm.

'Twas in the town of Jacksboro in the spring of seventy-three,
A man by the name of Crego came stepping up to me,
Saying, "How do you do, young fellow, and how would you like to go
And spend one summer pleasantly on the range of the buffalo?"

It's me being out of employment, this to Crego I did say,
"This going out on the buffalo range depends upon the pay.
But if you will pay good wages and transportation too,
I think sir, I will go with you to the range of the buffalo."

"Yes, I will pay good wages, give transportation too,
Provided you will go with me and stay the summer through;
But if you should grow homesick, come back to Jacksboro,
I won't pay transportation from the range of the buffalo."

It's now our outfit was complete, seven able-bodied men,
With navy six and needle gun, our troubles did begin;
Our way it was a pleasant one, the route we had to go,
Until we crossed Pease River on the range of the buffalo.

It's now we've crossed Pease River, our troubles have begun.
The first damned tail I went to rip, Christ! how I cut my thumb!
While skinning the damned old stinkers our lives they had no show,
For the Indians watched to pick us off while skinning the buffalo.

He fed us on such sorry chuck I wished myself most dead,
It was old jerked beef, croton coffee, and sour bread.
Pease River's as salty as hell fire, the water I could never go,
O God! I wished I had never come to the range of the buffalo.

Our meat it was buffalo hump and iron wedge bread,
And all we had to sleep on was a buffalo robe for a bed;
The fleas and gray-backs worked on us, O boys, it was not slow,
I'll tell you there's no worse hell on earth than the range of the buffalo.

Our hearts were cased with buffalo hocks, our souls were cased with steel
And the hardships of that summer would nearly make us reel.
While skinning the damned old stinkers our lives they had no show,
For the Indians waited to pick us off on the hills of Mexico.

The season being near over, old Crego he did say
The crowd had been extravagant, was in debt to him that day;
We coaxed him and we begged him and still it was no go,
We left old Crego's bones to bleach on the range of the buffalo.

Oh, it's now we've crossed Pease River and homeward we are bound,
No more in that hell-fired country shall ever we be found.
Go home to our wives and sweethearts, tell others not to go,
For God's forsaken the buffalo range and the damned old buffalo.

Git Along, Little Dogies

TRADITIONAL COWBOY SONG

Though your backs they are weak,
And your legs, they ain't strong,
Don't be scared, little dogies,
We'll get there 'fore long.
Hi yi yip, git along! [1]

OVER the mysterious highways and by-ways of the folk process, an old Irish song found its way to the western prairies and became one of the most popular cowboys songs of them all. Perhaps, like "Buffalo Skinners," the song followed the northern route through the lumber camps of Maine and Michigan and on to Texas in the memory of a lumberjack turned cowpuncher; or else, like "Streets of Laredo," it may have traveled a more southerly path, coming to the west, perhaps, via a restless Irish immigrant who forgot to stop in Boston or New York.

The original of this song is still very much alive in Ireland today, where a Dublin street musician may still sing:

As I was walkin' one evening for pleasure,
Down by the still river I joggled along.
I met an old man making sad lamentation,
And rocking the cradle, the child not his own.

Ee-i-o, my laddy, lie easy,
It's my misfortune and none of your own,
That she leaves me here weepin' and rockin' the cradle,
And nursing a baby that's none of my own.[2]

The cowboy song, as collected by John A. Lomax, is the first to use the term, "dogie." Howard Thorp believes that the term derives from the Spanish *dogal*, used by the Mexican cowboys to refer to the halter by which a calf was kept from its mother. Ranchers' lore, on the other hand, believes that the word is a short form of "dough-guts," by which cowmen referred to calves who were turned out to grass at a tender age because "its mammy is dead and its pappy ran off with another cow."

The song was used as a day-herding call, useful for driving the longhorns along the rough trail that led from Texas to Wyoming and beyond.

[1] "Cowboy Song," from *Ozark Folksongs*, Vol. 2, Vance Randolph.

[2] "The Old Man Rocking the Cradle," from the singing of Robin Roberts learned from Seamus Ennis in Dublin, Ireland.

GIT ALONG, LITTLE DOGIES

1. As I was a-walk-ing one morn-ing for pleas-ure, I spied a cow-punch-er a rid-ing a-long; His hat was throwed back and his spurs were a-jing-lin', As he ap-proached me a-sing-in' this song:___ Whoop-ee ti yi yo___ git a-long,___ lit-tle do-gies, It's

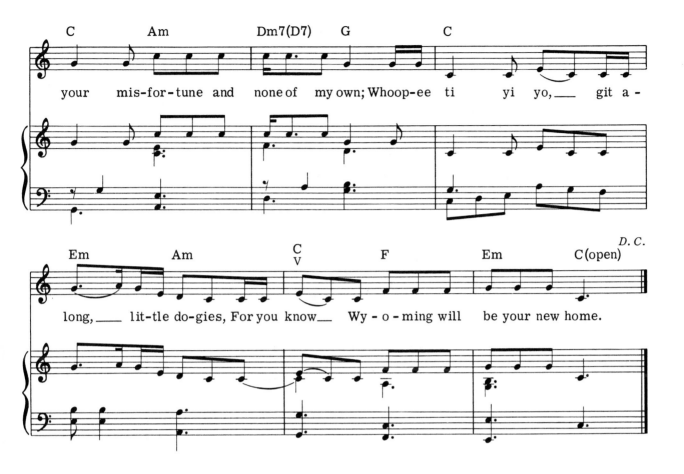

your mis-for-tune and none of my own; Whoop-ee ti yi yo,___ git a-

long,___ lit-tle do-gies, For you know___ Wy-o-ming will be your new home.

As I was a-walking one morning for pleasure,
I spied a cowpuncher a-riding along;
His hat was thrown back and his spurs were a-jinglin',
As he approached me a-singin' this song:

Chorus:

Whoopee ti yi yo, git along, little dogies,
It's your misfortune and none of my own;
Whoopee ti yi yo, git along, little dogies,
For you know Wyoming will be your new home.

Early in the springtime we'll round up the dogies,
Slap on their brands and bob off their tails;
Round up our horses, load up the chuck wagon,
Then throw those dogies upon the trail.

(Chorus)

It's whooping and yelling and driving the dogies,
Oh, how I wish you would go on,
It's whooping and punching and go on, little dogies,
For you know Wyoming will be your new home.

(Chorus)

175

Some of the boys goes up the trail for pleasure,
But that's where they git it most awfully wrong;
For you haven't any idea the trouble they give us,
When we go driving them dogies along.

(Chorus)

When the night comes on and we hold them on the bed-ground,
These little dogies that roll on so slow;
Roll up the herd and cut out the strays,
And roll the little dogies that never rolled before.

(Chorus)

Your mother she was raised way down in Texas,
Where the jimson weed and sandburs grow;
Now we'll fill you up on prickly pear and cholla,
Till you are ready for the trail to Idaho.

(Chorus)

Oh, you'll be soup for Uncle Sam's Injuns,
"It's beef, heap beef," I hear them cry.
Git along, git along, git along, little doggies,
You're going to be beef steers by and by.

(Chorus)

Cowboy's Gettin'-Up Holler

(MORNING GRUB HOLLER)

TRADITIONAL

After the singing of Pete Seeger (*Frontier Ballads*, Folkways Records FH5003), with additional words from other sources.

It was chuck-time on the round up, and we heard "Old Doughy" shout
"You had better come and get this or I'll throw the whole thing out."
So we headed for the wagon like a wild stampeded herd,
Fearful every minute lest the cook might keep his word.[1]

THE cowboy on a round up or on the trail was up at the crack of dawn; but the camp cook was up even earlier, making his fire, putting the coffee up, baking his hoecakes for the hungry cowpunchers who had a long day's work ahead of them. Many camp cooks were Negroes, ex-slaves who had drifted out west in search of fortune and an escape from the scenes of their bondage. With a singing tradition of centuries behind him, the Negro cook was also frequently the creator and preserver of the cowboy song.

It was a tough job, cooking for several dozen cowboys under difficult conditions. It was a long job, too, and a good cook earned his comparatively handsome pay.

In some of the smaller camps, there was no cook. Then the men would choose a cook by lot. It was a process which may have led to indigestion, but the system did not encourage complaints:

"You know the rules in a cowcamp when they have no regular cook? When anybody complains about the chuck, they have to do the cooking. One cowboy broke open a biscuit and he says: 'They are burnt on the bottom and top and raw in the middle and salty as hell, but shore fine. Just the way I like 'm.'"[2]

Sing without accompaniment, or use A-chord throughout.

[1] "Chuck-Time On The Round-Up," by Austin Corcoran, from *Songs of the Cowboys*, N. Howard Thorp.

[2] "A Corral Full of Stories," Joe M. Evans, quoted in *This Is The West*, Robert West Howard.

COWBOY'S GETTIN'-UP HOLLER

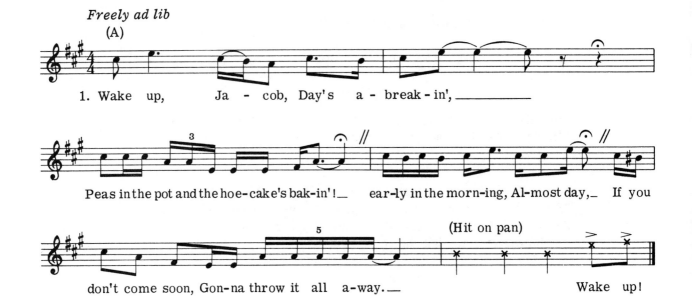

Freely ad lib
(A)

1. Wake up, Ja - cob, Day's a - break - in', _____

Peas in the pot and the hoe-cake's bak-in'! _ ear-ly in the morn-ing, Al-most day, _ If you

(Hit on pan)

don't come soon, Gon-na throw it all a-way. _   Wake up!

Wake up, Jacob,
Day's a-breakin',
Peas in the pot
And the hoecake's bakin'!

Early in the morning,
Almost day,
If you don't come soon,
Gonna throw it all away.

Wake up, Jacob!
Bacon in the pan,
Coffee in the pot,
Get up and get it—
Get it while it's hot.

178

Good-bye Old Paint

Text from *Songs of the Cowboys*, by N. Howard Thorp, who writes: "Heard this sung by a puncher who had been on a spree in Pecos City. He had taken a job temporarily as sheep-rustler for an outfit in Independence Draw, down the river, and was ashamed of the job. I won't mention his name."

Old Paint had a colt down on the Rio Grande,
And the colt couldn't pace, and they named it Cheyenne.[1]

FROM Texas to Wyoming and Montana—and back again—this was the pattern as the cowboy followed the grazing grass through the changing seasons. This is one of the oldest cowboy songs we know, a simple, haunting refrain and a hatful of easy-loping couplets. In the days when cattle-herding was still young, the song was already old. An ex-slave by the name of Charley Willis heard it on the Texas–Wyoming trail back in the heyday of the mighty cattle drives, and it was already a folk song then.

The song survived the cattle age, holding a place in the living traditions of the western country. In 1910, an Oklahoman told John Lomax:

"Out in my country, we do not dance 'Home Sweet Home' for the last waltz at a cowboy breakdown; instead we stop the music and all sing and dance, to slow waltz time, 'Good-bye Old Paint.'"[2]

[1] From the singing of Jess Morris, Dalhart, Texas, recorded by John A. Lomax, *Library of Congress* Record AAFS L28, *Cowboy Songs, Ballads and Cattle Calls*.

[2] Boothe Merrill, quoted in *Adventures of a Ballad Hunter*, John A. Lomax.

GOOD-BYE OLD PAINT

Chorus:

Good-bye, old Paint, I'm a-leavin' Cheyenne,
Good-bye, old Paint, I'm a-leavin' Cheyenne;
I'm a-leavin' Cheyenne, I'm off to Montana,
Good-bye, old Paint, I'm a-leavin' Cheyenne.

My foot in the stirrup, my pony won't stand,
Good-bye, old Paint, I'm a-leavin' Cheyenne.

(Chorus)

Old Paint's a good pony, he paces when he can,
Good-bye, little Annie, I'm off for Cheyenne.

(Chorus)

Oh, hitch up your horses and feed 'em some hay,
And seat yourself by me so long as you stay.

(Chorus)

My horses ain't hungry, they'll not eat your hay,
My wagon is loaded and rolling away.

(Chorus)

My foot in the stirrup, the reins in my hands,
Good morning, young lady, my horses won't stand.

(Chorus)

Corrido de Kansas

TRADITIONAL COWBOY SONG

From *Mexican Border Ballads*, Texas Folklore Publications XXI, 1946. Reprinted by permission of the Texas Folklore Society.

Come, all you old-timers, and listen to my song;
I'll make it short as possible and I'll not keep you long;
I'll relate to you about the time you all remember well,
When we with old Joe Garner drove a beef herd up the trail.[1]

The first cowboys in the west were the Mexican *vaqueros* who tended cattle on the west Texas plains several decades before the *gringos* were driving the herds along Jesse Chisholm's old wagon trail. Cowboy lore and song were fashioned in the shadow of the Spanish idiom, and the language of the range is rich in words of Spanish origin (remuda, lariat, stampede, rodeo, pinto, corral, buckaroo, and many others).

The narrative ballads of the Mexican cowboys were called *corridos* from the Spanish *correr* ("to run"), or a running account of an event. Sometime in the 1880's, a group of Mexican cowboys followed one of the old cattle trails north to Kansas and the railroads; one of them, an anonymous *vaquero* poet, made a ballad out of their trip, a *corrido* which became a part of the folklore of the southwest.

[1] "John Garner's Trail Herd," from *Songs of the Cowboys*, N. Howard Thorp.

Suggested guitar (arpeggio) style:

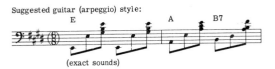

(exact sounds)

181

CORRIDO DE KANSAS

1. Cuan-do sa - li-mos pa' Kan-sas_____ Con u - na gran-de par -
ti - da_____ Nos de - cí - a el ca - po - ral:_____ No cuen -
to ni con mi vi - da._____

Cuando salimos pa' Kansas
Con una grande partida,
Nos decía el caporal:
—No cuento ni con mi vida.

Quinientos novillos eran
Pero todos muy livianos,
No los podíamos reparar
Siendo treinta mexicanos.

Cuando llegamos a Kansas
Un torito se peló,
Fue a tajarle un mozo joven
Y el caballo se volteó.

Cuando dimos vista a Kansas
Se vio un fuerte aguacero,
No los podíamos reparar
Ni formar un tiroteo.

Cuando dimos vista a Kansas
Era puritita correr,
Eran los caminos largos,
Y pensaba yo en volver.

La madre de un aventurero
Le pregunta al caporal:
—Oiga, déme razón de mi hijo,
Que no lo he visto llegar.

—Señora, le voy a decir
Pero no se vaya a llorar,
A su hijo le mató un novillo
En la puerta de un corral.

When we left for Kansas
With a large party,
The foreman said to us:
"I don't count on even my own life."

There were fifteen-hundred steers
And they were all very wild,
We could not keep them herded
Being only thirty Mexicans.

When we arrived in Kansas
A young steer took out (of the herd),
A young boy went to cut him off
And his horse fell down.

When we came in sight of Kansas
There was a heavy rain-shower,
We could not keep them herded
Nor get a shooting started.

When we came in sight of Kansas
It was nothing but running,
The roads were long,
And I thought about turning back.

The mother of a driver
Asks the foreman:
"Listen, give me news of my son,
As I have not seen him arrive."

"Lady, I will tell you,
But don't go and cry,
A steer killed your son
On the gate of a corral.

Treinta pesos alcanzó
Pero todo limitado,
Y trescientos puse yo
Pa' haberlo sepultado.

Todos los aventureros
Lo fueron a acompañar,
Con sus sombreros en las manos,
A verlo sepultar.

"Thirty *pesos* were left over
But it was all owed,
And I put in three hundred
To have him buried.

"All the drivers
Went to accompany him,
With their hats in their hands,
To see him buried."

Doney Gal

TRADITIONAL COWBOY SONG

Collected, adapted, and arranged by John A. and Alan Lomax. Copyright 1938 Ludlow Music Inc., New York, N. Y. Used by permission.

He was little and peaked and thin,
And nary a no-account horse,
Least that's the way you'd describe him
In case that the beast had been lost;
But for single and double cussedness
And double center-fired sin,
The horse never come out o' Texas
That was half-way knee-high to him.[1]

HERE'S one of the best of the songs about a cowboy's horse. The tune seems to evoke the very sound of lonely hoofbeats and the sweat-laden odor of a pony just off the trail. Alan Lomax believes that it is one of the last of the genuine cowboy songs, a haunting echo of the men who rode herd on the mighty longhorns who streamed along the cattle trails in the glory-days of the cow camp and the round up.

[1] "Speckles," by N. Howard Thorp, from *Songs of the Cowboys*, Thorp.

From the second G-chord on, begin each bar with G (third fret on sixth string) and play indicated chord on second beat.

Chorus (may be included as words for the verse part).

On the D and Bm chords, use left thumb *(on third fret, sixth string) for the G bass note.*

Here is how the opening bars of the chorus look musically and in guitar tablature:

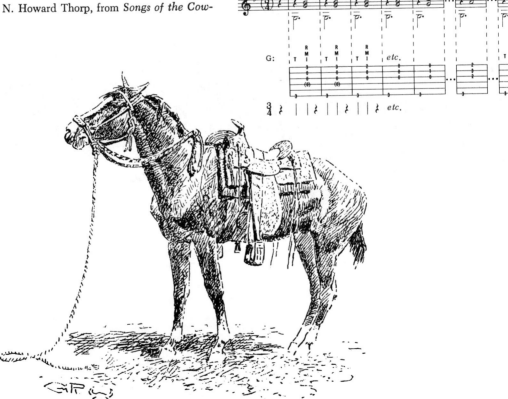

184

DONEY GAL

We're alone, Doney Gal, in the rain and hail,
Got to drive these dogies down the trail.

We'll ride the range from sun to sun,
For a cowboy's work is never done;
He's up and gone at the break of day,
Drivin' the dogies on their weary way.

Chorus:

It's rain or shine, sleet or snow,
Me and my Doney Gal are on the go.
Yes, rain or shine, sleet or snow,
Me and my Doney Gal are bound to go.

A cowboy's life is a weary thing,
For it's rope and brand and ride and sing;
Yes, day or night in the rain or hail,
He'll stay with his dogies out on the trail.

Rain or shine, sleet or snow,
Me and my Doney Gal are on the go;
We travel down that lonesome trail
Where a man and his horse seldom ever fail.

(Chorus)

We whoop at the sun and yell through the hail,
But we drive the poor dogies on down the trail,
And we'll laugh at the storms, the sleet and snow,
When we reach the little town of San Antonio.

Traveling up the lonesome trail
Where a man and his horse seldom ever fail;
Jogging along through fog and dew,
Wish for sunny days and you.

(Chorus)

Over the prairies lean and brown,
On through the wastes where there ain't no town;
Swimming the rivers across our way,
We fight on forward day-end on day.

Trailing the herd through mountains green,
We pen the cattle in Abilene.
Round the campfire's flickering glow,
We sing the songs of long ago.

(Chorus)

We're alone, Doney Gal, in the rain and hail,
Got to drive these dogies down the trail;
Get along, little dogie, on your way.

The Trail to Mexico

TRADITIONAL COWBOY SONG

Collected, adapted, and arranged by John A. and Alan Lomax. Copyright 1938
Ludlow Music, Inc., New York, N. Y. Used by permission.

> I met the boss; he wanted me to go
> Help drive his herd to Idaho.
> I told the boss it was out of my range,
> But if he had the price, I was about to change.[1]

THE cowboy was a roamer, a restless wanderer who chased a wild dream across a dozen states only to find himself playing nursemaid to a thousand cows.

The songs of the cowboy comprise a saga of travel. There is no end to a cattle trail, only a short stopover after payday in the Dodge City saloons, the Cheyenne gambling houses, or the Abilene brothels. And always the song is of the trail, following the longhorns to Idaho, Montana, Mexico, or "that crooked trail to Holbrook in Arizona."

Sometimes there was a girl, but she was more often imaginary than real. Sometimes the girl proved true, but that, too, was more fancy than fact. And the songs told it all. Like Joe Bowers' Sally, the girl of this song couldn't wait for her cowboy love. Perhaps, as Frank Dobie suggests, it was all part of a plot on the part of a rancher who didn't want his daughter marrying any no-account cowpuncher. True or not, it was the kind of song the cowboys loved to sing, a narrative that somehow summed up every broken dream of the men who followed the longhorn cows.

[1] "On the Trail to Idaho," from *Cowboy Songs,* Lomax.

THE TRAIL TO MEXICO

With energy and sentiment

change my way, Quit my crowd

way,_____ And quit my crowd _____ that was__ so

change my way, Quit my crowd

so ver-y gay,__ Leave that girl mm _____

gay, And_leave the girl _____ who'd prom-ised me her

so ver-y gay,__ Leave that girl

hand,_____ Head down south, hm _____

hand,_____ And head down south _____ of the Ri - o Grande.

hand,_____ Head down south head down south to the Ri - o

Chorus

unis.

I'm go - ing back _____

Go-in' back, go-in' back, go-in' back, go-in' back, go-in' back, go-in' back,

to Mex - i - co, _____ Where the long - horn

go - in' back, go - in' back, Go - in' back, go - in' back, go - in' back, go - in' back,

steers _____ and cac - tus grow,

go - in' back, go - in' back, go - in' back, go - in' back, Go - in' back, go - in' back,

Where the girls are good _____ day af - ter

go - in' back, go - in' back, go - in' back, go - in' back, go - in' back, go - in' back,

day _____ And do not

Girls are good, girls are good, girls are good, girls are good,

live _____ just for your pay. ____

Girls they don't, no they aren't liv - ing for, just for your pay. ____

It was in the year of eighty-three
That A. J. Stinson hired me.
He said, "Young feller, I want you to go
And drive this herd to Mexico."
I made up my mind to change my way,
And quit my crowd that was so gay,
And leave the girl who'd promised me her hand,
And head down south of the Rio Grande.

Chorus:

I'm going back to Mexico,
Where the longhorn steers and cactus grow,
Where the girls are good day after day
And do not live just for your pay.

And when I held her in my arms,
I thought she had ten thousand charms;
Her kisses were soft, her lips were sweet,
Saying, "We'll get married next time we meet."
And when I held her in my arms,
I knew she had ten thousand charms;
She promised then she would be true
And wait for me as lovers do.

(Chorus)

The first horse they gave me was an old black
With two big set-fasts on his back;
I padded him with gunnysacks and my bedding all,
He went up, then down, and I got a fall.
The next they gave me was an old gray,
I'll remember him till my dying day;
And if I had to swear to the fact,
I believe he was worse off than the black.

(Chorus)

Oh, it was early in the year
When I went on trail to drive the steer;

I stood my guard through sleet and snow
While on the trail to Mexico.
Oh, it was a long and toilsome go
As our herd rolled on to Mexico;
With laughter light and the cowboy's song,
To Mexico we rolled along.

(Chorus)

When I arrived in Mexico,
I wanted to see my love, but could not go;
So I wrote a letter, a letter to my dear,
But not a word from her could I hear.
When I arrived at my native home,
I called for the darling of my own;
They said she had married a richer life,
Therefore, wild cowboy, seek another wife.

(Chorus)

Oh, the girl is married I do adore,
And I cannot stay at home any more;
I'll cut my way to a foreign land
Or I'll go back West to my cowboy band.
I'll go back to the Western land,
I'll hunt up my old cowboy band
Where the girls are few and the boys are true
And a false-hearted love I never knew.

(Chorus)

"Oh, Buddy, Oh, Buddy, please stay at home,
Don't be forever on the roam.
There is many a girl more true than I,
So pray don't go where the bullets fly."
"It's curse your gold and your silver, too,
Confound a girl that won't prove true;
I'll travel West where the bullets fly,
I'll stay on the trail till the day I die."

(Chorus)

Cowboy's Life Is a Dreary, Dreary Life

TRADITIONAL COWBOY SONG

Text from *Songs of the Cowboys*, N. Howard Thorp, who says, "I first heard it at Kingston, New Mexico, sung by a man named Sam Jackson." Tune from the singing of Dave Frederickson, *Songs of the West* (Folkways Records, FH5259).

I have circle-herded, trail-herded, night-herded, and cross-herded, too,
But to keep you together that's what I can't do;
My horse is leg-weary and I'm awful tired,
But if you get away I'm sure to get fired.[1]

OLD-TIME cowboys say that there's more truth in this one song than in scores of stereotyped ballads which have created a sentimentalized romantic picture of life on the western prairies. Nineteenth-century America offered very few "cushy" jobs for the ordinary workingman, and the cowboy's job was tougher than most. The hours were long, the pay was low, and the working conditions were frequently abominable. The onslaught of bad weather aggravated the situation, for the cowboy had to tend the rancher's cattle before he could worry about taking care of himself.

Food was a gamble (more often than not a losing one), and good drinking water was hard to come by. One cowboy, asked if the drinking water in a particular draw was all right, replied:

"Yes, but it's pretty thick and you may have to chew it a little before you swallow it."

But most of all, the work was hard and the life was lonely. Sometimes it was enough to make a man a little saddle-happy; and when it got real tough, it might drive a man to pour out his heart and his troubles in a song.

Like many another cowboy song ("Buffalo Skinners," "Flat River Girl,") this song found its way into the cowboy repertoire from lumberjacks who drifted out west from Michigan and Maine. A shanty-boy song popular among the lumberjacks of the north went:

A shantyman's life is a drearisome life,
Though sometimes 'tis free from all care.
'Tis swinging an ax from morning till night
In the midst of the forest so drear.[2]

[1] "Night-Herding Song," *Songs of the Cowboys*, Thorp.

[2] "A Shantyman's Life," from *Lore of the Lumber Camps*, E. C. Beck.

COWBOY'S LIFE IS A DREARY, DREARY LIFE

As if riding a pony

1. A— cow-boy's life is a drear-y, drear-y life, Some say it's free from

care;— Round-ing up the cat-tle from morn-ing till— night On the

bald Prai-rie so bare.

2. Just a

A cowboy's life is a dreary, dreary life,
Some say it's free from care;
Rounding up the cattle from morning till night
On the bald prairie so bare.

Just about four o'clock old cook will holler out,
"Roll out, boys, it's almost day."
Through his broken slumbers the puncher he will ask,
"Has the short summer night passed away?"

The cowboy's life is a dreary, dreary life,
He's driven through the heat and cold;
While the rich man's a-sleeping on his velvet couch,
Dreaming of his silver and gold.

When the spring work sets in, then our troubles will begin,
The weather being fierce and cold;
We're almost froze, with the water on our clothes,
And the cattle we can scarcely hold.

The cowboy's life is a dreary, weary one,
He works all day to the setting of the sun;
And then his day's work is not done,
For there's his night guard to go on.

"Saddle up! Saddle up!" the boss will holler out,
When camped down by the Pecos stream,
Where the wolves and owls with their terrifying howls
Will disturb us in our midnight dream.

You are speaking of your farms, you are speaking of your charms,
You are speaking of your silver and gold;
But a cowboy's life is a dreary, dreary life,
He's driven through the heat and cold.

Once I loved to roam, but now I stay at home:
All you punchers take my advice;
Sell your bridle and your saddle, quit your roaming and your travels,
And tie on to a cross-eyed wife.

The Gal I Left Behind Me

TRADITIONAL COWBOY SONG

Text from *Songs of the Cowboys,* N. Howard Thorp; melody traditional.

I asked her if she would be willing for me to cross the plains;
She said she would be truthful until I returned again;
She said she would be faithful until death did prove unkind.
So we kissed, shook hands, and parted, and I left my girl behind.[1]

THE girl the cowboy left behind usually married another man. In most cases, she would have married the other man anyway. The cowboy had a great flair for self-dramatization and a penchant for stories which showed him the constant victim of hard luck. What better proof than the unfaithfulness of the girl who had promised to be true?

He handed me a letter which gave me to
  understand
That the girl I left in Texas had married another
  man.[2]

[1] "The Rambling Cowboy," *Cowboy Songs,* Lomax.
[2] *Ibid.*

But in one song, at least, the girl proved true, and that one, too, was a cowboy favorite. "The Gal I Left Behind Me" found its way to the western plains from the music hall stages of the east and from the oral tradition of the middle west. Originally a British soldier favorite with a history dating back at least to the early eighteenth century, the song was widely known in many versions throughout the United States before some cowboy poet adapted it to the life of the trail.

I suggest using the chords in parentheses; capo up if the chords in D are too difficult.

THE GAL I LEFT BEHIND ME

1. I struck the trail in sev-en-ty-nine, The herd strung out_ be - hind me; As I

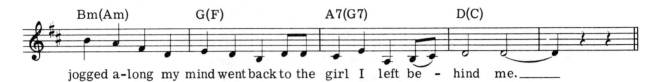

jogged a-long my mind went back to the girl I left be - hind me._____

Chorus

That sweet lit-tle gal, that true lit-tle gal, That gal I left be - hind me, That_

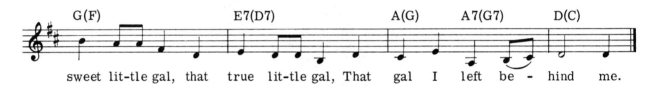

sweet lit-tle gal, that true lit-tle gal, That gal I left be - hind me.

I struck the trail in seventy-nine,
The herd strung out behind me;
As I jogged along my mind ran back
To the gal I left behind me.

Chorus:

That sweet little gal, that true little gal,
That gal I left behind me,
That sweet little gal, that true little gal,
That gal I left behind me.

If ever I get off the trail
And the Indians they don't find me,
I'll make my way straight back again
To the gal I left behind me.

(Chorus)

The wind did blow, the rain did flow,
The hail did fall and blind me;
I thought of that gal, that sweet little gal,
That gal I'd left behind me.

(Chorus)

She wrote ahead to the place I said,
I was always glad to find it;
She says, "I'm true, when you get through,
Ride back and you will find me."

(Chorus)

When we sold out, I took the train,
I knew where I would find her;
When I got back, we had a smack,
And that was no gol-darned liar.

(Chorus)

Utah Carroll

Cowboy song, author unknown
From *Singing Cowboy*, Margaret Larkin.

Once let the herd at its breath take fright,
Nothing on earth can stop their flight;
And woe to the rider, and woe to the steed,
That falls in front of their mad stampede.

THE stories of stampedes by rampaging cattle were told and retold at every cowboy campfire. Thunderstorms and the accompanying lightning were a frequent cause of stampedes, but most any sudden noise in the night might set off that unreasoned madness which sent the terrified longhorns on a path of senseless havoc and death.

"Obvious trivialities started more stampedes than anything else except storms: A stray dog sneaking up and smelling around a sleeping animal on the edge of the herd; a bunch of wild hogs rooting into the bed grounds; the sight of a haystack after dark in a field into which a herd of old and leery beeves had been turned for the night—'so that the boys could get some rest'; the cough of a cow; a human sneeze; the snapping of a twig; the sinking of a circling horse's foot in a prairie dog hole. It was the suddenness of a sound or movement rather than its unfamiliarity that made the drags wake up and forget all about sore feet. A polecat would come sashaying along in its nonchalant way into the edge of a herd; some steer, awake and investigative, would begin following the hopping creature. Then,

noticing the approaching monster, the little hairball would stop, pat its forefeet against the ground and go to jerking its tail with comical swiftness. Mr. Steer had never seen this performance before—and it was 'so sudden.' He would wheel and snort, having no intention of starting a stampede, but a moment later he was part of the panic terror he had caused. Like people, cattle are at their best when separated from the mob." [1]

Here is one of the best of the old stampede songs, a good narrative in the great tradition of the classical Anglo–American ballads set against a background of class lines, the cowboy's love for children, the self-sacrificing hero and sudden death. John Lomax passes along the report of J. T. Shirley, of San Angelo, Texas, who says that a cowboy on the Curve T Ranch in Schleicher County, Texas, wrote the song.

A good approach to this song might be to strum the bass string only once at the beginning of each bar, i.e., um-*pah-pah-pah,* um-*pah-pah-pah, etc.*

[1] J. Frank Dobie, *The Longhorns.*

UTAH CARROLL

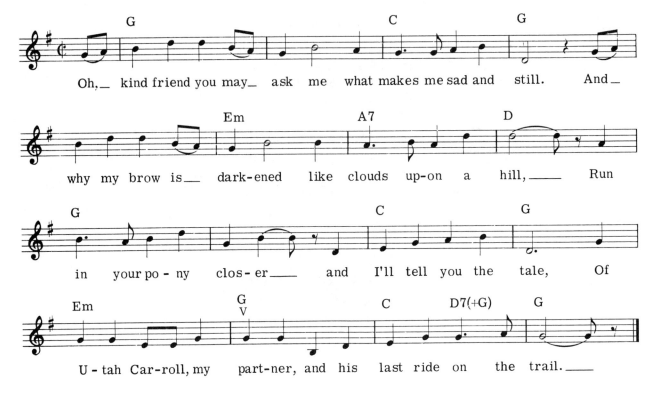

Oh, kind friend you may ask me what makes me sad and still,
And why my brow is darkened like clouds upon a hill,
Run in your pony closer and I'll tell you the tale,
Of Utah Carroll, my partner, and his last ride on the trail.

In a grave without a headstone, without a date or name,
Quietly lies my partner in the land from which I came,
Long, long we rode together, had ridden side by side,
I loved him as a brother, I wept when Utah died.

While rounding up one morning, our work was almost done,
The cattle quickly started on a wild and maddening run,
The boss's little daughter who was riding on that side,
Rushed in to stop the stampede, 'twas there poor Utah died.

Lenore upon her pony tried to turn the cattle right,
Her blanket slipped beneath her, but she caught and held on tight.
But when we saw that blanket each cowboy held his breath,
For should her pony fail her, none could save the girl from death.

When the cattle saw the blanket almost dragging on the ground,
They were maddened in a moment and charged with deafening sound,
The girl soon saw her danger; she turned her pony's face,
And bending in her saddle tried the blanket to replace.

Just then she lost her balance in front of that wild tide.
Carroll's voice controlled the round up, "Lie still, little girl," he cried.
And then close up beside her came Utah riding fast,
But little did the poor boy know that ride would be his last.

198

Full often from the saddle had he caught the trailing rope,
To pick her up at full speed was now his only hope.
He swung low from his saddle to take her to his arm,
We thought that he'd succeeded, that the girl was safe from harm.

Such a strain upon his saddle had never been put before,
The cinches gave beneath him and he fell beside Lenore.
When the girl fell from her pony, she had dragged the blanket down,
It lay there close beside her where she lay upon the ground.

Utah took it up again and to Lenore he said,
"Lie still," and quickly running waved the red thing o'er his head.
He turned the maddened cattle from Lenore, his little friend,
As the mighty herd rushed toward him he turned to meet his end.

And as the herd came on him his weapon quickly drew,
He was bound to die defended as all brave cowboys do.
The weapon flashed like lightning, it sounded loud and clear,
As the cattle rushed and killed him, he dropped the leading steer.

When I broke through that wide circle to where poor Utah lay,
With a thousand wounds and bruises his life blood ebbed away,
I knelt down close beside him and I knew that all was o'er,
As I heard him faintly whisper, "Good-bye, my sweet Lenore."

Next morning at the churchyard I heard the preacher say,
"Don't think our kind friend Utah was lost on that great day,
He was a much-loved cowboy, and not afraid to die,
And we'll meet him at the round up on the plains beyond the sky."

Bury Me Not on the Lone Prairie

TRADITIONAL COWBOY SONG

Version adapted by Earl Robinson from Lomax, Larkin, and Sandburg.

"O, bury me not in the deep, deep sea,"
The words came low and mournfully
From the pallid lips of a youth who lay
On his cabin couch at the close of day.[1]

THE living process of folk music is a constant interpenetration of the old and the new, of the traditional and the topical, of the familiar and the strange. The cowboy songs of oral tradition are almost invariably the result of a reworking of older materials under the new circumstances of prairie life.

Sometime in the 1870's or so, an anonymous cowboy poet (N. Howard Thorp says it was H. Clemons of Deadwood, South Dakota) refashioned a sentimental nineteenth-century parlor ballad called

[1] "The Ocean Burial," from *The Western Bell*, Perkins & Pease, 1857.

"The Ocean Burial" into this remarkably woeful and extremely popular cowboy song. The original is generally credited to the Reverend Edwin H. Chapin, a Universalist clergyman of a poetic bent. His verses were published in the *Southern Literary Messenger* in 1839. Several years later, George N. Allen composed a tune for the poem and, as performed by Ossian N. Dodge, it became popular around innumerable parlor pianos. Now, "The Ocean Burial" is a historical curiosity, while its cowboy parody has become a part of the American image, woven into the very fabric of the national idiom.

BURY ME NOT ON THE LONE PRAIRIE

Very slowly ♩ = ca 60

1. "Oh, bur-y me not on the lone prai-rie," Those words came low and mourn-ful-ly From the pal-lid lips of a youth who lay On his dy-ing bed at the close of day. "Oh, bur-y me not on the lone prai-rie,__Where the wild__ coy-otes will howl o'er me,_____ In a nar-row grave just

Chorus

201

six   by three.—   Oh, bur-y me not on — the lone prai-rie.—

"Oh, bury me not on the lone prairie,"
These words came low and mournfully
From the pallid lips of a youth who lay
On his dying bed at the close of day.

Chorus:

"Oh, bury me not on the lone prairie,
Where the wild coyotes will howl o'er me,
In a narrow grave just six by three.
Oh, bury me not on the lone prairie."

"It matters not, I've oft been told,
Where the body lies when the heart grows cold.
Yet grant, oh grant, this wish to me:
Oh, bury me not on the lone prairie."

(Chorus)

"I've always wished to be laid when I died
In the little churchyard on the green hillside;
By my father's grave there let mine be,
And bury me not on the lone prairie."

(Chorus)

"Let my death-slumber be where my mother's prayer
And a sister's tear will mingle there;
Where my friends can come and weep o'er me.
Oh, bury me not on the lone prairie."

(Chorus)

"Oh, bury me not"—and his voice failed there,
But we took no heed of his dying prayer.
In a narrow grave just six by three
We buried him there on the lone prairie.

(Chorus)

And the cowboys now as they roam the plain,
For they marked the spot where his bones were lain,
Fling a handful of roses o'er his grave
With a prayer to Him who his soul will save.

(Chorus)

"Oh, bury me not on the lone prairie,
Where the wolves can howl and growl o'er me.
Fling a handful of roses o'er my grave
With a prayer to Him who my soul will save."

(Chorus)

Spanish Is the Loving Tongue

(A BORDER AFFAIR)

WORDS: Charles Badger Clark, Jr.
MUSIC: Composer unknown

Text from *Songs of the Cowboys*, N. Howard Thorp; melody from the singing of Richard Dyer-Bennet, transcribed in *The People's Songs Bulletin* (Vol. 3, No. 11) and learned from Sam Eskin.

> I think we can all remember
> When a Mexican hadn't no show
> In Palo Pinto particular,
> It ain't very long ago.[1]

Of all the cowboy love songs which sang of sweethearts true and false, this touching literary ballad by the well-known western poet, Charles Badger Clark, Jr., has enjoyed the most sustained popularity. Written under the title, "A Border Affair," the poem struck a responsive note in a sentimental age. Its story of true love thwarted by the barrier of "racial" differences (a prejudice founded on a misconception that the Mexican was "less white" than his Caucasian neighbor to the north) had wide appeal in a romantic age. And long after many another cowboy ballad had been consigned to the printed page, "A Border Affair" was sung and declaimed by cowboys out on the range. For there is a sentiment which appeals to us all in this bittersweet ballad of the rough-hewn cowpuncher who doesn't "look much like a lover" and the señorita who whispered, "*Adiós, mi corazón!*"

[1] "The Texas Cowboy and the Mexican," from *Songs of the Cattle Trail and the Cow Camp*, Lomax.

SPANISH IS THE LOVING TONGUE

Soft and warm

Span - ish is the lov-ing tongue, Soft as mu - sic, light as spray:

'Twas a girl I learned it from, Liv-ing down So - no - ra way.

I don't look much like a lov- er, Yet I say her love words o-ver,—

Of - ten when I'm all a-lone— "Mi a -mor, mi co - ra-zón."

204

Spanish is the loving tongue,
Soft as music, light as spray
'Twas a girl I learned it from,
Living down Sonora way.
I don't look much like a lover,
Yet I say her love words over,
Often when I'm all alone—
"*Mi amor, mi corazón.*"

Nights when she knew where I'd ride
She would listen for my spurs,
Fling the big door open wide,
Raise them laughin' eyes of hers;
And my heart would nigh stop beating
When I heard her tender greeting,
Whispered soft for me alone—
"*Mi amor, mi corazón.*"

Moonlight in the patio,
Old Señora nodding near,
Me and Juana talking low
So the Madre couldn't hear;

How those hours would go a-flyin'!
And too soon I'd hear her sighin'
In her little sorry tone—
"*Adiós, mi corazón!*"

But one time I had to fly
For a foolish gamblin' fight,
And we said a swift goodbye
In that black unlucky night.
When I'd loosed her arms from clingin'
With her words the hoofs kept ringin'
As I galloped north alone—
"*Adiós, mi corazón!*"

Never seen her since that night—
I can't cross the Line, you know.
She was "Mex" and I was white;
Like as not it's better so.
Yet I've always sort of missed her
Since that last wild night I kissed her;
Left her heart and lost my own—
"*Adiós, mi corazón!*"

Little Joe, the Wrangler

WORDS: N. Howard Thorp
MUSIC: Adapted from "Little Old Log Cabin in the Lane"

Lightnin' rolls in hoops and circles,
Rain in sheets is comin' down,
Thunder rattles through the gulches,
As the hoof beats shake the ground.
Top hands ride like likkered Injuns,
Beggin' God for the break o' day.
A stampede beats the best camp meetin'
When it comes to gettin' men to pray.[1]

THE identity of the early cowboy ballad makers has, by now, been lost. The names of those range poets who wrote "Bury Me Not on the Lone Prairie," "Cowboy's Lament," and "I Ride an Old Paint" have been obscured in the dust of ten thousand trail herds from Texas to Montana.

Some of the best songs were composed toward the end of the cowboy era, and, in a few cases, the identities of their creators have been preserved.

One of the best of these latter-day cowboy song-smiths was N. Howard Thorp, many of whose ballads and poems found their way into the repertory of the range. His most popular song, adapted to the tune of "Little Old Log Cabin in the Lane," was "Little Joe, the Wrangler." Thorp, who was both ballad maker and song collector, wrote "Little Joe" in 1898 "on trail of herd of O Cattle from Chimney Lake, New Mexico, to Higgins, Texas."

The sentimentality of the early cowboy folk songs was embellished by the later poets who took a particular delight in depicting the "honor of the plains" and the soft hearts of their rugged cowboy heroes.

Stampedes were a frequent subject for cowboy songs, since the danger of a sudden cattle eruption was ever present on the trail, and since many a night-riding puncher sang to his cattle in order to keep them calm and quiet. "Little Joe" was a "wrangler," which is just about another way of saying he was an apprentice cowboy. The wrangler took care of the *remuda,* a term applied to all the horses in any particular outfit.

The song of "Little Joe" and his tragic death became an almost instantaneous Western favorite, quickly traveling from one cow camp to another all over the cattle country. So popular did it become, in fact, that a sequel was composed by some anonymous bard:

We could see that she'd been ridin', her little face
  was sad,
When she talked, her upper lip, it trembled so;
She was the livin' image, we all saw at a glance,
Of our little lost horse herder, Wrangler Joe.[2]

---

[1] "The Stampede," by Walt Cousins, quoted in *The Longhorns,* Dobie.

[2] "Little Joe the Wrangler's Sister Nell," from the singing of Harry Jackson, *The Cowboy* (Folkways Records FH-5723).

LITTLE JOE, THE WRANGLER

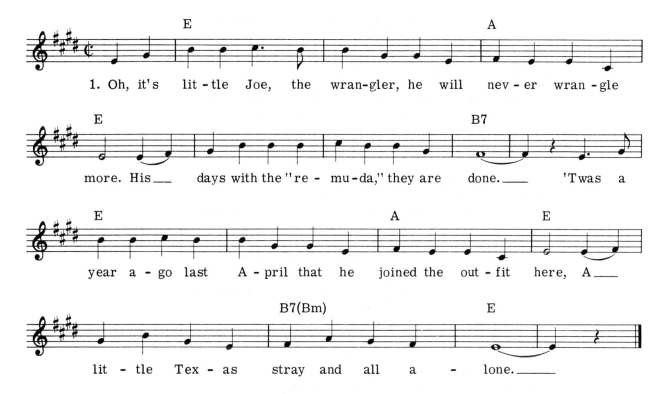

1. Oh, it's lit-tle Joe, the wran-gler, he will nev-er wran-gle more. His__ days with the "re - mu-da," they are done.___ 'Twas a year a - go last A - pril that he joined the out - fit here, A__ lit - tle Tex - as stray and all a - lone.____

Oh, it's Little Joe, the wrangler, he will never wrangle more,
His days with the "remuda," they are done.
'Twas a year ago last April he joined the outfit here,
A little Texas stray and all alone.

'Twas long late in the evening he rode up to the herd
On a little old brown pony he called Chaw;
With his brogan shoes and overalls, a harder looking kid
You never in your life had seen before.

His saddle was a southern kack built many years ago,
An O.K. spur on one foot idly hung,
While his "hot roll" in a cotton sack was loosely tied behind
And a canteen from the saddle horn he'd slung.

He said he had to leave his home, his daddy'd married twice,
And his new ma beat him every day or two;
So he saddled up old Chaw one night and "lit a shuck" this way—
Thought he'd try to paddle now his own canoe.

Said he'd try and do the best he could if we'd only give him work,
Though he didn't know "straight up" about a cow;
So the boss he cut him out a mount and kinder put him on,
For he sorter liked the little stray somehow.

Taught him how to herd the horses and learn to know them all,
To round 'em up by daylight, if he could;
To follow the chuck wagon and to always hitch the team
And help the "cosinero" rustle wood.

We'd driven to Red River and the weather had been fine;
We were camped down on the south side in a bend,
When a norther commenced blowing and we doubled up our guards,
For it took all hands to hold the cattle then.

Little Joe, the wrangler, was called out with the rest,
And scarcely had the kid got to the herd,
When the cattle they stampeded; like a hailstorm 'long they flew,
And all of us were riding for the lead.

'Tween the streaks of lightning we could see a horse far out ahead—
'Twas Little Joe, the wrangler, in the lead;
He was riding old "Blue Rocket" with his slicker 'bove his head,
Trying to check the leaders in their speed.

At last we got them milling and kinder quieted down,
And the extra guard back to the camp did go;
But one of them was missin', and we all knew at a glance
'Twas our little Texas stray, poor wrangler Joe.

Next morning just at sunup we found where Rocket fell,
Down in a washout twenty feet below;
Beneath his horse, mashed to a pulp, his spurs had rung the knell
For our little Texas stray—poor wrangler Joe.

PART 6

"The Farmer Is the Man"

Let sailors sing of ocean deep,
Let soldiers praise their armor,
But in my heart this toast I'll keep,
The Independent Farmer.[1]

[1] "The Independent Farmer," George F. Root, quoted in
Morris Brothers, Pell & Trowbridge's Songs (1860).

SALT CREEK, AT ASHLAND, NEB.,—LOOKING TOWARD THE PLATTE HILLS, FROM THE MILL HILL.

IOWA AND NEBRASKA LANDS.
What Time in the Year is it Best to Buy Them?
THE BURLINGTON AND MISSOURI RIVER RAILROAD

THE GREAT PLAINS which form the heartland of continental America have played host to many a historical traveler. The early explorer who followed the twists and turns of the Missouri, the haven-seeking Mormon, and the fortune-seeking '49er whose handcarts and covered wagons made the long, slow trek over the few well-worn trails, the Plains Indian who hunted the buffalo, the footloose cowboy who drove the longhorns from Texas to Montana and back again following the season and the grass—all these were heroic and memorable characters who played out the drama of their lives on the stage of the Great Plains. But all these only passed over the Plains. The true hero of this rugged frontier was the man who came to stay, the settler, the homesteader, the "sodbuster" who constructed his first home out of the tough earth of Kansas, Nebraska, Colorado, and the windswept Dakotas.

In 1849, when the gold seeker left Missouri on his way to Sacramento, the only sign of civilization he could expect to find en route was the Mormon settlement at Salt Lake. In the early fifties, Kansas and Nebraska were "settled" by political zealots determined to win these new states to either freedom or slavery. But the real settlement of this great section of the West does not begin until 1862, with the passage of the Homestead Act; and, after that, with the completion of the transcontinental railroad.

The history of the Great Plains is the history of the farmer and the railroad. Each was completely dependent on the other, and between them they settled the land and welded the nation into a single unit.

Until the railroad could guarantee outbound freight and inbound supplies, the frontier farmer could not pursue his hazardous dream of land he could call his own. And, once having spanned the continent with miles of track and steel, the railroads required the steady flow of traffic which only a permanently settled wheatland could provide. In fact, the railroads were the biggest promoters of land offerings of their time. Railroad agents offered innumerable inducements to prospective settlers on the Nebraska Plains, while railroad-published brochures and advertisements extolled the glories of the rich homesteads waiting to be plowed.

A pioneering people rose to the challenge. (In time, many would say that they fell for the bait.) From the Eastern seaboard, from the hill country of Kentucky and Tennessee and the Ozarks, from the rapidly developing frontier cities of Missouri and Illinois, and from all the lands of the old world they came—following their dream to the plains of Kansas, investing their lives in the vast fertile acreage of the Dakotas.

As with any people, they brought their stories and songs with them. Their music was of their church and the casual, public entertainments of

211

their day. The hymns of faith, the raucous minstrel songs, the sad, sweet songs of sentiment which they learned around the parlor piano—this was the music which came to the Plains in the 1860's and 1870's. In time, the men and women of the home-steads began to sing of the land they worked and the lives they led, fitting their new experiences to the old tunes. "Little Old Log Cabin In the Lane" became the "Little Old Sod Shanty on My Claim," while old songs like "Beulah Land" and "Year of Jubilo" were transformed into songs of greater immediacy.

It was a hard life, a life of struggle. The first struggle was against the land; then came the struggle against the railroads and the banks. And from these struggles came a new song, a farmer's song, nurtured by the fierce winds of the plains, sung in the shadow of violence and tragedy, pre-served in the folk memory which thrusts dreams in the teeth of the mid-winter frost.

The Homestead of the Free

(SONG OF THE KANSAS EMIGRANT)

WORDS: John Greenleaf Whittier
MUSIC: Anonymous

From *The Western Bell,* by Edward A. Perkins and Frederick H. Pease
(1857).

Ho, brothers! Come, brothers!
Hasten all with me:
We'll sing upon the Kansas plains
A song of liberty![1]

THE Kansas–Nebraska Act of 1854, paving the way for the admission of these two states to the Union, established the principle of "popular sovereignty" concerning slavery. The people of these territories would decide for themselves before applying for admission to the Union whether or not slavery would be legal in their states.

In 1855, the New England Emigrant Aid Company was organized in Massachusetts, with the avowed purpose of encouraging the settlement of persons and families of anti-slavery sentiments in Kansas. The company was largely responsible for the settlement of Lawrence, Kansas, and it is estimated that more than 2,000 people made the trip west under their auspices.

A supporter of the society and one of the most outspoken abolitionists of his day was the New England poet, John Greenleaf Whittier. The words to this song were penned by Whittier some time in 1854 upon the departure of a party of settlers for the Kansas plains.

This may fit your vocal and guitar chords better in C. If so, try transposing it down. It's easy. D becomes C, A₇ becomes G₇, Bm, Am and so on .

[1] From a Kansas newspaper of 1876, quoted in *Heritage of Kansas,* May, 1958.

213

THE HOMESTEAD OF THE FREE

1. We cross the prai-rie as of old, the pil-grims crossed the sea,___ To_

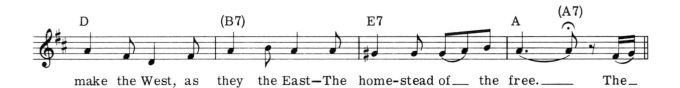

make the West, as they the East—The home-stead of__ the free.____ The_

Chorus

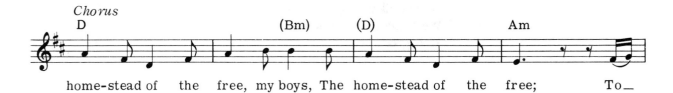

home-stead of the free, my boys, The home-stead of the free; To_

make the West as they the East, The_ home-stead of the free.____

We cross the prairie as of old
The pilgrims crossed the sea,
To make the West, as they the East—
The homestead of the free.

Chorus:

The homestead of the free, my boys,
The homestead of the free;
To make the West as they the East,
The homestead of the free.

We go to rear a wall of men
On freedom's southern line,
And plant beside the cotton bale
The rugged northern pine.

(Chorus)

We go to plant her common schools
On distant prairie swells;
And give the Sabbath of the wild
The music of her bells.

(Chorus)

Up-bearing, like the ark of old,
The Bible in our van;
We go to test the truth of God
Against the fraud of man.

(Chorus)

Uncle Sam's Farm

Words: Jesse Hutchinson, Jr.
Music: The Hutchinson Family

Text from *The Hutchinson Family's Book of Poetry;* music from *100 Comic Songs,* Turner (1858).

Broeder ve ha langt at go
Oever salte vaten,
Ok sa fins America
In vid andre stranden.[1]

Brothers we have far to go
Across the salty waters;
There we'll find America
On the other shore.

From 1820 to 1850 almost twenty million people responded to America's "general invitation to the people of the world" to find a new life in the mighty domain over the seas.

Of this total, the following comprised the main nationality groups: Germans, five million; Irish, three million; Scandinavians, one and a half million; English, Welsh and Scottish, three million; Slavic countries, two million; Italy, one million.

It was an age of hope and expanding frontiers, a time for men to claim the land for themselves and work it for their families. Most attractive of all were the vast virgin territories west of the Mississippi.

This song, so expressive of the mood of the times, is a Hutchinson Family composition (circa 1850). It was one of the Family's most popular numbers, drifting into folk tradition by way of both the original and countless parodies.

A strong six-note strum on every strong beat is strongly suggested:

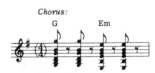

[1] Nineteenth-century Swedish immigrant song, from *Songs of the North Star State,* Gene Bluestein, (Folkways Records FA2112).

UNCLE SAM'S FARM

A dancing march

1. Of____ all the might-y na-tions in the East or in the West, O the
glo-ri-ous Yan-kee na - tion is the great - est and the best; We have
room for all cre - a - tion, and our ban - ner is un - furled, With a
gen-er - al in - vi - ta - tion to the peo - ple of the world.

Chorus
Then come a-long, come a - long, make no de-lay,
Come from ev - 'ry na - tion, come from ev - 'ry way; Our____
lands they are broad e - nough, don't be a-larmed, For____
Un - cle Sam is rich e-nough to give us all a farm.

Of all the mighty nations in the East or in the West,
The glorious Yankee nation is the greatest and the best;
We have room for all creation, and our banner is unfurled,
With a general invitation to the people of the world.

Chorus:

Then come along, come along, make no delay,
Come from every nation, come from every way;
Our lands they are broad enough, don't be alarmed,
For Uncle Sam is rich enough to give us all a farm.

St. Lawrence is our Northern line, far's her waters flow,
And the Rio Grande our Southern bound, way down in Mexico;
While from the Atlantic Ocean where the sun begins to dawn,
We'll cross the Rocky Mountains far away to Oregon.

(Chorus)

While the South shall raise the cotton, and the West the corn and pork,
New England manufactures shall do up the finer work;
For the deep and flowing waterfalls that course along our hills,
Are just the thing for washing sheep and driving cotton mills.

(Chorus)

Our fathers gave us liberty, but little did they dream
The grand results to follow in the mighty age of steam;
Our mountains, lakes and rivers are now in a blaze of fire,
While we send the news by lightning on the telegraphic wire.

(Chorus)

While Europe's in commotion and her monarchs in a fret,
We're teaching them a lesson which they never can forget;
And this they fast are learning, Uncle Sam is not a fool,
For the people do their voting and the children go to school.

(Chorus)

The brave in every nation are joining heart and hand,
And flocking to America, the real promised land;
And Uncle Sam stands ready with a child upon each arm,
To give them all a welcome to a lot upon his farm.

(Chorus)

A welcome warm and hearty do we give the songs of toil,
To come to the West and settle and labor on Free Soil;
We've room enough and land enough, they needn't feel alarm—
O! come to the land of Freedom and vote yourself a farm.

(Chorus)

Yes we're bound to lead the nations, for our motto's *"Go ahead,"*
And we'll carry out the principles for which our fathers bled;
No monopoly of kings and queens, but this is the Yankee plan:
Free Trade to Emigration and Protection unto man.

(Chorus)

217

The Little Old Sod Shanty on My Claim

WORDS: Anonymous
MUSIC: "Little Old Log Cabin in the Lane" (William S. Hays)

Lyrics from *Cowboy Songs*, Lomax; music from *The American Songbag*, Carl Sandburg.

Come, all you folks of enterprise who feel inclined to roam,
Beyond the Mississippi to seek a pleasant home;
Pray take a pioneer's advice, I'll point you out the best—
I mean the state of Kansas, the Lily of the West.[1]

WHEN the settler came to the Great Plains to stake out his homestead he needed a place to live. But there were no forests to provide lumber for a log cabin. There was only the tall prairie grass. At first, the homesteader dug into the side of a hill, fashioning a rude shelter out of the natural sod. In time, he would use the prairie sod to build his permanent home.

"With a spade he cut the sod furrows into three-foot lengths. Then it was like laying bricks—pile up the sod, chink the joints with earth, leave openings for a door and a window. Roof poles came from the willows a few miles up the creek. A layer of grass on the crisscrossed poles, a layer of sod on top, and it was done. Later he would get a door and window and his wife would cover the shaggy walls with sheets of newspaper.

This was the little old sod shanty on the claim, cool in summer, warm in winter, windproof, fireproof, but pervious to water. . . . Under a sod roof you got wet long after the rain was over. Saturated soil would drip for days. Sometimes a sodbuster's wife held an umbrella over the stove while she turned the pancakes."[2]

One settler composed a song about his prairie home, his "little old sod shanty." He borrowed the tune of William Shakespeare Hays' "Little Old Log Cabin in the Lane."

The chords in parentheses in the key of D are easier but not as interesting.

[1] "Lily of the West," Kansas adaptation of a traditional folksong, quoted in *Heritage of Kansas*, May 1961.

[2] Walter Havighurst, from *The Century Magazine* (Vol. 5), quoted in *This Is The West*, Robert West Howard.

218

THE LITTLE OLD SOD SHANTY ON MY CLAIM

I am looking rather seedy now while holding down my claim,
And my victuals are not always served the best;
And the mice play shyly round me as I nestle down to rest
In my little old sod shanty on my claim.

Refrain:

The hinges are of leather and the windows have no glass,
While the board roof lets the howling blizzards in,
And I hear the hungry coyote as he slinks up through the grass
Round the little old sod shanty on my claim.

Yet, I rather like the novelty of living in this way,
Though my bill of fare is always rather tame;
But I'm happy as a clam on the land of Uncle Sam
In the little old sod shanty on my claim.

(Refrain)

But when I left my Eastern home, a bachelor so gay,
To try and win my way to wealth and fame,
I little thought I'd come down to burning twisted hay
In the little old sod shanty on my claim.

(Refrain)

My clothes are plastered o'er with dough, I'm looking like a fright,
And everything is scattered round the room;
But I wouldn't give the freedom that I have out in the West
For the table of the Eastern man's old home.

(Refrain)

Still, I wish that some kind-hearted girl would pity on me take,
And relieve me from the mess that I am in;
The angel, how I'd bless her if this her home she'd make
In the little old sod shanty on my claim!

(Refrain)

And if fate should bless us with now and then an heir
To cheer our hearts with honest pride of fame,
Oh, then we'd be contented for the toil that we had spent
In the little old sod shanty on our claim.

(Refrain)

When time enough had lapsed and all those little brats
To noble man and womanhood had grown,
It wouldn't seem half so lonely as round us we should look
And we'd see the old sod shanty on our claim.

(Refrain)

Western Home

(HOME ON THE RANGE)

WORDS: Dr. Higley Brewster
MUSIC: Daniel E. Kelly

Text from the *Kirwin Chief* (Kirwin, Kansas), Feb. 26, 1876, reproduced in *Heritage of Kansas*, May, 1958; music adapted from the melody in *Cowboy Songs*, Lomax.

Come all who want to roam
   To Kansas.
Come all who want to roam
   To Kansas.
Come all who want to roam
And seek yourself a home
And be happy with your doom
   In Kansas.[1]

KANSAS in the 1870's was still a land of dugouts and sod shanties. Dr. Higley Brewster of Smith County, a prairie doctor with a literary bent wrote the words for this most famous of all Western songs in his dugout on the Kansas plains in 1873. A semiprofessional musician by the name of Daniel E. Kelly composed the tune. Aside from the fact that the text appeared in local newspapers several times during the seventies, there is no indication that the song was unusually popular. But the song remained with some and subsequently drifted into the oral tradition.

Years later, in 1910, John A. Lomax collected a variant on the song from a Negro trail cook in San Antonio. Lomax called the song "Home on the Range," by which title it has become the musical symbol of Western America.

[1] "In Kansas," from *Nebraska Folklore Pamphlets*, No. 16 (WPA Writer's Projert).

WESTERN HOME

Oh! give me a home where the buffalo roam,
Where the deer and the antelope play;
Where never is heard a discouraging word,
And the sky is not clouded all day.

Chorus:

A home! A home!
Where the deer and the antelope play;
Where seldom is heard a discouraging word,
And the sky is not clouded all day.

Oh! give me land where the bright diamond sand
Throws its light from the glittering streams,
Where glideth along the graceful white swan,
Like the maid to her heavenly dreams.

(Chorus)

Oh! give me a gale of the Solomon vale
Where the lifestreams with buoyancy flow;
On the banks of the Beaver, where seldom if ever
Any poisonous herbage doth grow.

(Chorus)

How often at night, when the heavens were bright,
With the light of the twinkling stars,
Have I stood here amazed and asked as I gazed
If their glory exceed that of ours.

(Chorus)

I love the wild flowers in this bright land of ours,
I love the wild curlew's shrill scream;
The bluffs and white rocks and antelope flocks,
That graze on the mountain so green.

(Chorus)

The air is so pure and the breezes so free,
The zephyrs so balmy and light,
That I would not exchange my home here to range
Forever in azures so bright.

(Chorus)

The Lane County Bachelor

(STARVING TO DEATH ON MY GOVERNMENT CLAIM)

WORDS: Anonymous
MUSIC: "Irish Washerwoman"

Text from *Heritage of Kansas*, May, 1961, "Kansas History and Folksong," by Bill and Mary Koch; music adapted from traditional sources.

To the West! To the West!
To the land of the free,
Where the mighty Missouri
Rolls down to the sea,
Where the young may exult
And the aged may rest,
Away! Far away!
To the land of the West.[1]

UNDER the terms of the Homestead Act of 1862, a man could claim 160 acres of land provided he worked and lived on his claim for a period of five years. "I've got a little bet with the government," the old homesteader would say. "They're betting me I can't live here for five years, and I'm betting them I can."

After the railroad propaganda had brought him to the plains of western Kansas, to the prairie counties of Lane and Lincoln and Logan and Ness, then the homesteader first saw "the elephant" of the plains. Many a man could not last his five years and headed back east. Others laughed in the face of adversity and burrowed in. One old bachelor made a song out of his troubles, and perhaps it helped him survive the drought, the insects, the loneliness, the mud and the long back-breaking day from "can't see to can't see" (before sunrise until after sundown) required to conquer the prairie soil.

[1] "To The West," Broadside songsheet, circa 1870, published by J. H. Johnson (Philadelphia).

THE LANE COUNTY BACHELOR

Coun - ty of Lane | Starv - ing to death on my
lev - el and plain, And I al - ways get wet when it

gov - ern-ment claim. My rain. But hur-
hap-pens to

rah for Lane Coun - ty, the land of the free, The

home of the grass-hop - per, bed - bug and flea, I'll

226

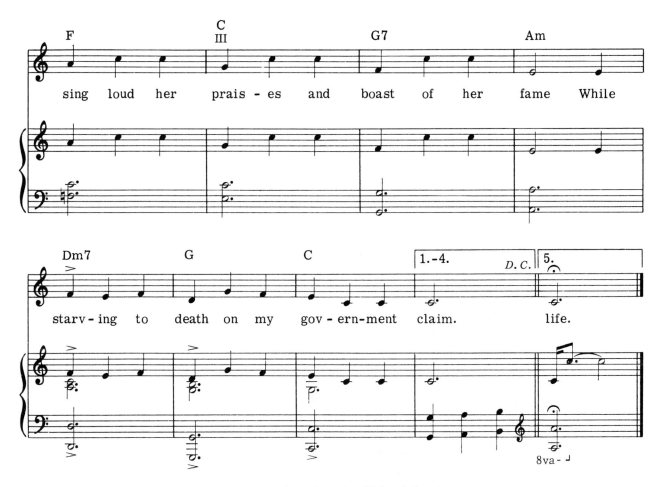

sing loud her prais - es and boast of her fame While

starv - ing to death on my gov - ern - ment claim. life.

My name is Frank Bolar, an old bachelor I am,
I'm keeping old batch on an elegant plan,
You'll find me out West in the County of Lane
Starving to death on my government claim;
My house it is built of the national soil,
The walls are erected according to Hoyle,
The roof has no pitch but is level and plain,
And I always get wet when it happens to rain.

But hurrah for Lane County, the land of the free,
The home of the grasshopper, bedbug and flea,
I'll sing loud her praises and boast of her fame
While starving to death on my government claim.

My clothes they are ragged, my language is rough,
My head is case-hardened, both solid and tough;
The dough it is scattered all over the room,
And the floor would get scared at the sight of a broom.
My dishes are dirty and some in the bed
Are covered with sorghum and government bread,
But I have a good time and live at my ease
On common-sop sorghum, old bacon and grease.

But hurrah for Lane County, the land of the West,
Where the farmers and laborers are always at rest,
Where you've nothing to do but sweetly remain,
And starve like a man on your government claim.

How happy am I when I crawl into bed,
And a rattlesnake rattles his tail at my head,
And the gay little centipede, void of all fear,
Crawls over my pillow and into my ear;
And the nice little bedbug, so cheerful and bright,
Keeps me a-scratching full half of the night,
And the gay little flea with toes sharp as a tack
Plays "Why don't you catch me?" all over my back.

But hurrah for Lane County where blizzards arise,
Where the winds never cease and the flea never dies,
Where the sun is so hot if in it you remain
'Twill burn you quite black on your government claim.

How happy am I on my government claim,
Where I've nothing to lose and nothing to gain,
Nothing to eat and nothing to wear,
Nothing from nothing is honest and square.
But here I am stuck and here I must stay,
My money's all gone and I can't get away;
There's nothing will make a man hard and profane
Like starving to death on a government claim.

Then come to Lane County, there's room for you all,
Where the winds never cease and the rains never fall,
Come join in the chorus and boast of her fame,
While starving to death on your government claim.

Now don't get discouraged you poor hungry men,
We're all here as free as a pig in a pen;
Just stick to your homestead and battle your fleas,
And pray to your Maker to send you a breeze.
Now a word to claim holders who are bound for to stay:
You may chew your hardtack till you're toothless and gray,
But as for me, I'll no longer remain
And starve like a dog on my government claim.

Farewell to Lane County, farewell to the West,
I'll travel back East to the girl I love best;
I'll stop in Missouri and get me a wife,
And live on corn dodgers the rest of my life.

Kansas Boys

TRADITIONAL KANSAS FOLK SONG

Words and music adapted from the singing of Tony Kraber. Additional lyrics from *Heritage of Kansas*, May 1961, "Kansas History and Folksong," by Bill and Mary Koch, and from *Nebraska Folklore*, Louise Pound.

Come all you Virginia gals and listen to my noise,
Neber you wed wid de Carolina boys,
For if dat you do your portion it will be,
Corn cake and harmony and Jango Lango tea.[1]

In the 1840's it was a minstrel song, sung in blackface on the music hall stages of New York and Philadelphia and Baltimore. Other minstrels added it to their repertoires, taking it along with their bag of ditties wherever Mr. Tambo and Mr. Bones trod the boards to entertain. In time, the song stayed with the audience and was taken out West along with the brindle cow and the feather quilt.

In the Ozarks, they told the Tennessee girls not to marry the Arkansas boys, while the Arkansas girls were similarly warned against the Missouri boys, and Louisiana girls were advised to guard against the Texas clan. Perhaps the song fit Kansas better than any place else, for it really took hold on the plains, kept alive by the early settlers and their children's children.

It was a song for the women folk, a riposte in rhyme by the female of the race. The plains pioneer saw more than his fair share of trouble; and the frontier woman shared her husband's lot, and more. One old-timer said: "Yeah, they had to stand what the men folks stood, and stand the men folks, too."

The song traveled to Wyoming, where young ladies were urged to scorn the Cheyenne boys, and out near the Great Salt Lake, the disciples of Brigham Young fashioned their own wry parody on themselves:

Come, girls, come, and listen to my noise,
Don't you marry the Mormon boys,
For if you do, your fortune it will be,
Johnnycakes and babies are all you'll see.[2]

[1] Minstrel song "De Free Nigger" (circa 1841) from the original sheet music in the Library of Congress.

[2] "Don't You Marry the Mormon Boys," as sung by Paul Anderson, Woods Cross, Utah, quoted in *Saints of Sage and Saddle*, Austin and Alta Fife.

KANSAS BOYS

1. Hel-lo girls,   lis-ten to my voice,   Don't you fall in love with no   Kan-sas boys,   For

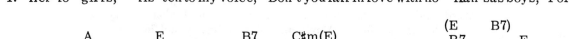

if   you do, your for-tune it will be   Hoe-cake, hom-i-ny, and sas-sa-frass tea.

Hello girls, listen to my voice,
Don't you fall in love with no Kansas boys,
For if you do, your fortune it will be
Hoecake, hominy, and sassafrass tea.

They'll take you out on a jet-black hill,
Take you there so much against your will,
Leave you there to perish on the plain;
That's the way with the Kansas range.

Some live in a cabin with a huge log wall,
Nary a window in it at all,
Sandstone chimney and a puncheon floor,
Clapboard roof and a buttoned door.

When they go to milk, they milk in a gourd,
Heave it in a corner and cover it with a board.
Some get plenty and some get none,
For that is the way with the Kansas run.

When they get hungry and go to make bread,
They kindle a fire as high as your head,
Rake around the ashes and in they throw,
The name they give it is "doughboy's dough."

When they go to meeting, the clothes that they wear
Is an old brown coat all picked and bare,
An old white hat more rim than crown,
A pair of cotton socks they wore the week around.

When they go to farming, you needn't be alarmed
In February they plant their corn,
The way they tend it I'll tell you now,
With a Texas pony and a grasshopper plow.

When they go a-fishing, they take along a worm,
Put it on a hook just to see it squirm,
The first thing they say when they get a bite
Is "I caught a fish as big as Johnny White."

When they go a-courting, they take along a chair.
First thing they say, "Has your daddy killed a bear?"
Second thing they say as they sit down,
"Madam, your johnnycake is baking brown."

When a young man falls in love,
First it's "honey," and then it's "Turtle dove."
After they're married, no such thing,
"Get up and get my breakfast you good-for-nothing

thing!"

The Wyoming Nester

TRADITIONAL

Learned from the singing of Jack Willis by J. Frank Dobie. From "More Ballads and Songs of the Frontier Folk," by J. Frank Dobie, in *Follow De Drinkin' Gou'd* (Texas Folklore Society Publications, Number VII). Reprinted by permission of the Texas Folklore Society.

The range's filled up with farmers an' there's fences ev'rywhere,
A painted house 'most ev'ry quarter mile;
They's raisin' blooded cattle an' plantin' sorted seed,
An' puttin' on a painful lot o' style.[1]

THE homesteaders moved west, following the railroad spurs, staking out their claims with barbed wire fences. By 1880, the settlers had left the eastern parts of Kansas and Nebraska behind and were beginning to drive their fence posts into the ground of the open range cattle country. It was a human tide of hungry land seekers which could not be denied. The ploughs dug up the prairie soil in western Kansas and Nebraska, in Colorado and Montana and Wyoming. And with every acre planted, the age of the once-proud cattlemen of the prairie and their colorful cowboys came closer to an end.

For more than a decade the settler and the cattleman fought, sometimes with threats and curses, sometimes with midnight murders, sometimes with open bloody war. In the end, as he had to, the settler won. Eventually, only the last, bitter song remained:

I'm going to leave old Texas now,
For they've got no use for the longhorn cow;
They've plowed and fenced my cattle range,
And the people there are all so strange.[2]

Play suggested bass line for guitar with chords as indicated; strum mainly on the second and fourth eighth-note beats of each measure:

Piano may play this down an octave.

[1] "The Old Cowboy's Lament," from *Cowboy Lyrics*, Robert V. Carr.

[2] "The Texas Song," from *Cowboy Songs*, Lomax.

THE WYOMING NESTER

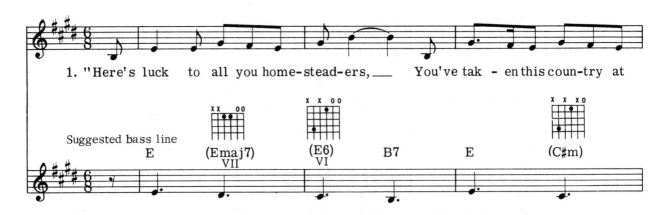

1. "Here's luck to all you home-stead-ers,____ You've tak-en this coun-try at

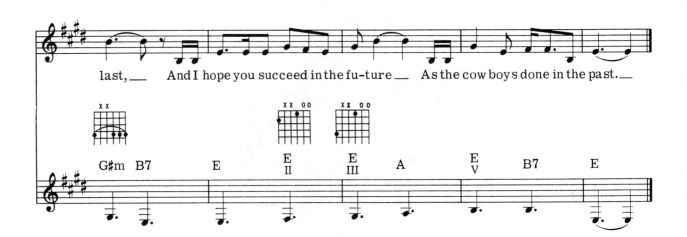

last,____ And I hope you succeed in the fu-ture____ As the cow-boys done in the past.____

"Here's luck to all you homesteaders,
You've taken this country at last,
And I hope you succeed in the future
As the cowboys done in the past.

"You've homesteaded all of this country,
Where the slicks and the mavericks did roam;
You've driven me far from my country,
Far from my birthplace and home.

"The cattle are still getting thinner,
And the ranches are shorter on men,
But I've got me a full quart of whiskey
And nearly a full quart of gin.

"You have taken up all of the water,
And all of the land that's nearby—"

And he took a big drink from his bottle
Of good old '99 rye.

He rode far into the evening,
His limbs at last had grown tired.
He shifted himself in his saddle,
And he slowly hung down his head.

His saddle he used for a pillow;
His blanket he used for a bed.
As he lay himself down for a night's slumber,
These words to himself he then said:

"I'm leaving this grand state forever,
This land and the home of my birth,
It fills my heart with sorrow,
But it fills your heart with mirth."

Dakota Land

WORDS: John A. Dean
MUSIC: "Beulah Land"

Words and music from *The American Songbag*, Carl Sandburg. See *Songs for the Toiler*, "Nebraska Land."

> In God we trusted,
> In Kansas we busted.[1]

THE plains country has a folklore of its own, legends of summer heat and winter frost, of drought and hail and the natural orneriness of the prairie soil. One pioneer felt that he was blessed:

"'Them the Lord loveth, he chasteneth.' Well, he ain't done very much for us Kansas fellers but chasten us with sand storms, chinch bugs, cyclones, dry weather, blizzards, and grasshoppers. He must love us a turrible sight." [2]

They called it "God's Country," and the same pioneer agreed, saying "There ain't much out here for anybody to be wicked on."

In Kansas, Nebraska, and the Dakotas, the story was the same. The land was rich, but nature was a savage adversary, and it took all a man's strength and will to draw his sustenance from this unplowed earth. Laughing at themselves, they took an old hymn called "Beulah Land" and fashioned it into a mocking comment on their own gullibility. Afterward, they began to sing of the bankers and the railroads who proved even fiercer enemies than nature.

Try a thumb strum, or four- or five-finger plucking, on every note to help give the march effect.

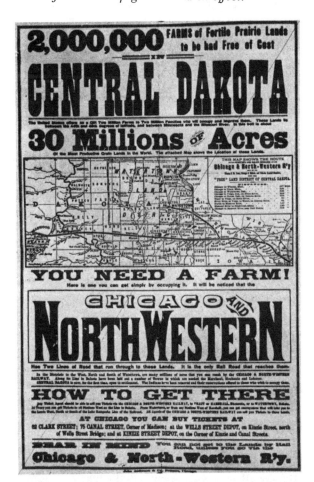

[1] Folk expression, quoted in *The Populist Movement in the United States*, Anna Rochester.
[2] From *Dodge City, Kansas*, Charles C. Lowtherm, quoted in *A Treasury of Western Folklore*, B. A. Botkin.

DAKOTA LAND

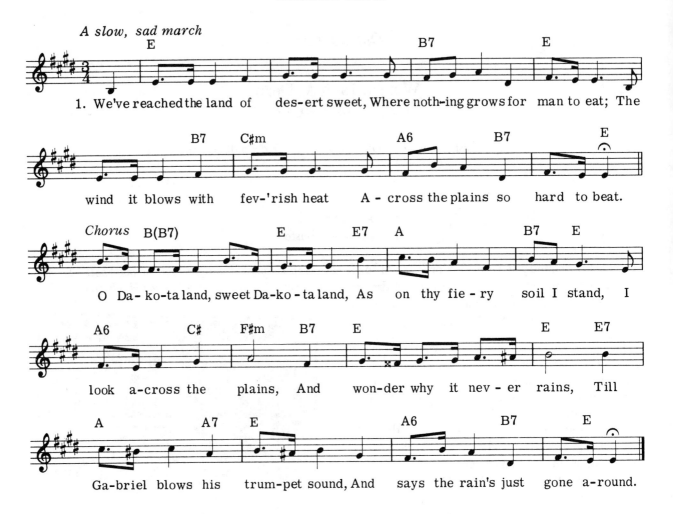

A slow, sad march

1. We've reached the land of des-ert sweet, Where noth-ing grows for man to eat; The wind it blows with fev-'rish heat A - cross the plains so hard to beat.

Chorus

O Da-ko-ta land, sweet Da-ko-ta land, As on thy fie-ry soil I stand, I look a-cross the plains, And won-der why it nev-er rains, Till Ga-briel blows his trum-pet sound, And says the rain's just gone a-round.

We've reached the land of desert sweet,
Where nothing grows for man to eat;
The wind it blows with feverish heat
Across the plains so hard to beat.

Chorus:

O Dakota land, sweet Dakota land,
As on thy fiery soil I stand,
I look across the plains
And wonder why it never rains,
Till Gabriel blows his trumpet sound
And says the rain's just gone around.

We've reached the land of hills and stones
Where all is strewn with buffalo bones.

O buffalo bones, bleached buffalo bones,
I seem to hear your sighs and moans.

(Chorus)

We have no wheat, we have no oats,
We have no corn to feed our shoats;
Our chickens are so very poor
They beg for crumbs outside the door.

(Chorus)

Our horses are of broncho race;
Starvation stares them in the face.
We do not live, we only stay;
We are too poor to get away.

(Chorus)

The Kansas Fool

WORDS: C. S. Whitney
MUSIC: "Beulah Land" (and "Dakota Land")

Text from *Songs for the Toiler*.

We have the land to raise the wheat,
And everything that's good to eat;
And when we had no bonds or debt,
We were a jolly, happy set,

Chorus:

Oh! Kansas fool! poor Kansas fool!
The banker makes of you a tool;
I look across the fertile plain,
Big crops made so by gentle rain;
But twelve-cent corn gives me alarm,
And makes me want to sell my farm,

With abundant crops raised everywhere,
'Tis a mystery, I do declare;
Why, farmers all should fume and fret,
And why we are so deep in debt.

(Chorus)

At first we made some money here,
With drouth and grasshoppers each year;
But now the interest that we pay
Soon takes our money all away.

(Chorus)

The bankers followed us out west,
And did in mortgages invest;
They looked ahead and shrewdly planned,
And soon they'll have our Kansas land.

(Chorus)

The Farmer Is the Man

TRADITIONAL

From a version collected by Waldemar Hille, *People's Songs Bulletin* (Vol. 2, No. 5).

We worked through spring and winter,
Through summer and through fall,
But the mortgage worked the hardest
And the steadiest of them all.
It worked on nights and Sundays;
It worked each holiday;
It settled down among us
And never went away.[1]

SOMEWHERE out in the plains country in the latter part of the nineteenth century, an unknown prairie poet fashioned a song out of the farmers' economic facts of life. Perhaps he had read that most revolutionary of English poems, Percy Bysshe Shelley's "Song to the Men of England":

> Men of England, wherefore plough
> For the lords who lay ye low?
> . . . .
> The seed ye sow, another reaps,
> The wealth ye find another keeps.

"The Farmer Is the Man" became a part of prairie folklore. Carl Sandburg heard a Galesburg, Illinois milkman (a one-time country fiddler) sing the song back in the 1890's. The theme is perennial. Half a century later, tenant sharecroppers in Arkansas would sing:

> Hungry, hungry are we,
> Just as hungry as hungry can be;
> We don't get nothing for our labor,
> So hungry, hungry are we.[2]

[1] "The Mortgage Worked the Hardest," from *Nebraska Folklore Pamphlets*, No. 16 (WPA Writer's Project).

[2] "Raggedy," by John Handcox, from *The People's Songs Bulletin*, Vol. 2, no. 1 (1947).

THE FARMER IS THE MAN

Bright; square-dance tempo

1. When the farm-er comes to town With his wag-on bro-ken down, Oh the

farm-er is the man who feeds them all._____ If you'll on - ly look and see, I_____

think you will a-gree That the farm-er is the man who feeds them all. The

Chorus

farm-er is the man, The farm-er is the man, Lives on cred-it till the

fall;_____ Then they take him by the hand And they lead him from the land, And the

mid-dle man's the man who gets it all._____

Interlude

D. C.

When the farmer comes to town
With his wagon broken down,
Oh the farmer is the man who feeds them all.
If you'll only look and see,
I think you will agree
That the farmer is the man who feeds them all.

Refrain:

The farmer is the man,
The farmer is the man,
Lives on credit till the fall;
Then they take him by the hand
And they lead him from the land,
And the middleman's the man who gets it all.

Oh the lawyer hangs around
While the butcher cuts a pound,
But the farmer is the man who feeds them all;
And the preacher and the cook
Go a-strolling by the brook,
But the farmer is the man who feeds them all.

Refrain:

The farmer is the man,
The farmer is the man,
Lives on credit till the fall;
With the interest rate so high,
It's a wonder he don't die,
For the mortgage man's the man who gets it all.

When the banker says he's broke
And the merchant's up in smoke,
They forget that it's the farmer feeds them all.
It would put them to the test
If the farmer took a rest,
Then they'd know that it's the farmer feeds them all.

Refrain:

The farmer is the man,
The farmer is the man,
Lives on credit till the fall;
His pants are wearing thin,
His condition, it's a sin,
He's forgot that he's the man who feeds them all.

The Hayseed

WORDS: Arthur L. Kellogg
MUSIC: Adapted from "Rosin the Beau" (see also "Acres of Clams")

Text from *Nebraska Folklore Pamphlets*, No. 18, "Nebraska Farmers' Alliance Songs of the 1890's," Federal Writers Project.

Come, boys, come! Let's down Monopoly!
Come, boys, come! From bankers set us free!
And vote no more for lawyers, but farmers they must be,
While we are marching through Kansas.[1]

THE homesteader had barely gained a handhold on the land, making his peace with the tyrannical natural conditions of the Great Plains, when he encountered other adversaries whose awesome power made even the fearful twisters of the Kansas prairie a blessing by comparison.

The prairie farmer grew his crops for market. But the markets in Omaha, Kansas City, and Chicago were hundreds of miles away, and the farmer shortly became dependent on a close-knit circle of entrepreneurs who controlled the shipping, the storage, and the trading apparatus. The elevator owner, the miller, the commission agent, and above all, the railroad company, called the turn.

Working together through interlocking directorates and mutual agreements, these various capitalists were able to exercise complete control over the farmers' crops. And slowly, surely moving into the picture was the banker who was willing to advance the farmer capital (at exorbitant rates of interest) against his next crop. By 1890, there were whole counties in Kansas, Nebraska, and the Dakotas where 90 per cent of the land was mortgaged to the banks.

In struggling against the abuses of the monopolies and the banks, the farmers formed a number of organizations. State farm associations, Granges, and local independent political parties all attempted to alleviate the worst conditions. Until 1890, the political activity of the farmers was con-

fined to attempts to influence the two major parties. But in time the farmer decided that both the Republican and Democratic party organizations were safely in the hands of the very financial interests who oppressed him. A new political awareness began to make itself felt:

All the way my party led me,
And they robbed me every day;
But I didn't see my folly
Till my home was took away.[2]

Political sophistication began to replace naïveté. The "new" farmer dismissed the differences between Democrat and Republican:

It's a sham, it's a sham,
It's a sham battle.
Watch the whole capoodle, boys,
While they divide the boodle,
For it's nothing but a sham battle.[3]

In 1892, the People's Party of the U.S.A. was formally organized. Better known as Populists, the party ran candidates for national office in the elections of 1892, their Presidential candidate polling over one million votes and almost ten per cent of the total. Its great strength, of course, was in the midwest, where the party carried Kansas, Idaho, Colorado, Nevada, and North Dakota.

The "hayseeds" came off the farms and went to the polls. And in the heated, singing campaign of 1892, this was their song.

[1] "Marching Through Kansas," Sam Berhers, from *Songs for the Toiler* (circa 1890).

[2] "My Party Led Me," S. T. Johnson, *ibid.*
[3] "The Sham Battle," H. W. Taylor, J. B. Herbert, *ibid.*

240

THE HAYSEED

band - ed to - geth-er____ To beat a poor hay - seed like

(C) (C III) F C V G7

H

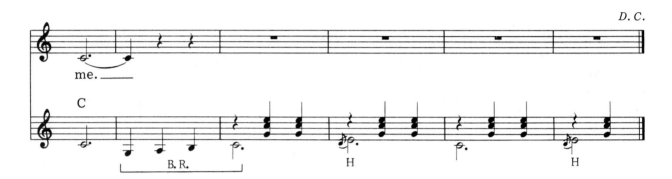

D. C.

me.____

C

B. R. H H

I once was a tool of oppression,
And as green as a sucker could be,
And monopolies banded together
To beat a poor hayseed like me.

    To beat a poor hayseed like me,
    To beat a poor hayseed like me,
    The monopolies banded together
    To beat a poor hayseed like me.

The railroads and old party bosses
Together did sweetly agree;
And they thought there would be little trouble
In working a hayseed like me.

    In working a hayseed like me, etc.

But now I've roused up a little
And their greed and corruption I see.
And the ticket we vote next November
Will be made up of hayseeds like me.

    Will be made up of hayseeds like me, etc.

_____

*I suggest an um-pah-pah accompaniment with bass
runs, hammer-ons on the D-string, etc. The bass line
only is given on the staff below the melody.*

The Independent Man

WORDS: Mrs. J. T. Kellie
MUSIC: "The Girl I Left Behind Me"

Text from *Nebraska Folklore Pamphlets*, No. 18, "Nebraska Farmers' Alliance
Songs of the 1890's," Federal Writers Project.

Then hurrah for the Demo–Republico party,
With abundant, unlimited, cast-iron gall;
This great combination, to capture the nation,
Is monopoly, whiskey, and the devil, this fall.[1]

A RECURRENT theme in the Populist songs of the 1890's is the duplicity of the two old political parties. Republican or Democrat, argued the Populist orators, it makes no difference; both parties are firmly in the hands of the railroads and the bankers. Only a new party, a farmer's party, a people's party, can save the nation. So they sang in 1892, their melodies echoing through the Grange and Alliance halls of the prairie towns. "Good-bye, my party, good-bye," they sang, and, mockingly, they described "Old Party Rallies":

They will meet but they will miss us,
There will be but vacant chairs,

They may linger for our coming
Till they climb the golden stairs.[2]

The political affiliations of decades were being swept away with the prairie winds; in place of the two old parties, a new banner, a new song, a new party was the hope and dream of the newly-independent man:

Oh the People's ticket; oh the People's ticket,
People's ticket I'm going to vote because it am so
   true;
Oh the Peoples ticket, oh the People's ticket,
People's ticket I'm going to vote in the fall of '92. [3]

[1] "Unlimited Gall," C. M. Maxson (circa 1890), from unpublished manuscript by Richard Stephenson, Lawrence, Kansas.

[2] "Old Party Rallies," from *The People's Songster*, C. S. White (1892).
[3] "The People's Ticket," *ibid.*

THE INDEPENDENT MAN

I was a party man one time,
The party would not mind me;
That's all for which I have to thank
The party's left behind me.

Chorus:

An older, sadder, poorer man
Sure every year did find me;
That's all for which I have to thank
The party left behind me.

I asked that from the railroad's clutch
A way out they should find me;
One party answered me, "Not much,"
The other would not mind me.

(Chorus)

I was to moneyed men a slave—
They said it was a fable;
One party would not try to save,
The other was not able.

(Chorus)

A true and independent man
You ever more shall find me;
I work and vote and ne'er regret
The party left behind me.

(Chorus)

The People's Jubilee

WORDS: C. S. White
MUSIC: "Kingdom Coming" ("Year of Jubilo") by Henry Clay Work

Text from *Songs for the Toiler*.

Don't you see the bankers squealing over yonder,
Where the grand old parties congregate?
But never you be frightened, they have lost their power,
And the Alliance, now, will seal their fate.[1]

For the farmers of the prairie, 1892 was a year of hope and dreams. Perhaps it would be the "Year of Jubilo." With a political organization that could speak for them, the farmers entered into the spirit of the election campaign with a fervor and a zeal which American political life had not seen for half a century. One historian of the movement wrote:

"It was a religious revival, a crusade, a pentecost of politics in which a tongue of flame sat upon every man, and each spake as the spirit gave him utterance. The farmers, the country merchants, the cattle-herders, they of the long chin-whiskers, and they of the broad-brimmed hats and heavy boots, had also heard the word and could preach the gospel of Populism." [2]

In speech and song, the Populists sounded forth, mincing no words, pouring out the hardship and frustration of three decades of victimization and exploitation by railroad and bank.

One frontier woman, of Irish descent, a mother of four and a self-trained lawyer to boot, traveled the length of Kansas in 1890. Her words were the overture to the upheavals of 1891 and 1892:

"Wall Street owns the country. It is no longer a government of the people, by the people and for the people, but a government of Wall Street, by Wall Street and for Wall Street. The great common people of this country are slaves and monopoly is the master. What you farmers need to do is to raise less corn and more *Hell!*" [3]

[1] "The Alliances Are Coming," *The People's Songster, op. cit.*
[2] From "The Populist Uprising," by Elizabeth N. Barr in *A Standard History of Kansas and Kansans,* quoted in *The*

Populist Revolt, John D. Hicks.
[3] From a speech by Mrs. Mary Elizabeth Lease, Kansas Populist organizer, quoted in Barr, *ibid.*

THE PEOPLE'S JUBILEE

Bright

1. Say— work-ers have you seen the bos-ses with— scared and pal-lid face, Go-ing

down the al-ley some-time this e-ven-ing To find a hid - ing place? They

saw the peo-ple cast their bal-lots And they knew their time had come; They

spent their boo-dle to get e-lect-ed But were beat-en by the peo-ple's men.

Chorus

The peo - ple laugh, ha ha! The bos - ses, Oh! how blue! It

must be now the ju - bi-lee is com-ing in the year of nine - ty - two.

Say, workers, have you seen the bosses
With scared and pallid face,
Going down the alley sometime this evening
To find a hiding place?
They saw the people cast their ballots
And they knew their time had come;
They spent their boodle to get elected
But were beaten by the people's men.

Chorus:

The people laugh, ha, ha!
The bosses, oh! how blue!
It must be now the jubilee is coming
In the year of ninety-two.

The bosses got to feeling so big,
They thought the world was their'n;
Of the starving people all over the land
They did not care to learn.
They blowed so much and called themselves leaders,
And they got so full of sin;
I spec' they try to fool the Almighty,
But Peter won't let them in.

(Chorus)

The working people are getting tired
Of having no home or land;
So now, they say, to run this government
They are going to try their hand.
There's gold and silver in the White House cellar,
And the workers all want some,
For they know it will all be counted out
When the People's Party comes.

(Chorus)

The election's over and the rings are beaten,
And the bosses have run away;
The people's army came out victorious
And have won the election day.
They cast their votes for truth and freedom,
Which are always bound to win;
Up to the polls they walked like freemen
And put their ballots in.

(Chorus)

PART 7

"Come All You Bold Fellers"

Well, I'm a wild cowboy,
I've roved the West o'er,
Roped the balls of lightning,
And shot up towns galore;
I've busted the wild broomtails,
With their heads plumb skinned,
And rode a slick saddle
From beginning to end.[1]

[1] "Wild Bronc Peeler," *Cowboy Songs*, Lomax.

THE OUTLAW is a natural folk hero. Symbol of defiance against law and landlord, the highwayman, the pirate, and the daring robber are characters with whom the Anglo–Saxon peasant and the plains cowboy could readily identify. Robin Hood, Captain Kidd, and Brennan on the Moor were the folk heroes of the old country. On the other side of the Atlantic, tradition kept the old heroes alive and new ones, like Tom Dooley, Stagolee and John Hardy came to birth in native ballads.

Out West, on the plains of Kansas and Colorado, true-to-life gunslinging outlaws like Jesse James, Sam Bass, and Billy the Kid took their places in the memory museums we call folk songs. Old-country ballads of violence and death were adapted to new-world settings, and the "Unfortunate Rake" of London became the dying cowboy of Laredo.

Incredible tales of great exploits by man and beast, of horses who could leap a mile and soft-talking bronc-busters who could ride them, became the subject of songs which were sung around lonely fires on a silent prairie.

The cowboy bard took over the old ballad form to create narratives in song of heroes, villains, cowards and fools whose exploits have become a permanent part of our folklore. Life on the prairie was hard, strenuous. It required men of stamina and patience to survive. Out of the struggle with nature and their fellow-man, these weather-bitten children of the plains created heroes who were larger than life. These heroes, their songs and their legends, outlasted their creators and are now an ineradicable part of the national image.

Jesse James

TRADITIONAL BALLAD

Authorship claimed by Billy Gashade. Composite text from a variety of traditional sources.

Jesse James was one of his names,
Another it was Howard.
He robbed the rich of every stitch,
You bet he was no coward.[1]

In the backwash of the Civil War, the western plains provided a stage for a breed of men who had learned to live by the gun. For many, like Frank and Jesse James, their training ground was that savage band of looters and marauders who traveled under the Confederate flag and went by the name of "Quantrill's Raiders."

When the war was over, Frank and Jesse James went into business for themselves. For fifteen years the notorious James brothers reigned as the scourge of Kansas and Missouri. Jesse James, the younger of the two, became the colorful mastermind and daring desperado of the gang.

"He stole from the rich and he gave to the poor," they sang in later years, after Jesse was gone, when the man had become a myth. And the folklore was based on fact. There wasn't much point to stealing from the poor. Not unless you could work out a system the way the landlords did. And Jesse undoubtedly gave to the poor, and won loyalty, safety and shelter in times of need.

To the hard-pressed plains farmers of the 1870's, Jesse James indeed may have appeared as the agent of destiny's vengeance. The outlaw's victims were usually those twin traducers of the farmers' labor and land—the railroads and the banks.

In April of 1882, Jesse James was murdered. His assassin was Robert Ford, a young man who had joined Jesse's band a short while before with the deliberate intent of killing the outlaw and claiming the $10,000 reward offered for the deed.

With Jesse's death (shot in the back of the head, unarmed, by a man he trusted as a friend), the legend was complete. Robin Hood betrayed by a woman, Brennan on the Moor likewise a victim of womanly treachery, these were the precedents from folklore and history which helped to create the Jesse James saga. All that was needed in order to enshrine the legend permanently was a ballad. Within a short time after Jesse's death, an otherwise unknown minstrel by the name of Billy Gashade created the ballad which has come to be Jesse James' lasting epitaph.

"Soon after the killing of James a ten-foot poem, set to music, came out and was sung on the streets of Springfield quite frequently. It told how Jesse James had a wife and she warned him all her life and the children they were brave and the dirty little coward who shot Mr. Howard and they laid poor Jesse in the grave. It caused tears to be shed; it was the Mark Antony eulogy at the bier of Caesar. An old blind woman used to stand in front of the court house in Springfield and sing it by the hour; mourners would drop coins in her tin can. She went up to Richmond, Mo., and was singing her sad song with tears in her voice when she found herself slapped and kicked into the middle of the street. Bob Ford's sister happened to be passing that way." [2]

With the passing years, the ballad became known throughout the country. Cowboys, lumberjacks, and

[1] From *Ballads and Songs Collected by the Missouri Folklore Society*, H. M. Belden.

[2] Robert L. Kennedy, an article in the Springfield (Mo.) *Leader* (1933), quoted in *Ozark Folksongs*, Vol. 2, Vance Randolph.

wandering troupers sang the song. The descendants of the plains farmers in the dust bowls of Kansas and Oklahoma in the 1930's still sang the old song of the daring outlaw whose six-shooter leveled class and caste with consummate urgency. One of these, Woody Guthrie, possibly the greatest ballad maker of our age, rewrote the old song to fit the bitter mood of the depression years (see "Jesse James" II). In later years, Woody completed the saga by retelling the story of Jesus to the Jesse James tune:

Jesus Christ was a man
That traveled through the land,
A hard-working man and brave.
He said to the rich,
"Give your goods to the poor,"
So they laid Jesus Christ in his grave.[3]

[3] "Jesus Christ," by Woody Guthrie, from *Sing Out!*, Vol. 10, No. 4.

JESSE JAMES (I)

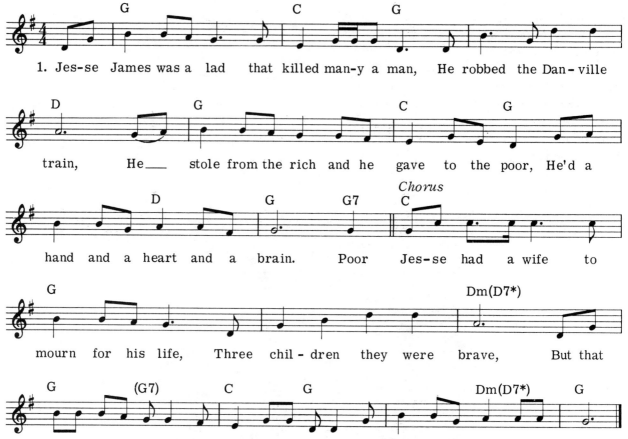

1. Jes-se James was a lad that killed man-y a man, He robbed the Dan-ville train, He__ stole from the rich and he gave to the poor, He'd a hand and a heart and a brain. *Chorus* Poor Jes-se had a wife to mourn for his life, Three chil-dren they were brave, But that dir-ty lit-tle cow-ard that shot Mis-ter How-ard Has laid Jes-se James in his grave.

* If Dm upsets you.

Jesse James was a lad that killed many a man,
He robbed the Danville train,
He stole from the rich and he gave to the poor,
He'd a hand and a heart and a brain.

Chorus:

Poor Jesse had a wife to mourn for his life,
Three children they were brave,
But the dirty little coward that shot Mr. Howard
Has laid Jesse James in his grave.

It was Robert Ford, that dirty little coward,
I wonder how he does feel,
For he ate of Jesse's bread and he slept in Jesse's bed,
Then he laid poor Jesse in his grave.

(Chorus)

Jesse James was a man, a friend to the poor,
He'd never see a man suffer pain;
And with his brother Frank, he robbed the Chicago bank,
And stopped the Glendale train.

254

(Chorus)

It was on a Wednesday night and the moon was shining bright,
They robbed the Glendale train,
And the people they did say for many miles away,
It was robbed by Frank and Jesse James.

(Chorus)

It was his brother Frank that robbed the Gallatin bank,
And carried the money from the town;
It was in this very place that they had a little race,
For they shot Captain Sheets to the ground.

(Chorus)

They went to the crossing not very far from there,
And there they did the same;
With the agent on his knees, he delivered up the keys
To the outlaws, Frank and Jesse James.

(Chorus)

It was on a Saturday night and Jesse was at home
Talking with his family brave,
Robert Ford came along like a thief in the night
And laid poor Jesse in his grave.

(Chorus)

The people held their breath when they heard of Jesse's death,
And wondered how he ever came to die.
It was one of the gang called little Robert Ford,
He shot poor Jesse on the sly.

(Chorus)

Jesse went to his rest with his hand on his breast,
The devil will be upon his knee.
He was born one day in the county of Clay,
And came from a solitary race.

(Chorus)

This song was made by Billy Gashade
As soon as the news did arrive;
He said there was no man with the law in his hand
Who could take Jesse James when alive.

(Chorus)

JESSE JAMES (II)

by Woody Guthrie

Jesse James and his boys rode that Dodge City Trail,
Held up the midnight Southern mail,
And there never was a man with the law in his hand
That could keep Jesse James in a jail.

It was Frank and Jesse James that killed a many a man,
But they never was outlaws at heart;
I wrote this song to tell you how it come
That Frank and Jesse James got their start.

They was living on a farm in the old Missouri hills,
With a silver-haired mother and a home;
Now the railroad bullies come to chase them off their land,
But they found that Frank and Jesse wouldn't run.

Then a railroad scab, he went and got a bomb,
And he throwed it at the door—
And it killed Mrs. James a-sleeping in her bed,
So Jesse grabbed a big forty-four.

    Yes, Frank and Jesse James was men that was game
    To stop that high-rolling train—
    And to shoot down the rat that killed Mrs. James,
    They was Two-Gun Frank and Jesse James.

Now a bastard and a coward called little Robert Ford,
He claimed he was Frank and Jesse's friend,
Made love to Jesse's wife and he took Jesse's life,
And he laid poor Jesse in his grave.

The people was surprised when Jesse lost his life,
Wondered how he ever came to fall,
Robert Ford, it's a fact, shot Jesse in the back,
While Jesse hung a picture on the wall.

They dug Jesse's grave and a stone they raised,
It says, "Jesse James lies here—
Was killed by a man, a bastard and a coward,
Whose name ain't worthy to appear."

Sam Bass

Author unknown

TRADITIONAL BALLAD

Text from *Songs of the Cowboys*, N. Howard Thorp; music from *Singing Cowboy*, Margaret Larkin.

Come listen to my tragedy,
Both people young and old,
I'll tell to you a story,
'Twill make your blood run cold.[1]

SAM Bass's permanent place in the folklore of the West grows out of one year of crime, mainly in the vicinity of Denton, Texas. In his year as leader of an outlaw gang, Sam Bass held up stagecoaches, trains, and banks, running up a total of hundreds of thousands of dollars in "primitive accumulation." The song tells his story, accurately and with all the colorful detail of folklore. Sam was killed in Round Rock, Texas, July 21, 1878, on his twenty-seventh birthday. Betrayed by a one-time friend and police agent, Jim Murphy, Sam Bass went to his death refusing to give the Texas Rangers information on the other members of his gang. The song, in the tradition of the come-all-ye narratives of English and American balladry, may have been written within days of Sam Bass's death. In the legend that grew up in later years, Sam became a hero like Jesse James (stealing from the rich, generous with the poor), and now the stories of these two outlaws are used interchangeably, living testimony to the class motivations of the folk process.

[1] "Henry Green," from *Ozark Folksongs*, Vol. 2, *op. cit.*

SAM BASS

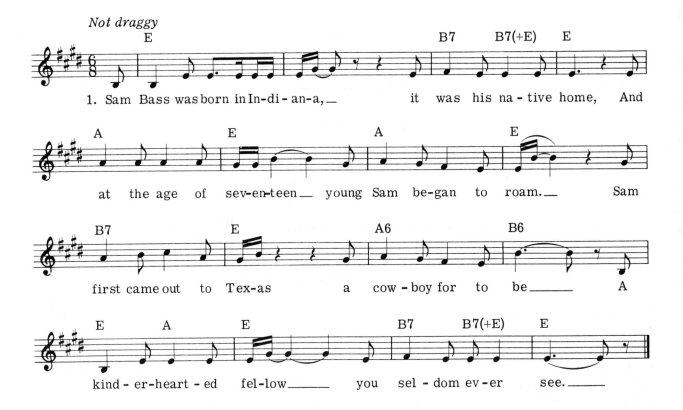

Not draggy

1. Sam Bass was born in In-di-an-a, — it was his na-tive home, And at the age of sev-en-teen — young Sam be-gan to roam. — Sam first came out to Tex-as a cow-boy for to be _____ A kind-er-heart-ed fel-low _____ you sel-dom ev-er see. _____

Sam Bass was born in Indiana, it was his native home,
And at the age of seventeen young Sam began to roam.
Sam first came out to Texas a cowboy for to be—
A kinder-hearted fellow you seldom ever see.

Sam used to deal in race stock, one called the Denton mare;
He matched her in scrub races and took her to the fair.
Sam used to coin the money, and spent it just as free;
He always drank good whiskey wherever he might be.

Sam left the Collins ranch, in the merry month of May,
With a herd of Texas cattle the Black Hills for to see;
Sold out in Custer City, and then got on a spree—
A harder set of cowboys you seldom ever see.

On their way back to Texas they robbed the U. P. train,
And then split up in couples and started out again;
Joe Collins and his partner were overtaken soon,
With all their hard-earned money they had to meet their doom.

Sam made it back to Texas, all right up with care,
Rode into the town of Denton with all his friends to share.
Sam's life was short in Texas, three robberies did he do;
He robbed all the passenger mail and express cars too.

Sam had four companions, four bold and daring lads,
They were Richardson, Jackson, Joe Collins and Old Dad;
Four more bold and daring cowboys the Rangers never knew,
They whipped the Texas Rangers and ran the boys in blue.

Sam and another companion, called "Arkansas" for short,
Was shot by a Texas Ranger by the name of Thomas Floyd;
Oh, Tom is a big six-footer and thinks he's mighty fly,
But I can tell you his racket—he's a deadbeat on the sly.

Jim Murphy was arrested and then released on bail;
He jumped his bond at Tyler and then took the train for Terrell;
But Mayor Jones had posted Jim and that was all a stall,
'Twas only a plan to capture Sam before the coming fall.

Sam met his fate at Round Rock, July the twenty-first,
They pierced poor Sam with rifle balls and emptied out his purse.
Poor Sam he is a corpse and six foot under clay,
And Jackson in the bushes trying to get away.

Jim had borrowed Sam's good gold and didn't want to pay,
The only shot he saw was to give poor Sam away.
He sold out Sam and Barnes and left their friends to mourn—
Oh, what a scorching Jim will get when Gabriel blows his horn.

And so he sold out Sam and Barnes and left their friends to mourn—
Oh what a scorching Jim will get when Gabriel blows his horn.
Perhaps he's got to heaven, there's none of us can say,
But if I am right in my surmise, he's gone the other way.

Billy the Kid

Author unknown

TRADITIONAL BALLAD

From *Cowboy Lore*, Jules Verne Allen.

Everyone claimed a woman,
Though none of their claims would stand
'Gainst the Kid, who was quicker than lightning
With a gun in either hand.[1]

THEY called him "Billy the Kid," and in his day no deadlier gunman existed in all the Southwest. By the time he was eighteen, he was a murderer with several corpses behind him. By the time he was nineteen, he had won a reputation as a cold-blooded killer. At the age of twenty he was a deadly profes-

[1] "Billy the Kid," by N. Howard Thorp, *Songs of the Cowboys*, Thorp.

sional gunman, and by the time he reached twenty-one he was the scourge of New Mexico. And then he was dead, shot to death by Sheriff Pat Garrett on July 14, 1881, in Fort Sumner, New Mexico. His body was not yet cold when the legend began, the legend of Billy the Kid, the boy bandit folk hero, a saint and a guardian of the poor.

The legend grew out of that natural affinity which the folk seem to have for the outlaw, for the man who can defy the power of authority; but in the case of Billy the Kid, it was a legend which had little basis in fact. For Billy was a cruel and blood-thirsty killer, a death-dealing homicidal maniac, a pint-sized gun-for-hire murderer who cast a ghastly giant shadow over his time and place.

Born on Rivington Street on the Lower East Side of New York City, November 23, 1859, Billy moved to Kansas with his family at the age of twelve. His life of crime began early. He was arrested frequently as a youngster and shortly became a jail-hardened outlaw. He lived in the image of his gun and developed a streak of cruelty which was known throughout the West. He was supposed to have killed twenty-one men by the age of twenty-one, but evidence suggests that the figure may actually have been much higher. Billy didn't count Indians and Mexicans, according to the racist prejudices of Southwestern lore.

In the end, he died by the gun. In ballad and song, a legend grew up. In recent years, however, history has begun to overtake the legend. It would be a symbolic act of poetic justice if, in the case of Billy the Kid, the folk process were to be reversed.

260

BILLY THE KID

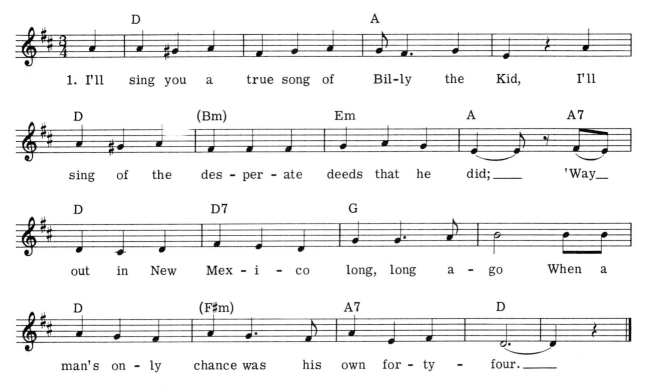

1. I'll sing you a true song of Bil-ly the Kid, I'll
sing of the des-per-ate deeds that he did; ____ 'Way __
out in New Mex-i-co long, long a-go When a
man's on-ly chance was his own for-ty-four. _____

I'll sing you a true song of Billy the Kid,
I'll sing of the desperate deeds that he did;
'Way out in New Mexico long, long ago,
When a man's only chance was his old forty-four.

When Billy the Kid was a very young lad,
In old Silver City, he went to the bad;
Way out in the West with a gun in his hand,
At the age of twelve years he killed his first man.

Fair Mexican maidens play guitars and sing,
A song about Billy, their boy bandit king;
How, ere his young manhood had reached its sad end,
Had a notch on his pistol for twenty-one men.

'Twas on the same night that poor Billy died,
He said to his friends, "I'm not satisfied;
There are twenty-one men I've put bullets through,
And Sheriff Pat Garrett must make twenty-two."

Now this is how Billy the Kid met his fate,
The bright moon was shining, the hour was late;
Shot down by Pat Garrett who once was his friend,
The young outlaw's life had come to its end.

There's many a man with face fine and fair,
Who starts out in life with a chance to be square;
But just like poor Billy, he wanders astray,
And loses his life the very same way.

The Zebra Dun

Author unknown

TRADITIONAL BALLAD

From the singing of Tony Kraber

Windy Bill was a Texas boy,
Said he could rope, you bet,
Said the steer he couldn't tie,
He hadn't met up with yet.[1]

AROUND campfires out on the open range, at way stations and stopping-places along the Chisholm trail, in the gin mills and brothels of Abilene and Dodge City, the men who worked the longhorn cows told their stories and sang their songs. Their ballads created a legend of mild-mannered men who turned out to be crackerjack riders and deadly shots, and of stately-looking horses and steers who were really the terrors of the cow country.

The best of these ballads concerned the horse they called "The Zebra Dun." Some folklorists believe that "Zebra" was really a corruption of "Z-Bar" since a "zebra dun" is a contradiction in terms. But that seems to be precisely the point of the narrative, since the horse of the narrative was indeed a rare creature, as rare, perhaps, as a "zebra dun."

[1] "Windy Bill," from *Singing Cowboy*, Larkin.

THE ZEBRA DUN

1. We was camped on the plains at the head of the Cim-ma-ron, When a-

long come a strang-er and stopped to ar-gue some, Well, he looked so ver-y fool-ish when he be-

gun to look a-round, For he seemed just like a green-horn just es-caped from town.

We was camped on the plains at the head of the Cimmaron,
When along come a stranger and stopped to argue some,
Well, he looked so very foolish when he begun to look around,
For he seemed just like a greenhorn just escaped from town.

We asked him had he been to chuck, he said he hadn't a smear,
So we opened up the chuckbox and said he could eat right here,
Well, he filled up on some coffee and some biscuits and some beans,
And started right in a-talking about the foreign kings and queens.

All about the foreign wars on the land and on the sea,
With guns as big as steers and ramrods big as trees,
About a fellow named Paul Jones, a fightin' son of a gun,
A fighter and the grittiest cuss that ever packed a gun.

Such an educated feller, his thoughts just come in herds,
He astonished all them cowboys with his highfalutin' words;
Well the stranger kept on talkin' till the boys they all got sick,
And begun to look around to see if they could play a trick.

Well, he said he'd lost his job upon the Seven-D,
Was tryin' to cross the range for to hit old Santa Fe,
He didn't say how come it, just some trouble with the boss,
But asked if he could borrow an old fat saddle horse.

Well, this tickled the boys near half to death, we laughed way down our sleeves,
We said we'd give him a fine horse, as fresh and fat as you please;
So Shorty grabbed his lariat and he roped the Zebra Dun,
And we give him to the stranger and waited for the fun.

Now old Dun he was an outlaw, had grown so awful wild,
He could paw the moon down, he could jump a mile,
Old Dun he stood right still, like as if he didn't know.
Till the stranger had him saddled and a-ready for to go.

263

When the stranger hit the saddle, then old Dun he quit the earth,
And started travelin' upwards for all that he was worth,
A-yellin' and a-squealin' and a-havin' warlike fits,
His hind feet perpendicular and his front feet in the bits.

We could see the tops of mountains under Dunny every jump,
But that stranger he was glued there just like the camel's hump,
The stranger sat upon him and he twirled his black moustache,
Just like a summer boarder waitin' for the hash.

Well, he thumped him in the shoulders and he spun him when he whirled,
And hollered to them cowboys, "I'm the wolf of the world!"
And when he had dismounted once more upon the ground,
We knowed he was a thoroughbred and not a gent from town.

The boss who was a-standin' by a-watchin' of the show,
Walked over to the stranger and said "You needn't go.
If you can use a lariat like you rode old Zebra Dun,
You're the man I've been waitin' for since the Year One."

There's one thing and a sure thing I've learned since I been born,
Every educated stranger ain't a plumb greenhorn.

El Toro Moro

(THE PURPLE BULL)

WORDS: Miguel de la Luna
MUSIC: Traditional

From "Folklore of the King Ranch Mexicans," by Frank Goodwyn, in *Southwestern Lore*, Dobie, Publications of the Texas Folklore Society, Number IX. Reprinted by permission of the Texas Folklore Society.

I am a vaquero by trade;
To handle my rope I'm not afraid.
I lass' an *otero* * by the two horns,
Throw down the biggest that ever was born.
Whoa! Whoa! Whoa! Pinto, whoa! [1]

MAN is dignified by the strength of his adversary— and folklore is filled with tales and songs of mighty beasts that only mighty men could tame. "The Derby Ram," "The Gray Goose," "The Zebra Dun" are all in this gallery of folk animals. So, too, is "El Toro Moro," the mighty purple bull captured on the King Ranch in Texas. This *corrido* may be based on an actual event, for there was a man named Euvence García on the King Ranch, and he is supposed to have roped and handled more wild cattle than any man in Texas. True or not, Euvence García and "El Toro Moro" are recorded for posterity in a song.

* "A steer as big as a mountain."
[1] "Pinto," from *Cowboy Songs and Other Ballads,* Lomax.

EL TORO MORO

Aquí me siento a cantar
con la voluntad de Dios.
Estos versos son compuestos
por la corrida del dos.

Señores, voy a cantar
con muchísimo decoro.
Estos versos son compuestos
al mentado Toro Moro.

I'll sit down here and sing
by the will of God. These
verses are composed by cow-camp
Number Two.

Sirs, I'm going to sing with a
lot of decoration. These
verses are composed about the
famous Purple Bull.

Es un torito moro, tiene el espinazo bajo. No lo han podido lazar, y echan la culpa al caballo.	He is a little purple bull. He has a dun (tan) back. They have not been able to rope him, and they blame it on the horse.
Buenos pollos lo han corrido, queriéndose aprovechar, pero en eso no han podido porque les entra al barral.	Expert birds have chased him, attempting to win favor. But in this they've not succeeded, for they are led into the thicket.
De becerro lo conocen. Desde que tenía tres años ahí anda en la Marcelina, completando los siete años.	Since he was a calf they have known him. Since he was a three-year-old he has been in the Marcelina pasture, and now he's completing his seventh year.
Se lo halló Euvence García, se lo enseño a su compadre; se pusieron a pensar y se les hizo muy tarde.	Euvence García found him, and showed him to his companion. They set themselves to planning, and this made them too late.
Y le decía su compadre con un cariño a lo bueno, "Lo echaremos por la brecha y por ahí esta Eugenio."	Euvence's companion said, with a most true affection: "We will chase him by the opening, and there Eugenio is waiting."
Eugenio como un territo, ya estaba en su agostadero, y al oir el primer grito fue y se hizo al corredero.	Eugenio, like a little terror, was there in his place. Upon hearing the first yell, he broke and made for the running place.
Cuando Eugenio lo vido al brincar la nopalera, desde ahí se lo fue entrando con su yegua Tesonera.	When Eugenio saw the bull jumping the prickly pear, he went after him on his Tesonera mare.
El toro se la fue en el punto de Placetitas, fue y les dijo a los demás que le truenan las pezuñitas.	The bull got away from him at the point known as Placetitas. He went and told the other hands that its hooves were making the ground thunder.
Decía Manuel Rosas en su caballo Cupido, ¡"Ojalá que se topara Este torito conmigo!"	Then Manuel Rosas, on his horse Cupido, said: "Oh, that this little bull would meet up with me!"
Otro día se lo topó en ese Plan del Jardín. El toro, al brincar la brecha ahí le pintó un violín.	On another day Manuel did meet him on the Plain of the Garden. When the bull jumped past the opening, he painted Manuel like a fiddle.

Manuel Rosas lo corrió,
diciendo, ¡"Ora si lo lazo!"
Pero jamás le tocó
el polvo del espinazo.

Manuel Rosas lo corrió
por todo el Plan del Jardín;
El caballo se voltió,
y no lo pudo seguir.

Manuel se arrendó a la brecha
y topó con su tocayo.
"Se me fue por hay ansina
porque se voltió el caballo."

Decía Manuel la Changa,
que era un hombre de valor,
"Échenmelo por aquí
para hacerles un favor."

Por toditita la brecha
se veía una polvadera;
era la Changa diciendo,
"Yo ya perdí esta carrera."

Más allá iba Chon Cortinas,
corriendo y moviendo un brazo,
"Ese toro tiene espinas;
por eso yo no lo lazo."

Dijo Macario Mayorgua,
viéndolo tan apurado,
"Voy a ver a mi compadre
ya tendrá el rodeo dado."

Cuando Euvence lo vido
ya venía muy ajilado,
con sonrisas nos decía,
"El torito está amarrado."

Decía Eugenio Cantú
en la orilla de un mogote,
"Échenmelo por aquí
pa doblarle un calabrote."

Eugenio se lo lazó
por no verlos batallar,
fue y les dijo a los demás
que lo fueran a llevar.

Manuel Rosas chased him, saying,
"Now I'll rope him!" But the dust
on the bull's back wasn't even brushed
off.

Manuel Rosas chased him all along the
Plain of the Garden. His horse
turned a somersault, and he couldn't
follow farther.

Manuel went back to the opening, and
there he met his namesake.*
"The bull got away from me over yonder
because my horse turned over."

Then said Manuel the Monkey, who was a
man of valor: "Just chase him around
this way that I may do you a favor."

All along through the opening was
raised a cloud of dust. It was the
Monkey saying, "This is a race I have
lost."

Farther on, Chon Cortinas entered the
chase, running and waving his arm.
"This bull has thorns; that's why I
don't rope him."

Then said Macario Mayorgua, seeing him
so played out, "I'm going back to my
partner. By now he has a round up
made."

When Euvence saw him (Macario) coming
to the round up with such speed, he
said to us, smiling, "The little bull
is now roped and tied."

Then said Eugenio Cantu, who was at
the edge of a little thicket, "Chase
him to me around this way that I may
dab a loop on him."

Eugenio roped him so as to prevent
the other hands from bothering
themselves. Then he went and told
them to go and bring the bull out.

* His namesake was Manuel la Changa, Manuel the
Monkey, so called on account of his comic pranks.

Decía Euvence García
en el tordillo grandote,
"Mancuérnenmelo con los bueyes,
llévenlo pa'l Tecolote."

Por todo lo de la brecha
el fuego está cerrado.
Le dijeron al patrón
que el toro estaba amarrado.

Lo llevamos para Norias;
lo embarcamos pa' For Wes.
Ya se fué el Torito Moro;
ya no volverá otra vez.

Y con esta me despido
y sin dilación ninguna.
Él que compuso estos versos
se llama Miguel de la Luna.

Then Euvence García on his big gray
horse said, "Neck him to the oxen
and take him to the Tecolote Trap." °

All along the opening the game is
now closed. The men told the boss
(the *patrón* is over the *corporal*)
that the bull was roped.

We took the bull to Norias: we
shipped him to Fort Worth. Now the
Purple Bull is gone. He'll never
come back.

And now I beg dismissal without
further delay. He who composes
these verses is named Miguel
de la Luna.

° Oxen, trained to lead and kept for such purposes, are
used to bring in outlaw animals that have been roped
and tied out in the brush. Tie a wild animal by the neck
to one of these "neck oxen" and he will bring it in.

Corrido de Heraclio Bernal

TRADITIONAL CORRIDO
Text and melody from *El Corrido Mexicano*, Mendoza.

He stole from the rich and he gave to the poor,
He'd a hand and a heart and a brain.[1]

THE outlaw heroes of the West were to be found not only in Kansas and Colorado; the Spanish counterparts for Jesse James and Sam Bass roamed the badlands of northern Mexico and the border country. Heraclio Bernal, Valentin Manceras, and

"Jesse James," from this collection.

Benito Canales were among the most famous of these Mexican Robin Hoods. Of them all, Bernal enjoys the greatest popularity in Mexican folklore —perhaps because he was betrayed and killed in the tradition of bandit heroes, perhaps because this corrido has helped to keep his story alive.

CORRIDO DE HERACLIO BERNAL

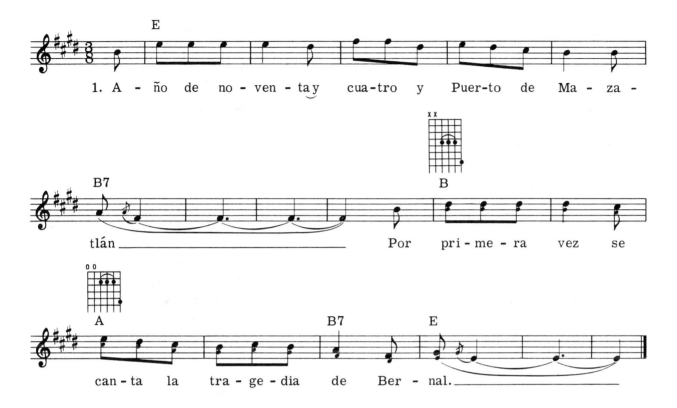

1. A - ño de no - ven - ta y cua-tro y Puer-to de Ma - za -

tlán _____ Por pri - me - ra vez se

can - ta la tra - ge - dia de Ber - nal. _____

Año de mil ochocientos	In the year of eighteen hundred,
ochenta y cinco al contado,	Eighty five, exactly,
murió Heraclio Bernal	Heraclio Bernal died
por el Gobierno pagado.	At the hands of a paid Government agent.
Estado de Sinaloa,	The State of Sinaloa,
Gobierno de Culiacán,	The Government of Culiacan,
ofrecieron diez mil pesos	Offered ten thousand pesos
por la vida de Bernal.	For the life of Bernal.
La tragedia de Bernal	The tragedy of Bernal
en Guadalupe empezó,	Began in Guadalupe
por unas barras de plata	Over a few bars of silver
que dicen que se robó.	Which it was said he stole.
Heraclio Bernal gritaba	Heraclio Bernal shouted
que era hombre y no se rajaba,	That he was a man and wouldn't back down.
que subiéndosa a la sierra	That, climbing up in the hills,
poleaba con la Acordada.	He would fight with the Acordada.
¿Qué es aquello que relumbra	What is that that shines
por todo el camino real?	All along the main highway?
—Son las armas del "Dieciocho"	—They are the arms of the "Eighteenth"
que traen a Heraclio Bernal.	Being brought to Heraclio Bernal.

¿—Qué dice, Heraclio Bernal?
—No vengo de roba-bueyes,
yo tengo plata sellada
y en ese Real de los Reyes.

Heraclio Bernal gritaba
en su caballo alazán:
—No pierdo las esperanzas
de pasearme en Culiacán.

Heraclio Bernal decía,
cuando estaba muy enfermo:
—Máteme usted, compadrito,
pa' que le pague el Gobierno.

—Aprevengan su Acordada
y su escuadrón militar,
y les damos diez mil pesos,
yo les entrego a Bernal.

Decía don Crispín García,
muy enhadado de andar;
—Si me dan los diez mil pesos,
yo les entrego a Bernal.

Le dieron los diez mil pesos,
los recontó en su *mascada*,
y le dijo al comandante:
—Alísteme una Acordada.

What says Heraclio Bernal?
—I haven't come as a cattle thief,
I have genuine silver money
And it's back in 'Real de los Reyes.'

Heraclio Bernal shouted
From his chestnut horse:
—I haven't given up hope
Of taking Culiacan.

Heraclio Bernal said
When he was very sick:
—Kill me, little godfather,
So the government will pay you.

—Apprehend their organization
And their military squadron,
And we'll give you ten thousand pesos
For the head of Bernal.

Don Crispín García said,
Disgusted with so much marching,
—If you give me the ten thousand pesos
I'll deliver you Bernal.

They gave him the ten thousand pesos,
Which he put in his neckband,
And he said to the commander:
—Get me together a command.

Custer's Last Charge

Author unknown

From the singing of Warde H. Forde, Central Valley, California, 1938. Recorded by Sidney Robertson. Transcribed by Ruth Crawford Seeger, Archive of American Folk Song, Library of Congress, Record #4199 B. From *A Treasury of Western Folklore*, B. A. Botkin.

We're marching off for Sitting Bull
And this is the way we go;
Forty miles a day on beans and hay,
In the Regular Army-O.[1]

BEFORE the settlers came—the homesteaders, the sodbusters, the cowboys, the ranchers, the gold-seekers—the Indians ruled and roamed the western plains. Relentlessly, like a raging flood which no dam could stay, the white men took the Indian land. Sometimes they took the land by forced treaty and by money. But mostly, they took the land by bloodshed, treachery, and outright aggrandizement. It was a process, perhaps, which was as inevitable as death, but it was likewise ruthless and inhuman. In the history of America, it is a chapter of shame, and most of us conveniently keep the story out of sight and out of mind. But it is there on the national conscience, nevertheless, an infamy never to be completely forgotten, a grim reminder that we Americans must temper our pride in our land and people with an awareness of the scars on our national soul.

In the process of "winning the West" from the Indians, battles were fought, lives were lost, legends were created. Among the most famous of the battles was the one at the Little Bighorn River in Montana, June 25, 1876. Here, General George A. Custer and a contingent of 264 United States soldiers were annihilated by an overwhelming force of Sioux Indians under the leadership of Chiefs Sitting Bull and Crazy Horse. It was a battle which left no American survivors and ended the short, brilliant and controversial career of General Custer, one of the great cavalry soldiers of United Sates history.

Perhaps the Sioux recalled Custer's Washita campaign, where American troops under his command massacred thousands of unarmed Indian men, women, and children in one of those violent episodes of madness which drenched the frontier in blood. Perhaps the Sioux at Little Big Horn realized that there would never be an end to the white man's demand on their lands and property, and that only a vengeance of murder would tell their story for history.

In any event, the massacre at Little Bighorn became history and legend. Custer emerged as the boy hero of the plains and the tale of his famous last stand has become folklore. The Western air still rang with the war whoops of the victorious Sioux when the first of Custer's song memorials appeared:

The bugle called to duty a brave and noble band,
Three hundred gallant soldiers, the bravest of our land;
They marshalled for the battle, with Custer at their head,
To meet the treacherous foemen who come with stealthy tread.[2]

[1] U. S. Army Marching Song from the Sioux Campaign, quoted in *This Is The West,* Howard.

[2] "Custer's Last Charge," orginal song by William H. Long and H. T. Martin (1876).

273

CUSTER'S LAST CHARGE

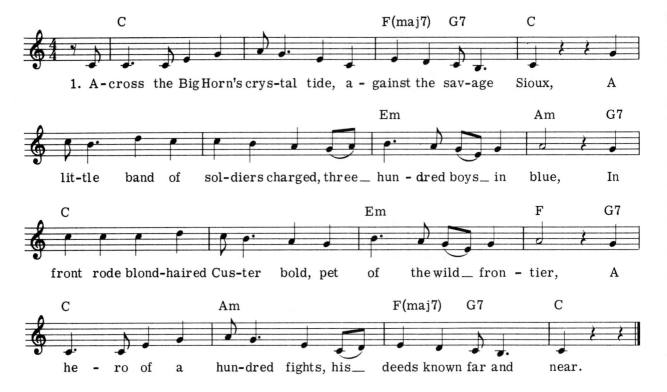

1. A-cross the Big Horn's crys-tal tide, a - gainst the sav-age Sioux, A

lit-tle band of sol-diers charged, three— hun-dred boys— in blue, In

front rode blond-haired Cus-ter bold, pet of the wild— fron - tier, A

he - ro of a hun-dred fights, his— deeds known far and near.

Across the Bighorn's crystal tide, against the savage Sioux,
A little band of soldiers charged, three hundred boys in blue,
In front rode blond-haired Custer, pet of the wild frontier,
A hero of a hundred fights, his deeds known far and near.

"Charge, comrades, charge! There's death ahead, disgrace lurks in our rear!
Drive rowels deep! Come on, come on!" came his yells with ringing cheer.
And on the foe those heroes charged; there rose an awful yell,
It seemed as though those soldiers stormed the lowest gates of hell.

Three hundred rifles rattled forth, and torn was human form;
The black smoke rose in rolling waves above the leaden storm.
The death groans of the dying braves, their wounded piercing cries,
The hurling of the arrows fleet did cloud the noonday skies.

The snorting steeds with shrieks of fright, the firearms' deafening roar;
The war song sung by the dying braves who fell to rise no more.
O'er hill and dale the war song waved 'round craggy mountain side,
Along down death's dark valley ran a cruel crimson tide.

Our blond-haired chief was everywhere 'mid showers of hurling lead,
The starry banner waved above the dying and the dead.
With bridle rein in firm-set teeth, revolver in each hand,
He hoped with his few gallant boys to quell the great Sioux band.

Again they charged, three thousand guns poured forth their last-sent ball;
Three thousand war whoops rent the air; gallant Custer then did fall.
And all around where Custer fell ran pools and streams of gore,
Heaped bodies of both red and white whose last great fight was o'er.

The boys in blue and their savage foe lay huddled in one mass,
Their life's blood ran a-trickling through the trampled prairie grass,
While fiendish yells did rend the air and then a sudden hush,
While cries of anguish rise again as on the mad Sioux rush.

O'er those strewn and blood-stained fields those goading redskins fly;
Our gang went down three hundred souls, three hundred doomed to die,
Those blood-drunk braves sprang on the dead and wounded boys in blue,
Three hundred bleeding scalps ran high above the fiendish crew.

Then night came on with sable veil and hid those sights from view,
The Bighorn's crystal tide was red as she wound her valleys through.
And quickly from those fields of slain those gloating redskins fled—
But blond-haired Custer held the field, a hero with his dead.

Roy Bean

WORDS: Charles J. Finger
MUSIC: "Tramp, Tramp, Tramp" (George F. Root)

Judge Roy Bean of Vinegarroon
Held high court in his own saloon,
Fer a killin' or a-thievin' or other sech fracas,
Bean was the law west of the Pecos.[1]

JESSE James, Cole Younger, Sam Bass, and Billy the Kid earned their places in the folklore of the West as outlaws. Wild Bill Hickok and Wyatt Earp were celebrated as lawmen. But a unique niche in the history of the West is held by a colorful character, a combination saloon-keeper and justice of the peace in the little town of Langtry in southwest Texas, the self-appointed "Law West of the Pecos," Judge Roy Bean.

A one-time '49er who never found gold, a one-time pony express rider, Roy Bean was actually elected justice of the peace in 1885 for Precinct Three of Val Verde County in Texas. For the next two decades, with his own saloon as his courthouse, Bean made the law for his vast domain.

His "courtroom procedure," his unique sentences, his subtle and not-so-subtle bending of the law for personal convenience and his own irreverent sense of justice and fair play, his passions and his prejudices, have all become a part of folklore.

One of his passions was the then-famous actress Lillie Langtry. Bean named his town for her and invited her to visit the hamlet. At first, Miss Langtry declined the honor, but offered to donate an ornamental water fountain to the town as a token of her appreciation. Saloon-keeper Bean replied immediately that "the only thing the citizens of Langtry did not drink was water." Eventually, the actress did visit Langtry, and a legend grew up that she and Roy Bean were lovers, a legend which does not seem to be supported by ascertainable evidence.

Roy Bean's prejudices were equally famous—and typical of his era. He refused to convict a rancher for murdering a Chinese laborer, holding that Texas law made it a crime to kill another human being, but said nothing about killing Chinese. Indians and Mexicans likewise expected (and received) little justice in Roy Bean's court.

It was Bean's practice to declare frequent recesses in court so that all present could purchase liquid refreshments from Bean's bar. Once, so the story goes, a juryman declined the invitation with thanks, only to be notified that his refusal was considered "contempt of court" with a fine of ten dollars to go with the sentence. The fines, let it be said, went to pay for Langtry's "administration of justice."

Perhaps the most famous story of all is the one told in this song. The story itself is now folklore, but the ballad was created by folk-song collector Charles J. Finger who believed that the old rascal deserved to be remembered in song.

The use of two even eighth notes as a contrast to the quarter-eighth bouncy rhythm could occur at almost any place in the singing of a song like this. It depends on which words the singer chooses to emphasize.

[1] "The Ballad of Roy Bean," S. Omar Barker, from *Law West of the Pecos,* Everett Lloyd.

ROY BEAN

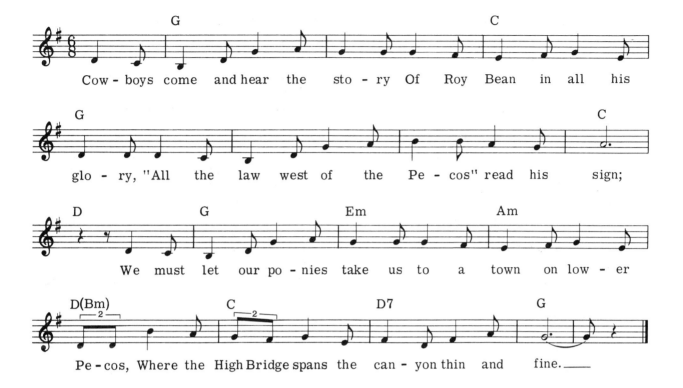

Cow - boys come and hear the sto - ry Of Roy Bean in all his
glo - ry, "All the law west of the Pe - cos" read his sign;
We must let our po - nies take us to a town on low - er
Pe - cos, Where the High Bridge spans the can - yon thin and fine.____

Cowboys come and hear the story
Of Roy Bean in all his glory,
"All the law west of the Pecos" read his sign;
We must let our ponies take us
To a town on lower Pecos,
Where the High Bridge spans the canyon thin and fine.

He was born one day near Toyah
Where he learned to be a lawyer
And a teacher and a barber and the Mayor,
He was cook and old shoe mender,
Sometimes preacher and bartender,
And it cost two bits to have him cut your hair.

He was right smart of a hustler,
And considerable a rustler,
And at mixing up an eggnog he was grand,
He was clever, he was merry,
He could drink a Tom and Jerry,
On occasion at a round up took a hand.

Though the story isn't funny,
There was once he had no money,
Which was for him not very strange or rare,
So he went to help Pap Wyndid,
But he got so absent-minded
That he put his RB brand on old Pap's steer.

As Pap was right smart angry
Old Roy Bean went down to Langtry,
Where he opened up an office and a store,
There he'd sell you drink or buttons,
Or another rancher's muttons,
Though the latter made the other fellow sore.

Once there came from Austin city
A young dude reported witty,
Out of Bean he sort of guessed he'd take a rise,
And he got unusual frisky
As he up and called for whisky,
Saying, "Bean, now hurry up, goldurn your eyes."

Then a-down he threw ten dollars,
Which the same Roy quickly collars,
Then the same Roy holds to nine and hands back one
So the stranger gave a holler
As he saw that single dollar,
And at that began the meriment and fun.

The dude he slammed the table
Just as hard as he was able,
That the price of whiskey was too high he swore,
Said Roy Bean, "For all that fussin'
And your most outrageous cussin',
You are fined the other dollar by the law.

"On this place I own a lease, sir,
I'm the Justice of the Peace, sir.
The law west of the Pecos all is here,
And you've acted very badly."
Then the dude he went off sadly
While down his lily cheeks there rolled a tear.

One fine day they found a dead man
Who in life had been a redman,
So it's doubtless he was nothing else than bad,
They called Bean to view the body,
First he took a drink of toddy,
Then he listed all the things the dead man had.

For a redman he was tony
For he had a pretty pony,
And a dandy bit and saddle and a rope,
He'd a fine Navajo rug
And a quart within his jug,
And a bronco that was dandy on the lope.

So the find it was quite rare-o,
For he'd been a "cocinero,"
And his pay day hadn't been so far away,
He'd a brand-new fine white Stetson
And a silver Smith and Wesson,
While a purse of forty dollars jingled gay.

Said Roy Bean, "You'll learn a lesson
For you have a Smith and Wesson,
And to carry implements of war is very wrong.
Forty dollars I will fine you,
For we couldn't well confine you
As already you've been laying 'round too long."

So you boys have heard the story
Of Roy Bean in all his glory,
He's the man who was the Justice and the Law,
He was handy with his hooks,
He was ornery in his looks,
And just now I ain't a-telling any more.

The Streets of Laredo

TRADITIONAL COWBOY BALLAD

From the singing of Tony Kraber.

As I was a-walking down by St. James Hospital,
I was a-walking down there one day,
What should I spy but one of my comrades
All wrapped up in flannel though warm was the day.[1]

WHERE does a folk song begin? By what mysterious process do the "folk" choose a song, a ballad, a poem, and keep it alive from generation to generation, adapting it, rewriting it, making it over to fit the needs and climate and circumstances of their lives?

A partial answer, perhaps, may be found in the classic ballad of the dying cowboy on the streets of Laredo, whose tragic fate has become an indelible part of the folklore of the West.

An Irish street ballad, "The Unfortunate Rake," provided the plot and the imagery for a score of American and British variants, known among cowboys as "The Streets of Laredo," or "The Cowboy's Lament." Folklorists date the original back to the 1790's and the story of a dying British soldier "cut down in the height of my prime" by "a handsome young woman" who infected him with syphilis.

In one of the earliest versions, London's St. James Hospital provides the setting for the narrative. But the unknown ballad maker, who penned the original song, with a gift of poetic insight, decorated his tale with the image of a ceremonial funeral which has become the hallmark of all subsequent descendants:

Get six young soldiers to carry my coffin,
Six young girls to sing me a song,
And each of them carry a bunch of green laurel,
So they don't smell me as they bear me along.[2]

"The Unfortunate Rake" passed into history as a song in its own right, but first it inspired a host of variants which have survived through the oral tradition, the most widely known of which have been the cowboy ballad and the early Negro jazz ballad, "St. James Infirmary."

As "The Trooper Cut Down In His Prime," "The Sailor Cut Down In His Prime," "The Bad Girl's Lament," and "St. James Hospital," the song survived the passage of time and was adapted to varying regional and occupational environments.

Then beat the drum slowly and play your fife lowly,
And sound the dead march as you carry me along;
And fire your bundooks right over my coffin,
For I'm a young trooper cut down in my prime.[3]

We'll beat the big drums and we'll play the pipes merrily,
Play the dead march as we carry him along,
Take him to the churchyard and fire three volleys o'er him,
For he's a young sailor cut down in his prime.[4]

When I was a young girl I used to seek pleasure,
When I was a young girl I used to drink ale;
Right out of the alehouse and into the jailhouse,
Out of a barroom and into my grave.[5]

Somehow, through lumberjacks turned cowboys or southern Negroes who became camp cooks on the range, the old ballad was transplanted on western soil. The frontier town of Laredo, Texas, with a history dating back to 1757, became the setting

[1] "The Unfortunate Rake," from the singing of A. L. Lloyd, Folkways Records, *The Unfortunate Rake*, FS3805.
[2] *Ibid.*

[3] "The Trooper Cut Down In His Prime," from the singing of Ewan MacColl; *ibid.*
[4] "The Young Sailor Cut Down In His Prime," from the singing of Harry Cox; *ibid.*
[5] "One Morning In May," from the singing of Hally Wood; *ibid.*

for the tragedy. The soldier became a cowboy, his fatal "disorder" became a shot in the breast, and his pallbearers likewise changed to suit the Texas clime. But the story was the same—and the dying request for a ceremonial death procession remained the heart of the ballad.

In later years, the song provided the base for parodies by railroaders, lumberjacks, and longshoremen; and in more recent times, even college professors and undergraduates have been immortalized in the form of the old ballad (see "Professor's Lament," and "Ballad of Sherman Wu," also in the record album, *The Unfortunate Rake,* Folkways FS3805).

More significant, perhaps, were the adaptations made by early Negro blues and jazz singers, who may have been inspired by the cowboy song rather than by variants of the original. The key is the ceremonial funeral. In "St. James Infirmary," the dying gambler sings:

I want six crap shooters for pall bearers,
A chorus girl to sing me a song;

Put a jazz band on my hearse wagon,
Raise hell as I stroll along.[6]

The unknown ballad maker who first composed the tale of the disordered young man never knew how well he had wrought. His song, created for a penny broadsheet audience two centuries ago, has given birth to several dozen folk songs, not the least of which is this classic cowboy ballad.

For guitar, I suggest an um-*pah technique similar to* "Doney Gal," *keeping the G in the bass (3d fret on low E) throughout, but adding another string to the* um *and playing the* pah *with middle, ring, and little fingers.*

Here is how the first few bars would look in tablature:

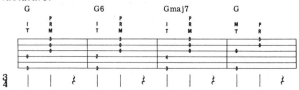

[6] "Gambler's Blues," from the singing of Dave Van Ronk; *ibid.*

THE STREETS OF LAREDO

1. As I walked out in the streets of La - re - do, As I walked out in La - re - do one day,____ I spied a poor cow - boy wrapped up in white lin - en, All wrapped in white

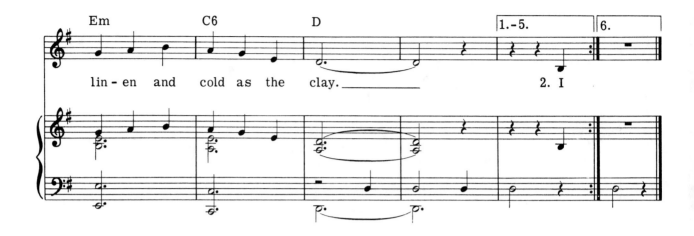

lin - en   and   cold   as   the   clay.＿＿＿＿＿＿   2. I

As I walked out in the streets of Laredo,
As I walked out in Laredo one day,
I spied a poor cowboy wrapped up in white linen,
All wrapped up in white linen and cold as the clay.

"I see by your outfit that you are a cowboy,"
These words he did say as I proudly stepped by,
"Come sit down beside me and hear my sad story,
Got shot in the breast and I know I must die.

" 'Twas once in the saddle I used to go dashing,
'Twas once in the saddle I used to go gay;
'Twas first to drinkin', and then to card-playing,
Got shot in the breast and I'm dying today.

"Let six jolly cowboys come carry my coffin,
Let six pretty gals come carry my pall;
Throw bunches of roses all over my coffin,
Throw roses to deaden the clods as they fall.

"Oh beat the drum slowly, and play the fife lowly,
And play the dead march as you carry me along,
Take me to the green valley and lay the earth o'er me,
For I'm a poor cowboy and I know I've done wrong."

Oh we beat the drum slowly and we played the fife lowly,
And bitterly wept as we carried him along,
For we all loved our comrade, so brave, young and handsome,
We all loved our comrade although he done wrong.

Tying Ten Knots in the Devil's Tail

WORDS: Gail Gardner
MUSIC: Adapted by Bill Simon

From the singing of Tony Kraber, with apologies to Gail Gardner, for a good song travels fast and pretty soon belongs to all who sing it.

"I was born full-growed with nine rows of jaw teeth and holes bored for more. There was spurs on my feet and a rawhide quirt in my hand, and when they opens the chute I come out a-riding a panther and a-roping the long-horned whales. I've rode everything with hair on it . . . and I've rode a few things that was too rough to grow any hair.

"I've rode bull moose on the prod, she-grizzlies and long bolts of lightning. Mountain lions are my playmates and when I feels cold and lonesome, I sleeps in a den of rattlesnakes, 'cause they always makes me nice and warm.

"To keep alive I eat stick dynamite and cactus. The Grand Canyon ain't nothin' but my bean hole.

When I get thirsty I drink cyanide cut with Alkali. When I go to sleep I pillow my head on the Bighorn Mountains, I lay my boots in Colorado and my hat in Montana. I can stretch out my arms clean out from the Crazy Woman Fork plumb over to the Upper Grey Bull River. My bed tarp covers half of Texas and all of old Mexico.

"But there's one thing for sure and certain, and if you boys want to know, I'll tell you that I'm still a long way short of being the daddy of 'em all . . . 'cause he's full-growed and as any man that really knows can see—well, boys, I ain't nothing but a young 'un." [1]

[1] "Cowboy Brag Talk," from Harry Jackson, *The Cowboy*, Folkways Records, FH5723.

283

TYING TEN KNOTS IN THE DEVIL'S TAIL

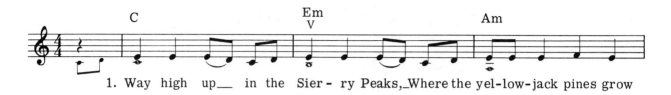

1. Way high up__ in the Sier - ry Peaks,__Where the yel-low-jack pines grow

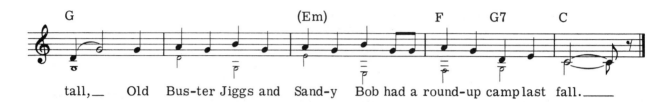

tall,__ Old Bus-ter Jiggs and Sand-y Bob had a round-up camp last fall.____

Way high up in the Sierry * Peaks
Where the yellow-jack pines grow tall,
Old Buster Jiggs and Sandy Bob
Had a round-up camp last fall.

Well, they took along their running irons,
Maybe a dog or two,
And they 'lowed they'd brand every long-eared calf
That came within their view.

Now every little long-eared dogie
That didn't push up by day,
Got his long ears whittled and his old hide scorched
In a most artistic way.

One fine day, says Buster Jiggs,
As he threwed his seago down,
"I'm tired of cowpiography,
And I think I'm a-goin' into town."

Well they saddled up their ponies and they hit a lope,
For it warn't no sight of a ride,
And them was the days that a good cow-punch
Could oil up his insides.

Well they started in at Kentucky Bar,
At the head of Whiskey Row,
And they wound her up at the Depot House
About forty drinks below.

Well they sets 'em up and they turns around,
And they started in the other way,
And to tell the God-forsaken truth
Them boys got drunk that day.

* Sierra.

284

They was on their way, goin' back to camp,
A-packin' that awful load,
Who should they meet but the Devil himself
Come a-traipsin' down the road.

He says, "You ornery cowboy skunks,
You better go hunt for your hole,
'Cause I've come up from Hell's rim rock
To gather in your souls."

"The Devil be damned," says Buster Jiggs,
"Us boys is a little bit tight,
But you don't go gatherin' no cowboys souls
Without one helluva fight."

Now Buster Jiggs could ride like hell,
Throw a lasso, too,
So he threw it over the Devil's horns
And he took his dallies * true.

Now Sandy Bob was a reata ** man,
With his gut-line coiled up neat,
But he shook her out and he builds a loop
And he roped the Devil's hind feet.

Well they stretches him out and they tails him down,
While the runnin'-irons were gettin' hot,
And they cropped and swallow-forked his ears
And they branded him up a lot.

Well they trimmed his horns way down to his head,
Tied ten knots in his tail for a joke,
And then they went off and left him there
Tied up to a little pin oak.

Now when you're way high up in the Sierry Peaks,
And you hear one hell of a wail,
Well you'll know it's just the Devil himself
Yellin' about them knots in his tail.

---

* A half-hitch around the saddle horn with a rope after a catch is made, the loose
end being held in the roper's hand so that he can let it slip in case of an emergency,
or take it up shorter.
** A rope which ties one animal to another.

I Will Win

PART 8

"Roll On, Columbia"

Well the world has seven wonders
That the travelers always tell,
Some gardens and some towers,
I guess you know them well;
But now the greatest wonder's
In Uncle Sam's fair land,
It's the King Columbia River
And the Big Grand Coulee Dam.[1]

[1] "Grand Coulee Dam," words by Woody Guthrie to the tune of "Wabash Cannonball," © 1958 Guthrie Children's Trust Fund.

THE NEW WEST—the twentieth-century West—has given us a different song. In the age of the industrial West, the gold-rush broadside and the cowboy song have become memories, the populist parody and the bad-man ballad are now echoes of other times and other men. The folk songs of the twentieth-century West are of hoboes and Wobblies, of copper miners and Klondike miners, of logging men and the great industrial power complex of the Northwest.

A strain of contrary individualism and collective anarchism runs through Western song tradition. From the topical–political songs of early San Francisco to the Populist songs of the 1890's the element of protest has played a significant role in indigenous songs of the West. Cowboy griping songs, Mexican anti-gringo ditties, scores of outlaw ballads contributed to a tradition that reached its peak in the second decade of the twentieth century when the IWW (Industrial Workers of the World) became one of the significant forces in the American West.

Organized in 1905, the IWW was an anarcho–syndicalist organization devoted to a belief in violent class struggle, industrial unionism and the O.B.U. ("One Big Union") to which every worker would belong. Its strength rested primarily among unskilled and migratory copper miners, agricultural workers, lumberjacks, longshoremen, and seamen.

Through an unusual combination of circumstances and talents, the "Wobblies" developed songs and singing as one of their chief propaganda and organizing tools. Their *Little Red Songbook* was published annually with a new batch of songs (invariably parodies on popular songs of the day) in each issue. The lyrics were frank political tracts for the IWW program:

> Conditions they are bad,
> And some of you are sad,
> You cannot see your enemy,
> The class that lives in luxury.
> You workingmen are poor—
> Will be forevermore—
> As long as you permit the few
> To guide your destiny.
>
> Shall we still be slaves and work for wages?
> It is outrageous—has been for ages;
> This earth by right belongs to toilers,
> And not to spoilers of liberty.[1]

Industrialism came to the West in giant boots, Rockefellers scooping the profits out of the copper and silver mines of Colorado, Paul Bunyans striding through the virgin forests of Washington and Idaho. The songs that come out of the hearts and experiences of people become fewer and fewer,

[1] "Workingmen Unite!" by E. S. Nelson to the tune of "Red Wing," from *The Little Red Songbook*.

as machine-produced music heralds the age of mass production. But some men still feel the need to sing from their hearts for themselves. And the hoboes and lumberjacks and miners continue to make their own songs.

In the pages that follow are some of these songs of the most recent West. They are not popular songs in the juke box sense of that word—but in the true interchangeable meaning of "folk" and "popular" they are popular songs of our own age. Their meaning and substance are in the songs of Woody Guthrie, who has given us an anthem to sum up our experiences as a people and a nation:

> This land is your land,
> This land is my land,
> From California to the New York Island,
> From the redwood forests
> To the Gulf Stream waters,
> This land was made for you and me.[2]

[2] "This Land Is Your Land," words and music by Woody Guthrie, © 1956 by Ludlow Music Inc.

The Big Rock Candy Mountain
Words and music by Mac McClintock

This version from *The People's Songs Bulletin* (Vol. III, No. 6-7, July–August, 1948).

In Poor Man's Heaven, we'll have our own way,
There's nothing up there but good luck.
There's strawberry pie that's twenty foot high,
And whipped cream they bring in a truck.[1]

IMMIGRANTS, wanderers, and hoboes—necessity travelers and professional roamers—have a song literature of their own. One of the archetypes of the hobo song is the "Utopia dream," with the fantasy ballad of the "Big Rock Candy Mountain" the best-known living example of the genre. Mac McClin-

tock, a professional busker and old-time Wobbly, created the original which subsequently spread via word of mouth to become, along with "Hallelujah, I'm a Bum" (also credited to McClintock), the theme song of all the homeless wanderers and hoboes who rode the rods from Omaha to 'Frisco and from Seattle to St. Paul.

[1] "Poor Man's Heaven," from *Sing Out!* (Vol. 11, No. 3).

THE BIG ROCK CANDY MOUNTAIN

box - cars all are emp - ty And the sun shines ev - 'ry

day, Oh, the birds and the bees And the cig - ar - ette trees, The

rock-'n rye springs Where the whang doo-dle sings In the Big Rock Can - dy

Moun-tain.

2. In the

294

Introduction:

One evening as the sun went down,
And the jungle fires were burning,
Down the track came a hobo hiking,
And he said, "Boys, I'm not turning.
I'm headed for a land that's far away
Beside the crystal fountain.
I'll see you all this coming fall
In the Big Rock Candy Mountain.

Verse:

In the Big Rock Candy Mountain,
There's a land that's fair and bright,
Where the handouts grow on bushes
And you sleep out every night;
Where the boxcars all are empty
And the sun shines every day,
Oh, the birds and the bees
And the cigarette trees,
The rock 'n rye springs
Where the whang doodle sings
In the Big Rock Candy Mountain.

In the Big Rock Candy Mountain,
All the cops have wooden legs,
And the bulldogs all have rubber teeth
And the hens lay soft-boiled eggs.
The farmer's trees are full of fruit
And the barns are full of hay,

Oh, I'm bound to go
Where there ain't no snow,
Where the sleet don't fall
And the wind don't blow,
In the Big Rock Candy Mountain.

In the Big Rock Candy Mountain,
You never change your socks,
And the little streams of alcohol
Come trickling down the rocks.
The shacks all have to tip their hats,
And the railroad bulls are blind,
There's a lake of stew,
And of whiskey, too,
And you can paddle all around
In a big canoe,
In the Big Rock Candy Mountain.

In the Big Rock Candy Mountain,
The jails are made of tin,
And you can bust right out again,
As soon as they put you in.
There ain't no short-handled shovels,
No axes saws or picks—
I'm a-goin' to stay
Where you sleep all day,
Where they boiled in oil
The inventor of toil,
In the Big Rock Candy Mountain.

The Ludlow Massacre

Words and music by Woody Guthrie

Now folks, let me tell you a story,
About a terrible crime,
That was done in Ludlow, Colorado,
To men that work in the mine.[1]

THE wealth and power of the West came out of the bowels of the earth. Rich deposits of gold, silver, lead, copper, and zinc brought the people in search of easy and sudden riches—and they stayed to work the mines and railroads and settle the land.

Coal was also in the earth, rich deposits in Colorado to supplement the great fields of Kentucky and Pennsylvania. But coal, unlike gold and silver, was more than wealth. It was trade, commerce, industrial power.

Along with coal came the latest techniques of mining, and the cheating managers and operators, and the company towns and company stores—and over it all hovered the figure of John D. Rockefeller.

The miners say that "there is blood on the coal," remembering the many thousands who have gone down into the pits never to return. And sometimes the blood comes from one of those outbursts of horror when the naked power of the entire system is directed against workingmen trying to carve out a fairer share of the pie.

In 1914, in the mining town of Ludlow in Southern Colorado, occurred one of those outbursts

—a pitiless bloodbath engineered by the coal company resulting in the murder of twenty men, women and children and the wounding and maiming of scores of others. History has come to call it "The Ludlow Massacre," and the miners themselves have memorialized it in song.

The date was April 20, 1914. Coal-company thugs, deputized by the Governor and the National Guard, attacked the camp of the striking miners. (The miners had been evicted from their company-owned homes when they first went on strike.) A pitched battle ensued. Children were shot without mercy. Captured union prisoners were put to death. At the end of the day, the miners abandoned their camp and the company troops burned it to the ground. In the morning's ashes, the miners found the bodies of two women and their eleven children, burned to death in the flames.

One tragic incident in time; one event, Ludlow, Colorado. But the Ludlow Massacre is a symbol, as well, reminding us that the sound of the West was pioneers, and horses, and steers, and railroads—and also the haunting cries of little children and poor men caught in the grinding machinery of the profit system.

[1] "The Ludlow Massacre," from "Songs of the Ludlow Massacre," by John Greenway, in *The United Mine Workers Journal*, reprinted in *Sing Out!* (Vol. 8, No. 3).

THE LUDLOW MASSACRE

1. It was ear - ly spring-time____ that the strike was on,____ They drove us
min - ers out of doors, Out from the hous-es____ that the com-pa-ny
owned,____ We moved in-to tents____ up at old Lud - low.

It was early springtime that the strike was on,
They drove us miners out of doors,
Out from the houses that the company owned,
We moved into tents up at old Ludlow.

I was worried bad about my children,
Soldiers guarding the railroad bridge;
Every once in a while a bullet would fly,
Kick up gravel under my feet.

We were so afraid you would kill our children,
We dug us a cave that was seven feet deep;
Carried our young ones and a pregnant woman
Down inside the cave to sleep.

That very night you soldiers waited
Until us miners was asleep;
You snuck around our little tent town,
Soaked our tents with your kerosene.

You struck a match and the blaze it started;
You pulled the triggers of your Gatling guns;
I made a run for the children but the fire wall
   stopped me,
Thirteen children died from your guns.

I carried my blanket to a wire fence corner,
Watched the fire till the blaze died down;

I helped some people grab their belongings
While your bullets killed us all around.

I never will forget the look on the faces
Of the men and women that awful day,
When we stood around to preach their funerals
And lay the corpses of the dead away.

We told the Colorado governor to phone the President,
Tell him to call off his National Guard;
But the National Guard belonged to the governor,
So he didn't try so very hard.

Our women from Trinidad they hauled some potatoes
Up to Walsenburg in a little cart;
They sold their potatoes and brought some guns back
And put a gun in every hand.

The state soldiers jumped us in the wire fence corner;
They did not know that we had those guns;
And the red-neck miners mowed down them troopers,
You should have seen them poor boys run.

We took some cement and walled the cave up,
Where you killed these thirteen children inside;
I said, "God bless the Mine Workers' Union,"
And then I hung my head and cried.

The Preacher and the Slave

WORDS: Joe Hill
MUSIC: "In the Sweet By and By"

From *Songs of Joe Hill*, Barrie Stavis and Frank Harmon.

There's a land that is fairer than day,
And by faith we can see it afar,
For the Father waits over the way,
To prepare us a dwelling place there.

In the sweet by and by,
We shall meet on that beautiful shore,
In the sweet by and by,
We shall meet on that beautiful shore,[1]

HE was born Joel Emanuel Hagglund. The date was October 7, 1879; the place, the little seaport town of Gavle, Sweden.

In 1901, like hundreds of thousands of his fellow-Scandinavians before him, he migrated to the "land of wealth and opportunity," the United States. His name was Americanized to Joseph Hillstrom. In time, this was shortened to Joe Hill.

For close to a decade he worked at odd jobs, eventually winding up in San Pedro, California, where he worked as a longshoreman and a seaman. Sometime around 1910, Joe Hill joined the IWW.

A gifted, untrained musician, Joe Hill played almost any kind of musical instrument. He had a special talent, however, for improvising satirical parodies to familiar songs. As a Wobbly, Joe Hill turned his gifts to the class struggle and the O.B.U.

In the years from 1910 to 1915, Joe Hill turned out more than a score of IWW propaganda songs, among them "Casey Jones," "Mister Block," "The Tramp," "The Rebel Girl," and a biting parody on Navy life, "Stung Right."

His best song, however, the one which has survived over the years, was a mocking takeoff on the popular hymn, "In the Sweet By and By." Joe Hill called his song "The Preacher and the Slave," although it is better known by the phrase which has since become a part of the American idiom, "Pie in the Sky."

Among the hazards encountered by the IWW in its organizing activities throughout the West was the competition offered by the Salvation Army. Since both the Army and the Wobblies were seeking the same souls—the homeless, uprooted migratory and unemployed workers of the western towns—a natural rivalry developed. The Salvation Army, with its trumpets sounding forth the call of God, frequently had the better of the encounter. But the Wobblies decided that there was no reason for God to have all the good tunes, so they "borrowed" the Army's melodies and, with caustically irreverent satires, held forth on street corners in San Francisco, Denver, Seattle, and Salt Lake City. Joe Hill's contribution to this effort was "The Preacher and the Slave."

In 1915 Joe Hill was arrested in Salt Lake City on a charge of murder. A grocer had been killed in a holdup, and the police, unable to find the killers,

[1] "In the Sweet By and By," Bennet & Webster, from the original music quoted in *Fireside Book of Favorite American Songs*, Boni.

arrested Joe Hill as a convenient scapegoat. A prejudiced prosecution, a traitorous defense lawyer, and a jury inflamed by an atmosphere of hysteria helped convict the "singing Wobbly." A "case" with world-wide repercussions ensued. Despite appeals by President Wilson, the Swedish ambassador, the American Federation of Labor, and tens of thousands of others, the State of Utah put Joe Hill before a firing squad on November 19, 1915, and killed him.

In an "open letter to the people of the State of Utah," shortly before his execution, Joe Hill wrote:

"I have always worked hard for a living and paid for everything I got, and my spare time I spent painting pictures, writing songs and composing music. Now if the people of the State of Utah want to shoot me without giving me half a chance to state my side of the case, then bring on your firing squads—I am ready for you. I have lived like an artist and I shall die like an artist." [2]

And in a last letter to the fiery IWW leader, Bill

[2] From *Letters of Joe Hill*, Philip S. Foner.

Haywood, he penned the words which have become an immortal slogan of the labor movement:

Don't waste any time mourning—organize!

In the years following his death, Joe Hill became a legend. For millions of workingmen in the birth pangs of industrial organization, his life and death became symbols of struggle and dedication. The legend of the martyred singing Wobbly has outlasted his executioners. More than a decade after the firing squad had disposed of Joe Hill, a poet and a composer memorialized him for the ages with a song which would be sung on picket lines and in union halls from coast to coast—and, eventually, in almost every language in the world:

I dreamed I saw Joe Hill last night
Alive as you and me,
Says I, "But Joe, you're ten years dead,"
"I never died," says he.
"I never died," says he.[3]

[3] "Joe Hill," Alfred Hayes and Earl Robinson, from *The People's Songbook*, Hille.

THE INTERNATIONAL

ONE BIG UNION

TORCH OF FREEDOM

I.W.W. SONGS TO FAN THE FLAMES OF DISCONTENT

JOE HILL
MEMORIAL EDITION

PUBLISHED BY
I.W.W. PUBLISHING BUREAU
112 HAMILTON AVE., CLEVELAND, OHIO
U.S.A

THE PREACHER AND THE SLAVE

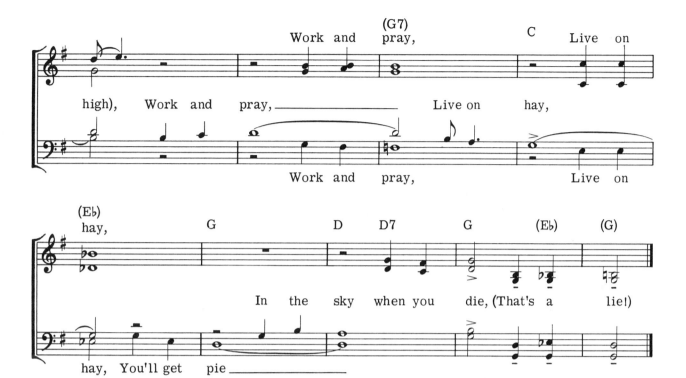

Long-haired preachers come out every night,
Try to tell you what's wrong and what's right;
But when asked about something to eat,
They will answer with voices so sweet
  (Oh so sweet):

Chorus:

You will eat, by and by,
In that glorious land above the sky,
  (Way up high),
Work and pray,
Live on hay,
You'll get pie in the sky when you die,
  (That's a lie!)

And the starvation army they play,
And they sing and they clap and they pray,
Till they get all your coin on the drum,
Then they'll tell you when you're on the bum:

(Chorus)

Holy Rollers and jumpers come out,
And they holler, they jump and they shout.

"Give your money to Jesus," they say,
"He will cure all diseases today."

(Chorus)

If you fight hard for children and wife,
Try to get something good in this life,
You're a sinner and bad man, they tell,
When you die you will sure go to hell.

(Chorus)

Workingmen of all countries unite,
Side by side we for freedom will fight!
When the world and its wealth we have gained,
To the grafters we'll sing this refrain:

Final chorus:

You will eat, by and by,
When you've learned how to cook and to fry,
Chop some wood,
'Twill do you good,
And you'll eat in the sweet by and by.
  (That's no lie!)

The Commonwealth of Toil

Words: Ralph Chaplin
Music: "Darling Nelly Gray"

Lyrics from *IWW Songs (The Little Red Songbook)*; music from *Lift Every Voice*, Irwin Silber.

In our hands is placed a power greater than their hoarded gold,
Greater than the might of armies, magnified a thousand-fold.
We can bring to birth a new world from the ashes of the old,
For the Union makes us strong.[1]

The Wobbly was a visionary—and a revolutionary. Unlike any previous American movement, the IWW (Industrial Workers of the World) believed that it was necessary completely to transform society in order to correct the ills and abuses of an unjust world. They had only contempt for "reformers" who tried to patch up the sores of society without getting to the cause of the disease. And that basic cause, according to the IWW philosophy, was the capitalist system itself.

They have taken untold millions that they never
    toiled to earn,

[1] "Solidarity Forever," by Ralph Chaplin, from *IWW Songs (The Little Red Songbook)*.

But without our brain and muscle not a single
    wheel can turn.
We can break their haughty power, gain our
    freedom when we learn
That the Union makes us strong.[2]

Joe Hill's great gift as a songwriter was in his ability to individualize his themes. He could write about *Mister Block* or *The Rebel Girl* or *Scissor Bill* or *Casey Jones*, the scab. It was Ralph Chaplin's special talent to be able to capture the essence of the IWW in song—and to produce great hymns of revolutionary faith.

[2] *Ibid.*

In the gloom of mighty cities
Mid the roar of whirling wheels,
We are toiling on like chattel slaves of old,
And our masters hope to keep us
Ever thus beneath their heels,
And to coin our very lifeblood into gold.

Chorus:

But we have a glowing dream
Of how fair the world will seem
When each man can live his life secure and free;
When the earth is owned by Labor
And there's joy and peace for all
In the Commonwealth of Toil that is to be.

They would keep us cowed and beaten
Cringing meekly at their feet,
They would stand between each worker and his
    bread.
Shall we yield our lives up to them

For the bitter crust we eat?
Shall we only hope for heaven when we're dead?

(Chorus)

They have laid our lives out for us
To the utter end of time,
Shall we stagger on beneath their heavy load?
Shall we let them live forever
In their gilded halls of crime
With our children doomed to toil beneath their
    goad?

(Chorus)

When our cause is all triumphant
And we claim our Mother Earth,
And the nightmare of the present fades away,
We shall live with Love and Laughter,
We, who now are little worth,
And we'll not regret the price we have to pay.

(Chorus)

THE COMMONWEALTH OF TOIL

In the gloom of might-y cit-ies, 'mid the roar of whirl-ing wheels, We are toil-ing on like chat-tel slaves of old,— And our mas-ters hope to keep us ev-er thus be-neath their heels, And to coin our ver-y life-blood in-to gold.—

Chorus
But we have a glow-ing dream of how fair the world will seem When each man can live his life se-cure and free,— When the earth is owned by La-bor and there's joy and peace for all, in the Com-mon-wealth of Toil that is to be.—

* Play this E second fret on D string.

Too Ree Ama

WORDS: Author unknown
MUSIC: "Barnyards of Delgaty"

Text from J. Barre Toelken, "Northwest Ballads" in *Northwest Review* (Winter 1962); music from the singing of Ewan MacColl. Variations in the tune as sung by Mr. Toelken are indicated by smaller notes below.

When the lumberman comes down,
Every pocket bears a crown,
And he wanders, some pretty girl to find;
If she's not too sly,
With her dark and rolling eye,
The lumberman is pleased in his mind.[1]

SOME men came to the great Northwest in search of gold; some came hungry for virgin land; some came to fish, some to trap, and some men came to follow the cry of "timber" in the great forests of Idaho and Washington and British Columbia. The loggers brought their axes and their heavy mackinaws from back east—and they also brought their songs. In the logging camps of Michigan and Maine they had sung of the "Lost Jimmie Whalen" and the "Jam on Gerry's Rocks" where the foreman, Young Monroe, had died. And these songs came to the Northwest. Once in a while, some lumberjack poet would come up with a new rhyme that was particularly of the new country.

An old Scottish bothy ballad, "The Barnyards of Delgaty," provided the tune for this lively Idaho lumberjack song. Like its logger descendant, the Scottish original was a wild, boasting song with an infectious refrain. Perhaps some old woodsman, not so far removed from the Scottish soil, remembered the old song while hauling timber in the Idaho woods and set these rambunctious words to the tune.

If you have trouble with the F's and B♭'s try this in E or D. For higher voices try G or A.

[1] "The Lumberman In Town," from *The Maine Woods Songster*, Phillips Barry.

TOO REE AMA

Happy, snappy

1. My eyes look like dried up rai-sins, My nose is a pur - ple red,

I wear a coat of man - y col - ors and it smells of some-thing dead.

Too ree a - ma, too ree a - ma, Too ree a - ma, too ree - ay.

Too ree a - ma, too ree a - ma, Too ree a - ma, too ree - ay.

*Small notes indicate singing style of Barre Toelkin.

My eyes look like dried up raisins,
My nose is a purple red,
I wear a coat of many colors
And it smells like something dead.

Chorus:

Too ree ama, too ree ama,
Too ree ama, too ree-ay.
Too ree ama, too ree ama,
Too ree ama, too ree-ay.

I can tame a wild hoot'nanny,
I can chop a redwood tree,
I dip snoos ° and chew tobaccy:
Will you marry me, me, me?

(Chorus)

° Snuff

I went down to see my honey,
When I got there she was sick;
In her gut they found a peavy,†
Three pulaskis ‡ and a pick.

(Chorus)

I can drink and not get drunken,
I can fight and not get slain,
I can kiss another man's girlie
And be welcome back again.

(Chorus)

† A stout, hooked pole for turning logs in the water.
‡ A fire-fighting tool with an axe blade on one side of its head and a narrow mattock on the other.

The Frozen Logger

Words and music by James L. Stevens

Paul Bunyan, the lumberman, came from St. Paul,
He owned a big ox that was eleven feet tall.
He mowed the trees as the farmers mow hay,
And the crew was at work before break of day.[1]

THE railroad construction gangs of the South created a giant of a legend as their symbol, and they called him John Henry. The riverboat men of the mighty Mississippi told tales of Mike Fink who could out-fight, out-cuss, and out-work any six men along the river. The deep-sea sailors had old Captain Stormalong, while the cowhands of Arizona, when asked about the greatest cowboy of them all, would tell the story of Pecos Bill.

In the lumber camps of the Northwest they told the tales of Paul Bunyan and Babe, his mighty blue ox. Or did they?

[1] "Paul Bunyan," from the singing of Gene Bluestein, *Songs of the North Star State* (Folkways Records FA2132).

Sometimes folklore becomes literature; and sometimes literature becomes folklore. The myth which is now Paul Bunyan was more the work of a writer by the name of James Stevens than the folklore of the logging camps. Not that it matters much any more. Paul Bunyan belongs to our culture now, no matter who created him. And lumberjacks have come to accept him as their own.

Stevens had the feel for folklore. Among his works is the ballad of "The Frozen Logger," as fine a piece of "folkliar" hokum as the folk themselves have produced.

Play the first and last verse in slow waltz rhythm, other verses faster; singer ad lib.

THE FROZEN LOGGER

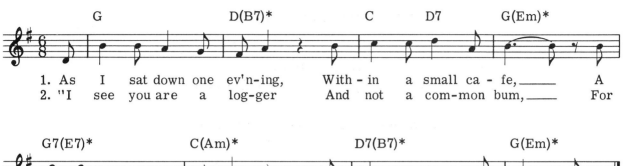

1. As I sat down one ev'n-ing, With-in a small ca-fe,_____ A
2. "I see you are a log-ger And not a com-mon bum,_____ For

for-ty-year-old wait-ress To me these words did say:_____
no one but a log-ger Stirs his cof-fee with his thumb._____

*Suggested "dramatic" chord variation for verses 9. and 10.

As I sat down one evening,
Within a small café,
A forty-year-old waitress
To me these words did say:

"I see you are a logger
And not a common bum,
For no one but a logger
Stirs his coffee with his thumb.

"My lover was a logger,
There's none like him today,
If you poured whiskey on it,
He'd eat a bale of hay.

"He never shaved the whiskers
From off of his horny hide,
But he drove them in with a hammer
And bit them off inside.

"My logger came to see me
On one freezing day,
He held me in a fond embrace
That broke three vertebrae.

"He kissed me when we parted,
So hard he broke my jaw,

I could not speak to tell him
He'd forgot his mackinaw.

"And so my logger left me,
A-sauntering through the snow,
Going gaily homeward
At forty-eight below.

"The weather tried to freeze him,
It tried its level best;
At one hundred degrees below zero,
He buttoned up his vest.

"It froze clean through to China,
It froze to the stars above,
At one thousand degrees below zero
It froze my logger love.

"They tried in vain to thaw him,
And if you'll believe me, sir,
They made him into axe-blades
To chop the Douglas Fir.

"And so I lost my lover,
And to this café I come,
And here I wait till someone
Stirs his coffee with his thumb."

Fifty Thousand Lumberjacks

Author unknown
Music adapted by Earl Robinson

From *IWW Songs (The Little Red Songbook).*

The Revolution started, so the judge informed the mayor,
Now Baker paces back and forth, and raves and pulls his hair,
The waterfront is tied up tight, the Portland newsboy howls,
And not a thing is moving, only Mayor Baker's bowels.[1]

FROM 1912 through the late 1920's, the most powerful industrial force in the West was the IWW. The Wobblies attempted to organize every trade, every occupation, every working man into "one big union." In the years shortly after World War I, they organized the lumber camps of Washington and Oregon into the IWW, and when the time was right, they called an industry-wide strike throughout their territory. This is the song of that strike.

[1] "The Portland Revolution," from *The Little Red Songbook.*

308

FIFTY THOUSAND LUMBERJACKS

Fif - ty thou-sand lum-ber jacks, fif - ty thou-sand packs,

Fif - ty thou-sand dirt - y rolls of ___ blan-kets on their backs,

Fif - ty thou-sand minds made up to strike and strike like men; For

fif - ty years they've "packed" a bed, but nev - er will a - gain.

Chorus

"Such a lot of dev - ils," That's ___ what the pa - pers say, "They've

gone on strike for short-er hours and ___ some in-crease in pay. They

left the camps, the la - zy tramps, they all walked out as one; They

say they'll win the strike and put the bos - ses on the bum."

Fifty thousand lumberjacks, fifty thousand packs,
Fifty thousand dirty rolls of blankets on their backs,
Fifty thousand minds made up to strike and strike like men;
For fifty years they've "packed" a bed, but never will again.

Chorus:

"Such a lot of devils," that's what the papers say,
"They've gone on strike for shorter hours and some increase in pay.
They left the camps, the lazy tramps, they all walked out as one;
They say they'll win the strike or put the bosses on the bum."

Fifty thousand wooden bunks full of things that crawl;
Fifty thousand restless men have left them once for all.
One by one they dared not say, "Fat, the hours are long."
If they did they'd hike—but now they're fifty thousand strong.

(Chorus)

Men who work should be well paid—"A man's a man for 'a that."
Many a man has a home to keep same as yourself, Old Fat.
Mothers, sisters, sweethearts, wives, children, too, galore,
Stand behind the men to win this bread-and-butter war.

(Chorus)

When the Ice Worms Nest Again

WORDS: Attributed to Robert Service
MUSIC: Composer unknown

From *Canada's Story in Song*, by Edith Fowke, Alan Mills, and Helmut Blume.

Tell my friends and tell my enemies, if you ever reach the East,
That the Dawson City region is no place for man or beast;
That the land's too elevated and the wind too awful cold,
And the hills of South Dakota yield as good a grade of gold.[1]

THE magic power of gold is a bright thread running through the fabric of the history of the West. Gold brought the Spanish to Mexico and the pioneers of '49 to California. Half a century after gold was discovered at Sutter's Mill, the fabulous Klondike Gold Rush opened the farthest reaches of the cold Alaska country to the "benefits" of civilization.

The mining town of Dawson, in the heart of the Klondike region, became the center for the fortune hunters from California, British Columbia, and all points east who crowded onto ocean steamers in Seattle and Vancouver headed for the gold country in Alaska.

Oh, come to the place where they struck it rich,
Come where the treasure lies hid,
Where your hat full of mud is a five-pound note,
And a clod on your heel is a quid.

Klondike, Klondike,
Label your luggage for Klondike,
For there ain't no luck in the town today,
There ain't no work down Moodyville way,
Pack up your traps and be off, I say,
Off and away to the Klondike.[2]

More than 25,000 prospectors came to Alaska in the heady days of the Klondike gold fever. Only a handful of these found their fortunes in the snow and mud of the frozen north; and many a man who struck it rich in the Alaska hills squandered his fortune in the gambling houses of Dawson City.

Some of the lucky ones—and some of the busted ones—made their way back home to warmer climes. But thousands stayed in the fabulous land of the midnight sun, rising to the challenge of the frozen North to build a new civilization in the shadow of the Arctic.

The musical symbol for those who stayed was the song, probably written originally by Robert Service, "When the Ice Worms Nest Again." Not only the song, but the ice worms themselves were also Service's creation.

Old prospectors, so the story goes, annoyed with the "sourdough" airs affected by an English dude who had arrived in Klondike country only a week earlier, decide to initiate the British gentleman in the mysteries of an ice-worm cocktail. Intrigued and dubious, the Englishman asks what an ice worm is. He is told that the beast is unique to the Mountain of the Blue Snow, where it flourishes until caught and pickled for sourdough cocktails. The dude remains skeptical, so the bartender proceeds to make up four ice-worm cocktails for the party. The old prospectors immediately down their liquid delicacies, but the Englishman blanches at the prospect of swallowing the "grey and greasy things." When, after screwing up his courage, Percy finally drinks, he discovers that the ice worm is "a stick of stained spaghetti with two red ink spots for eyes."

In the northern reaches of Saskatchewan and Manitoba, the old-time trappers and their lively bands still sing and play the catchy song about the inevitable nesting of those mysterious creatures of the northern snows—the ice worms of Alaska.

[1] "Just From Dawson," from *American Ballads and Folk Songs*, Lomax.
[2] "The Klondike Gold Rush," from *Canada's Story In Song*, Edith Fowke, Alan Mills, and Helmut Blume.

311

WHEN THE ICE WORMS NEST AGAIN

1. There's a husk-y, dusk-y maid-en in the Arc-tic, And she waits for me but it is not in vain,____ For some day I'll put my muk-luks on and ask her____ If she'll wed me when the ice worms nest a - gain.____

Chorus

In the land of the pale blue snow Where it's nine-ty - nine be - low, And the po - lar bears are roam-ing o'er the plain,____ In the shad-ow of the Pole I will clasp her to my soul, We'll be mar-ried when the ice worms nest a - gain.____

last time the am en chords

There's a husky, dusky maiden in the Arctic,
And she waits for me but it is not in vain,
For some day I'll put my mukluks on and ask her
If she'll wed me when the ice worms nest again.

Chorus:

In the land of the pale blue snow
Where it's ninety-nine below,
And the polar bears are roamin' o'er the plain,
In the shadow of the Pole
I will clasp her to my soul,
We'll be happy when the ice worms nest again.

For our wedding feast we'll have seal oil and blubber;
In our kayaks we will roam the bounding main;
All the walruses will look at us and rubber,
We'll be married when the ice worms nest again.

(Chorus)

And when the blinken icebergs bound around us,
She'll present me with a bouncing baby boy.
All the polar bears will dance a rumba 'round us,
And the walruses will click their teeth with joy.

Final Chorus:

When some night at half-past two
I return to my igloo,
After sitting with a friend who was in pain,
She'll be waiting for me there
With the hambone of a bear,
And she'll beat me till the ice worms nest again.

Roll On, Columbia

Words and music by Woody Guthrie

Well the world has seven wonders that the travelers always tell,
Some gardens and some towers, I guess you know them well;
But now the greatest wonder's in Uncle Sam's fair land,
It's the King Columbia River and the Big Grand Coulee Dam.[1]

IN 1941, when the United States government undertook to harness the power of the Columbia River to provide electricity for home and industry, some intelligent soul in the Department of the Interior decided to hire Woody Guthrie, the great folk poet and Dust Bowl balladeer, to make up songs about the project. Woody went up to the Northwest country and, inspired by the natural beauty of the rivers and the land, as well as the dream of a better life for the people of the area, he composed twenty-six ballads in less than a month. Amazingly enough, at least half a dozen of these have already become lasting classics of American folk song. One of the best is Woody's historical ballad which has since become the unofficial state song of Washington—"Roll On, Columbia."

"I saw the Columbia River and the big Grand Coulee Dam from just about every cliff, mountain, tree, and post from which it can be seen. I made up twenty-six songs about the Columbia and about the dam and about the men, and these songs were recorded by the Department of Interior, Bonneville Power Administration out in Portland. The records were played at all sorts and sizes of meetings where people bought bonds to bring the power lines over the fields and hills to their own little places. Electricity to milk the cows, kiss the maid, shoe the old mare, light up the saloon, the chili joint window, the schools, and churches along the way, to run the factories turning out manganese, chrome, bauxite, aluminum and steel."[2]

[1] "Grand Coulee Dam," from *California to the New York Island*, Woody Guthrie.

[2] *Ibid.*

ROLL ON, COLUMBIA

Bright and confident

1. Green Doug - las Fir where the wa - ters cut through,

Down her wild moun-tains and can-yons she flew, Ca - na - dian North-

west to the o - cean so blue, It's roll on, Co - lum - bia, roll

316

Green Douglas fir where the waters cut through,
Down her wild mountains and canyons she flew,
Canadian Northwest to the ocean so blue,
It's roll on, Columbia, roll on.

Chorus:

Roll on, Columbia, roll on,
Roll on, Columbia, roll on,
Your power is turning our darkness to dawn,
So roll on, Columbia, roll on.

Other great rivers add power to you,
Yakima, Snake and the Klickitat, too.
Sandy Williamette and Hood River, too,
Roll on, Columbia, roll on.

(Chorus)

Tom Jefferson's vision would not let him rest,
An empire he saw in the Pacific Northwest,
Sent Lewis and Clark, and they did the rest,
Roll on, Columbia, roll on.

(Chorus)

It's there on your banks we fought many a fight,
Sheridan's boys in the blockhouse that night,
They saw us in death, but never in flight,
Roll on, Columbia, roll on.

(Chorus)

At Bonneville now there are ships in the locks,
The waters have risen and cleared all the rocks.
Shiploads of plenty will steam past the docks,
So roll on, Columbia, roll on.

(Chorus)

And on up the river is Grand Coulee Dam,
The mightiest thing ever built by a man,
To run the great factories and water the land,
It's roll on, Columbia, roll on.

(Chorus)

These mighty men labored by day and by night,
Matching their strength 'gainst the river's wild flight,
Through rapids and falls they won the hard fight,
Roll on, Columbia, roll on.

(Chorus)

318

BIBLIOGRAPHY

A. BOOKS

C. E. Abbott and Helena Huntington Smith. *We Pointed Them North*. New York, Farrar & Rinehart, 1939.

Andy Adams. *Log of a Cowboy*. New York, Doubleday & Co., 1902.

Ramon F. Adams. *Western Words: A Dictionary of the Range, Cow Camp and Trail*. Norman, Okla., Univ. of Oklahoma Press, 1946.

Francis D. Allan. *Allan's Lone Star Ballads; a collection of Southern Patriotic Songs made during Confederate Times*. Galveston, Tex., J. D. Sawyer, 1874.

Eleanor Allen. *Canvas Caravans; based on the journal of Esther Belle McMillan Hanna, who with her husband, Rev. Joseph A. Hanna, brought the Presbyterian Colony to Oregon in 1852*. Portland, Oreg., Binfords & Mort, 1946.

Jules Verne Allen. *Cowboy Lore*. San Antonio, Tex., Naylor Co., 1933, 1950.

The Alliance Songster; a collection of labor and comic songs for the use of grange, alliance and debating clubs. Compiled by H. Leopold Vincent. Winfield, Kan., H. & L. Vincent, 1891.

Margaret Blake Alverson. *Sixty Years of California Song*. Oakland, California, M. V. Alverson, 1913.

American War Songs. Published under the supervision of the National Committee for the Preservation of Existing Records of the National Society of the Colonial Dames of America. Privately printed. Philadelphia, 1925.

John Bargate Appleton. *The Pacific Northwest: A Selected Bibliography, 1930–1939*. Portland, Ore., Northwest Regional Council, 1939.

The Arkansas Traveler's Songster. New York, Dick & Fitzgerald, 1863.

Herbert Asbury. *The Barbary Coast*. New York, Alfred Knopf, 1933.

Washington Baily. *A Trip to California in 1853; recollections of a gold-seeking trip by ox train across the plains and mountains by an old Illinois pioneer*. LeRoy, Ill., LeRoy Journal Printing Co., 1915.

C. Stanley Banks and Grace T. McMillan. *The New Texas Reader*. San Antonio, Tex., Naylor Co., 1947, 1960.

Phillips Barry. *The Maine Woods Songster*. Cambridge, Mass., Powell Printing Co., 1939.

Beadle's Half-Dime Singer's Library (Nos. 1–42). New York, Beadle & Adams, 1878–1879.

Delilah L. Beasley. *The Negro Trail Blazers of California*, Los Angeles, 1919.

Earl Clifton Beck. *Lore of the Lumber Camps*. Ann Arbor Mich., Univ. of Michigan Press, 1948.

H. M. Belden. *Ballads and Songs Collected by the Missouri Folklore Society*. Columbia, Mo., Univ. of Missouri Studies, 1940, 1955.

Major Horace Bell. *Reminiscences of a Ranger*. Santa Barbara, Calif., Wallace Hubbard, 1927.

Bella Union Melodeon Songster. San Francisco, D. E. Appleton Co., 1860.

Bella Union Songster; popular songs of the day and all the songs that have been sung by Sheridan and Reilly at the Bella Union Theater. San Francisco, n.d.

Ben Cotton's Own Songster #2. San Francisco, D. E. Appleton Co., 1864.

General John Bidwell. *Echoes of the Past*. Published originally by the *Chico Advertiser*, Chico, California. Reprinted, New York, Citadel Press, 1962.

Cantell A. Bigly (G. W. Peck). *Aurifodina; or Adventures in the Gold Region; a satire*. New York, Baker & Scribner, 1849.

Ray Allen Billington. *The Far Western Frontier (1830–1860)*. New York, Harper & Bros., 1956.

Billy Emerson's New Comic Songster, containing a

319

choice collection of new comic Ethiopian and Eccentric Songs as sung by the renowned comic vocalist, Billy Emerson. New York, Dick & Fitzgerald, 1868.

Billy Warner's Clown Songster. San Francisco, Francis & Valentine, 1874.

Eleanora Black and Sidney Robertson. *The Gold Rush Song Book.* San Francisco, Colt Press, 1940.

George E. Blankenship. *Lights and Shades of Pioneer Life on Puget Sound.* Olympia, Wash., 1923.

The Blue and Gray Songster. San Francisco, 1871.

Mody C. Boatright. *Mexican Border Ballads and Other Lore.* Publications of the Texas Folklore Society, No. 21, Austin, Tex., 1946.

Mody C. Boatright, William M. Hudson, and Allen Maxwell. *Folk Travelers: Ballads, Tales, and Talk.* Publications of the Texas Folklore Society, No. 25, Dallas, Tex., Southern Methodist Univ. Press, 1953.

————*Singers and Storytellers.* Publications of the Texas Folklore Society, No. 30, Dallas, Tex., Southern Methodist Univ. Press, 1961.

————*Texas Folk and Folklore.* Publications of the Texas Folklore Society, No. 26, Dallas, Tex., Southern Methodist University Press, 1954.

Bobby Newcomb's San Francisco Minstrel Songster; a first-rate collection of song ballads and choruses, humorous, pathetic, witty; including all the new sensations. Adapted to very popular and well-known airs and choruses. New York, Robert M. De Witt, 1868.

Margaret Bradford Boni. *Fireside Book of Favorite American Songs.* New York, Simon & Schuster, 1952.

————*Fireside Book of Folk Songs.* New York, Simon & Schuster, 1947.

B. F. Bonney. *Across the Plains by Prairie Schooner; a personal narrative of his trip to Sutter's Fort, California, in 1846, and of his pioneering experiences in Oregon during the days of Oregon's Provisional Government.* Eugene, Oreg., Fred Lockely, n.d.

Booth Campaign Songster. San Francisco, Alta Calif. General Printing House, 1871.

Sam Booth. *Local Lyrics.* San Francisco, Bruce's Printing House, 1872.

J. D. Borthwick. *The Gold Hunters; a first-hand picture of Life in California Mining Camps in the Early Fifties.* Printed in Scotland, 1857.

B. A. Botkin. *A Treasury of Western Folklore.* New York, Crown, 1951.

Boyd's Songster and San Francisco Pictorial: Vol. I, Nos. 2, 4, 5, 6. San Francisco, 1868.

Oscar Brand. *Singing Holidays.* New York, Alfred A. Knopf, 1957.

Carl W. Breihan. *Badmen of the Frontier Days.* New York, Robert M. McBride, 1957.

Paul G. Brewster. *Ballads and Songs of Indiana.* Bloomington, Ind., Indiana Univ. Publications, 1940.

Carol Brink. *Harps in the Wind. The Story of the Singing Hutchinsons.* New York, The Macmillan Company, 1947.

Paul Frederick Brissenden. *The IWW, a study of American Syndicalism.* New York, Columbia Univ. Press, 1920.

Frank C. Brown. *Collection of North Carolina Folklore,* 5 vols. Durham, N. C., Duke Univ. Press, 1952.

Walter Noble Burns. *The Saga of Billy the Kid.* New York, Doubleday, Page & Co., 1926.

Olive Wooley Burt. *American Murder Ballads.* New York, Oxford Univ. Press, 1958.

California Broadsides. From the collection in the Bancroft Library, Univ. California, Berkeley, Calif.

The California Songster, containing a selection of California and other popular songs. San Francisco, D. E. Appleton Co., 1855.

California Valentine Writer; a collection of entirely new and original valentines and amatory effusions for the especial use of Cupid's votaries in the Golden State, by TREM (pseud.). San Francisco, D. E. Appleton Co., 1863.

Arthur Leon Campa. *Spanish Folk-Poetry in New Mexico.* Albuquerque, N. Mex., Univ. of New Mexico Press, 1946.

Robert V. Carr. *Black Hills Ballads.* Denver, Colo., Reed Pub. Co., 1902.

————*Cowboy Lyrics* Chicago, W. B.. Conkey Co., 1908.

E. S. Carter. *Life and Adventures (including a trip across the plains and mountains in 1852, Indian Wars in the early days of Oregon).* St. Joseph, Mo., Combe Printing Co., 1896.

Norman Cazden. *The Abelard Folk Song Book.* New York, Abelard–Schuman, 1958.

Champagne Charlie and Coal Oil Tommy Songster. San Francisco, D. E. Appleton Co., 1868.

Gilbert Chase. *America's Music: from the Pilgrims to the Present.* New York, McGraw–Hill, 1955.

E. P. Christy. *Christy and White's Ethiopian Melodies.* Philadelphia, T. B. Peterson & Bros., 1854 (?)

————*Christy's Minstrels Song Book.* 2 volumes. London, Boosey & Sons, n.d.

————*Christy's Plantation Melodies.* 3 volumes. New York, Fisher & Bros., 1851, 1853.

Charles Badger Clark. *Sun and Saddle Leather.* Boston, R. G. Badger, 1920.

George W. Clark. *The Liberty Minstrel.* New York, Saxton & Miles, and Myron Finch. 1845.

Kenneth S. Clark. *The Cowboy Sings; songs of the ranch and range.* New York, Paull–Pioneer Music Corp., 1932.

Thomas D. Clark. *The Rampaging Frontier.* Indianapolis, Ind., Bobbs–Merrill, 1939.

Sarah M. Clarke. *Songs of Labor for the People.* San Francisco, A. M. Slocum, 1880.

Stanton A. Coblentz. *Villains and Vigilantes.* New York, Thomas Yoseloff, 1936.

Joanna C. Colcord. *Songs of American Sailormen.* New York, W. W. Norton, 1938, Oak Publications, 1964 (Reprint edition).

Rufus A. Coleman. *The Golden West in Story and Verse.* New York, Harper & Bros., 1932.

John Harrington Cox. *Folk Songs of the South.* Cambridge, Mass., Harvard Univ. Press, 1925.

Capt. Jack Crawford. *Campfire Sparks.* Chicago, Charles H. Kerr & Co., 1893.

George W. Cronyn. *The Path on the Rainbow; an anthology of songs and chants from the Indians of North America.* New York, Boni & Liveright, 1918.

Ralph Herbert Cross. *The Early Inns of California, 1844–1869.* San Francisco, Cross & Brandt, 1954.

Homer Croy. *Last of the Great Outlaws.* New York, Duell, Sloan & Pearce, 1956.

General George A. Custer. *My Life on the Plains.* New York Citadel Press, 1962.

Carl C. Cutler. *The Greyhounds of the Sea; the story of the American Clipper Ship.* Annapolis, Md., U.S. Naval Institute, 1930, 1960.

Rev. Owen da Silva (O.F.M.). *Mission Music of California; a collection of old California mission hymns and masses.* Los Angeles, Warren F. Lewis, 1941.

Joe Davis. *Tip Top Songs of the Roaming Ranger.* New York, Joe Davis Inc., 1935.

M. C. Dean. *Flying Cloud and 150 other old-time songs and ballads of outdoor men, sailors, lumberjacks, soldiers, men of the Great Lakes, railroadmen, miners, etc.* Virginia, Minn., The Quickprint, 1922.

Alonzo Delano. *Life on the Plains and Among the Diggings; being scenes and adventures of an overland journey to California; with particular incidents of the route, mistakes and sufferings of the emigrants, the Indian tribes, the present and the future of the Great West.* New York, Miller, Orton & Co., 1857.

———*Old Block's Sketch Book.* Drawings by Charles Nahl. Santa Ana, Calif., Fine Arts Press (reprint), 1947.

Harry Dichter and Elliott Shapiro. *Early American Sheet Music; Its Lure and Its Lore, 1768–1889.* New York, R.R. Bowker Co., 1941.

J. Frank Dobie. *Follow De Drinkin' Gou'd.* Publications of the Texas Folklore Society, No. 7, Austin, Tex., 1928.

———*The Longhorns.* New York, Grosset & Dunlap, 1941.

———*Southwestern Lore.* Publications of the Texas Folklore Society, No. 9, Austin, Tex., 1931.

———*Tone The Bell Easy.* Publications of the Texas Folklore Society, No. 10, Austin, Tex., 1932.

William Main Doerflinger. *Shantymen and Shantyboys.* New York, The Macmillan Company, 1951.

Edward Arthur Dolph. *"Sound Off"—Soldier Songs.* New York, Cosmopolitan Book Corp., 1929.

Fairfax Downey. *Indian-Fighting Army.* New York, Charles Scribner's Sons, 1941.

Harry Sinclair Drago. *Red River Valley.* New York, Clarkson N. Potter, 1962.

Harold E. Driver. *Indians of North America.* Chicago, Univ. of Chicago Press, 1961.

Richard A. Dwyer and Richard E. Lingenfelter, *The Songs of the Gold Rush,* Berkeley and Los Angeles, Univ. of California Press, 1964.

Mary O. Eddy. *Ballads and Songs from Ohio.* New York, J.J. Augustin, 1939.

George Cary Eggleston. *American War Ballads and Lyrics.* 2 Vols. New York, G. P. Putnam's Sons, 1889.

Albert G. Emerick. *Songs for the People; comprising national, patriotic, sentimental, comic, and naval songs.* Boston, Oliver Ditson Co., 1852.

Aurora Esmerelda (Ella Sterling Mighels). *Life and Letters of the Forty-Niner's Daughter.* San Francisco, Harr Wagner Pub. Co., n.d.

Farmer's Alliance Songs. A collection of songs for Alliance meetings, farmers' institutes, etc., by E. O. Excell and Dr. D. Reid Parker. Chicago, E. O. Excell, 1890

Federal Writers Project—Idaho. *Idaho Lore.* Caldwell, Idaho, Caxton Printers, 1939.

Federal Writers Project—Montana. *Copper Camp; stories of the world's greatest mining town, Butte, Montana.* New York, Hastings House, 1943.

Federal Writers Project—Nebraska. *Nebraska Folklore: Pamplet #16—Ballads; #18—Farmer's Alliance Songs of the 1890's; #20—More Farmers' Alliance Songs of the 1890's (1938 and 1939).*

Benjamin G. Ferris. *Utah and the Mormons. The History, Government, Doctrines, Customs and Propects of the Latter-Day Saints from Personal Observations during a Six-Months' Residence at Great Salt Lake City.* New York, Harper & Bros., 1856.

Austin and Alta Fife. *Saints of Sage and Saddle.* Bloomington, Ind., Indiana Univ. Press, 1956.

Charles J. Finger. *Frontier Ballads.* Garden City, N.Y., Doubleday, Page & Co., 1927.

Philip S. Foner, *The Letters of Joe Hill.* New York, N. Y., Oak Publications, 1965.

The Forget Me Not Songster, containing a choice collection of old ballad songs as sung by our grandmothers. New York, Nafis & Cornish (c. 1843).

Foster-Harris. *The Look of the Old West.* New York, Viking Press, 1960.

Edith Fowke, Alan Mills, and Helmut Blume. *Canada's Story in Song*. Toronto, W. G. Gage, 1960.

The Free Soil Minstrel. New York, Martin & Ely, 1848.

The Freemen's Glee Book, a collection of songs, odes, glees and ballads with music, original and selected, harmonized and arranged for each. Published under the auspices of the Central Fremont & Dayton Glee Club of the City of New York, and dedicated to all, who, cherishing Republican liberty, consider Freedom Worth a Song. New York and Auburn, Miller, Orton & Mulligan, 1856.

Hugo Frey. *American Cowboy Songs*. New York, Robbins Music, 1936.

Albert B. Friedman. *The Viking Book of Folk Ballads of the English-Speaking World*. New York, Viking Press, 1956.

James J. Fuld. *American Popular Music, 1875–1950*. Philadelphia, Musical Americana, 1955.

Harvey H. Fuson. *Ballads of the Kentucky Highlands*. London, The Mitre Press, 1931.

Emelyn Elizabeth Gardner and Geraldine Jencks Chickering. *Ballads and Songs of Southern Michigan*. Ann Arbor, Mich., Univ. of Michigan Press, 1939.

George B. German. *Cowboy Campfire Ballads*. Yankton, S. Dak., 1929.

Captain Willard Glazier. *Peculiarities of American Cities*. Philadelphia, Hubbard Bros., 1886.

Robert W. Gordon. *Folk Songs of America*. National Service Bureau WPA, 1938.

Philip Graham. *Early Texas Verse (1835–1850)*. Austin, Tex., The Stock Co., 1936.

Roland Palmer Gray. *Songs and Ballads of the Maine Lumberjacks*. Cambridge, Mass., Harvard Univ. Press, 1924.

The Great Emerson New Popular Songster containing songs sung by the "Great Emerson," "Vivian," and "Milburn." San Francisco, S. C. Blake, 1872.

Elisabeth Bristol Greenleaf. *Ballads and Sea Songs of Newfoundland*. Cambridge, Mass., Harvard Univ. Press. 1933.

John Greenway. *American Folksongs of Protest*. Philadelphia, Univ. of Pennsylvania Press, 1953.

Wesley S. Griswold. *A Work of Giants. Building the First Transcontinental Railroad*. New York, McGraw-Hill, 1962.

Erwin G. Gudde. *1,000 California Place Names, Their Origin and Meaning*. Berkeley and Los Angeles, Univ. of California Press, 1949.

Woody Guthrie. *California to the New York Island*. New York, Guthrie Children's Trust Fund, 1960.

Eleanor Hague. *Spanish-American Folk-Songs*. New York, The American Folklore Society, 1917.

Handy Andy's Budget of Songs. New York, William H. Murphy (Circa 1848).

Joseph Mills Hanson. *Frontier Ballads*. Chicago, A. C. McClurg & Co., 1910.

Frederick Pease Harlow. *Chanteying Aboard American Ships*. Barre, Mass., Barre Gazette, 1962.

Charles Haywood. *A Bibliography of North American Folklore and Folksong*. New York, Greenberg, 1951.

William D. Haywood. *Autobiography*. New York, International Publishers, 1929.

Harold Hersey. *Singing Rawhide—A Book of Western Ballads*. New York, George H. Doran, 1926.

John D. Hicks. *The Populist Revolt. A History of the Farmers' Alliance and The People's Party*. Univ. of Minnesota Press, 1931.

Waldemar Hille, *The People's Songbook*. New York, Oak Publications, 1948, 1962.

Hitchcock's Half-Dime Series of Music for the Millions. New York, B.W. Hitchcock, 1869.

Stewart H. Holbrook. *The Story of American Railroads*. New York, Crown, 1947.

Hooley's Opera House Songster, containing a choice collection of sentimental, comic and Ethiopian songs. San Francisco, D.E. Appleton Co., 1863.

John Tasker Howard. *Our American Music*. New York, Thomas Y. Crowell Co., 1946, 1954.

———*A Treasury of Stephen Foster*. New York, Random House, 1946.

Robert West Howard. *The Great Iron Trail. The Story of the First Transcontinental Railroad*. New York, G. P. Putnam's Sons, 1962.

———*This Is The West*. New York, Rand McNally & Co., 1957.

Lester Hubbard. *Ballads and Songs from Utah*. Salt Lake City, Utah, Univ. of Utah Press, 1961.

Arthur Palmer Hudson. *Folksongs of Mississippi*. Chapel Hill, N.C., Univ. of North Carolina Press, 1936.

Stan Hugill. *Shanties from the Seven Seas*. New York, E.P. Dutton & Co., 1961.

Archer Butler Hulbert. *Forty-Niners; the Chronicle of the California Trail*. Boston, Little, Brown, 1932.

John W. Hutchinson. *Hutchinson's Republican Songster for the Campaign of 1860*. New York, O. Hutchinson, 1860.

Hutchinson Family. *The Granite Songster; Songs of the Hutchinson Family (without the music)*. Boston, A.B. Hutchinson, 1847.

———*Hutchinson Family Book of Words*. Boston, J.S. Potter & Co., 1855.

———*Hutchinson Family's Book of Poetry, containing 67 of their most popular songs*. Boston, S. Chism-Franklin Prntg. House, 1858.

IWW Songs—Songs of the Workers (The Little Red Songbook). Chicago, Industrial Workers of the World, various editions 1912–1936.

George Stuyvesant Jackson. *Early Songs of Uncle Sam*. Boston, Bruce Humphries, 1933.

322

William Henry Jackson. *The Old West Speaks*. Englewood Cliffs, N. J., Prentice–Hall, 1956.

John Brown and the "Union Right or Wrong" Songster containing all the celebrated "John Brown" & "Union Songs" which have become so immensely popular throughout the Union. San Francisco, D.E. Appleton Co., 1863.

Helen Kendrick Johnson. *Our Familiar Songs and Those Who Made Them*. New York, Henry Holt & Co., 1881, 1909.

Willis E. Johnson. *South Dakota Community Songbook*. Brookings, S. Dak., 1922.

Johnson's Original Comic Songs. San Francisco, Presko & Appleton Co., 1858.

Johnson's New Comic Songs No. 2. San Francisco, D. Appleton & Co., 1863.

Johnson's Original Comic Songs No. 3. San Francisco, D.E. Appleton Co., 1864.

Philip D. Jordan. *Singin' Yankees*. Minneapolis, Minn., Univ. of Minnesota Press, 1946.

———and Lillian Kessler. *Songs of Yesterday*. Garden City, N.Y., Doubleday, Doran & Co., 1941.

T. S. Kenderdine. *A California Tramp—and Later Footprints, or Life on the Plains and in the Golden State Thirty Years Ago*. Newton, Pa., 1888.

Lowell Klappholz. *Gold! Gold!* New York, Robert M. McBride, 1959.

Henry Herbert Knibbs. *Songs of the Last Frontier*. Boston, Houghton Mifflin, 1930.

Winifred I. Knox. *Folksongs from the Olympic Peninsula and Puget Sound*. Unpublished master's thesis, Juilliard School of Music, 1945.

George Korson. *Coal Dust on the Fiddle; songs and stories of the Bituminous Industry*. Philadelphia, Univ. of Pennsylvania Press, 1943.

Margaret Larkin. *Singing Cowboy*. New York, Alfred A. Knopf, 1931; Oak Publications 1964 (Reprint edition).

David Lavender. *Land of Giants; The Drive to the Pacific Northwest, 1750–1950*. New York, Doubleday and Co., 1958.

Malcolm G. Laws, Jr. *American Balladry from British Broadsides*. Philadelphia, American Folklore Society, 1957

———*Native American Balladry*. Philadelphia, American Folklore Society, 1964.

MacEdward Leach. *The Ballad Book*. New York, Harper & Bros., 1955.

Cornel Lengyel. *History of Music in San Francisco: Vol. 1—Music of the Gold Rush Era. Vol. 2— A San Francisco Songster 1849–1939*. San Francisco, Work Progress Administration, Northern California, 1939.

Everett Lloyd. *Law West of the Pecos; The Story of Roy Bean*. San Antonio, Tex., Naylor Co., 1936.

Fred Lockley. *Oregon's Yesterdays*. New York, Knickerbocker Press, 1928.

Arthur Loesser. *Humor In American Song*. New York, Howell, Soskin, 1942.

Alan Lomax. *The Folk Songs of North America*. Garden City, N.Y., Doubleday & Co., 1960.

John A. Lomax. *Adventures of a Ballad Hunter*. New York, The Macmillan Company, 1947.

———*Songs of the Cattle Trail and Cow Camp*. New York, Duell, Sloan & Pearce, 1919, 1947.

John A. Lomax and Alan Lomax. *American Ballads and Folk Songs*. New York, The Macmillan Company, 1934. (Dover, 1994.)

———*Cowboy Songs and Other Frontier Ballads*. New York, The Macmillan Company, 1957 edition.

———*Folk Song U.S.A.* New York, Duell, Sloan & Pearce, 1947.

———*Our Singing Country*. New York, The Macmillan Company, 1949.

Charles F. Lummis. *The Land of Poco Tiempo*. New York, Charles Scribner's Sons, 1893.

Edwin Markham. *California Songs and Stories*. Los Angeles, Powell Pub., 1931.

Frank Marryat. *Mountains and Molehills*. London, Longman, Brown, Green & Longmans, 1855.

Edward Winslow Martin. *History of the Grange Movement; or The Farmer's War Against Monopolies, being a full and authentic account of the struggles of the American farmers against the extortion of the railroad companies; with a history of the rise and progress of the order of Patrons of Husbandry*. Philadelphia, Nat'l Publishing Co., 1873.

William Audley Maxwell. *Crossing the Plains (Days of '57); a narrative of early emigrant travel to California by the Ox-Team method*. San Francisco, Sunset Pub., 1915.

William M'Carty. *National Songs, Ballads & Other Patriotic Poetry, chiefly relating to the War of 1846*. Philadelphia, William M'Carty, 1846.

E. S. McComas. *A Journal of Travel*. Portland, Oreg., Champoeg Press, 1954.

Hugh F. McDermott. *Poems: Epic, Comic and Satiric, dedicated to free-lunchers and noddle-headed scribblers*. San Francisco, published by the author, 1857.

Edward Washington McIlhany. *Recollections of a '49er; a quaint and thrilling narrative of a trip across the plains, and life in the California gold fields during the stirring days following the discovery of gold in the far west*. Kansas City, Mo., Hailman Printing Co., 1908.

Vicente T. Mendoza. *El Corrido Mexicano*. Letras Mexicanas, 1954.

Minstrel Songs Old and New. Boston, Oliver Ditson Co., 1882.

The Monthly Popular Songster, publisher and proprietor, A. A. McLean. San Francisco, 1872.

Madison Berryman Moorman. *The Journal of (1850–51)*. Calif. Historical Society, 1948.

George G. W. Morgan. *Selections of Poetic Waifs*. San Francisco, 1869.

Paul Morgan. *Texas Ballads and Other Verses*. Dallas, Tex., Tandy Pub. Co., 1934.

Music in Denver and Colorado. Denver Public Library, 1927.

The National Minstrel, embracing a collection of the most popular and approved national, patriotic, moral, love, sentimental, comic and Negro songs, compiled expressly for the publisher. Buffalo, N.Y., Phinney & Co., 1858.

Daniel O'Connell. *Songs from Bohemia*. San Francisco, A. M. Robertson, 1900.

Old Folks at Home Songster. Philadelphia, Fisher & Bros., 1851.

One Hundred Comic Songs, music and words; to which have been added many valuable copyright pieces by J. W. Turner, E. T. Bates and others. Boston, Oliver Ditson & Co., 1858.

Ernest Staples Osgood. *The Day of the Cattleman*. Chicago, Univ. of Chicago Press, 1929, 1957.

The Pacific Songbook, containing all the songs of the Pacific Coast and California, by various authors such as John A. Stone (Old Put,) Dr. Robinson, Jack the Grumbler, J. Swett, Mart Taylor, Johnson (comic singer). San Francisco, D. E. Appleton Co., 1861.

Priscilla Post Parker. *California Song Book (A Brief History of California)*. Lancaster, Calif., 1950.

Dailey Paskman and Sigmund Spaeth. *"Gentlemen Be Seated!" A Parade of the Old-Time Minstrels*. Garden City, N.Y., Doubleday, Doran & Co., 1928.

Edward A. Perkins and Frederick H. Pease. *The Western Bell*. Boston, Oliver Ditson Co., 1857.

Pioneer Songs. Compiled by Daughters of the Utah Pioneers. Salt Lake City, Utah, 1932.

Popular California Songs. Collection in the Bancroft Library, Univ. of California, Berkeley, Calif.

Popular Songs and Ballads, No. 1. W. F. Shaw, 1882.

Populist and Silver Songs. Words by Henry W. Taylor, Music by J. B. Herbert. Chicago, S. Brainard's Sons, 1896.

Louise Pound. *American Ballads and Songs*. New York, Charles Scribner's Sons, 1922.

————*Folk Song of Nebraska and the Central West*. Nebraska Academy of Sciences Publications, 1915.

————*Nebraska Folklore*. Lincoln, Nebr., Univ. of Nebraska Press, 1959.

Milo Milton Quaife. *Pictures of Gold Rush California*. Chicago, The Lakeside Press, 1949.

Vance Randolph. *Ozark Folksongs*. 4 vols. Columbia, Mo., State Historical Society, 1946.

Georgia Willis Read and Ruth Gaines. *The Journals, Drawings and Other Papers of J. Goldsborough Bruff*. New York, Columbia Univ. Press, 1944.

Felix Reisenberg, Jr. *The Golden Road; the story of California's Spanish Mission Trail*. New York, McGraw–Hill, 1962.

Frederic Remington. *Frederic Remington's Own West*. New York, Dial Press, 1960.

Republican Campaign Songster: A collection of lyrics, original and selected, specially prepared for the friends of freedom in the campaign of fifty-six. New York and Auburn, Miller, Orton & Mulligan, 1856.

LeRoy Rice. *Monarchs of Minstrelsy*. New York, Kenny Pub. Co., 1911.

Franz Rickaby. *Ballads and Songs of the Shanty-Boy*. Cambridge, Mass., Harvard Univ. Press, 1926.

John Donald Robb. *Hispanic Folk Songs of New Mexico, with selected songs collected, transcribed and arranged for voice and piano*. Albuquerque, N. Mex., Univ. of New Mexico Press, 1954.

Sidney H. Robertson. *Check List of California Songs*. Folk Music Project, WPA, Berkeley, Calif., 1940.

Dr. D. G. Robinson. *Comic Songs; or Hits at San Francisco*. San Francisco, Commercial Book & Job Office, 1853.

Anna Rochester. *The Populist Movement in the United States*. New York, International Publishers, 1943.

Rocky Mountain Collection. Salt Lake City, Utah, Intermountain Folk Music Council, 1962.

Frederic W. Root and James R. Murray. *The Pacific Glee Book*. Chicago, Root & Cady, 1869.

The Rough and Ready Songster, embellished with 25 splendid engravings, illustrative of the American victories in Mexico, by an American Officer. New York, Nafis & Cornish (circa 1848).

Constance Rourke. *Troupers of the Gold Coast, or the rise of Lotta Crabtree*. New York, Harcourt, Brace & Co., 1928.

S. J. Sackett and William E. Koch. *Kansas Folklore*. Lincoln, Neb., Univ. of Nebraska Press, 1961.

Carl Sandburg. *The American Songbag*. New York, Harcourt, Brace & Co., 1927.

Mari Sandoz. *Love Song to the Plains*. New York, Harper & Bros., 1961.

Lorenzo Sawyer. *Way Sketches; containing incidents of travel across the plains from St. Joseph to California in 1850, with letters describing life and conditions in the gold region*. New York, Edward Eberstadt, 1926.

Pete Seeger. *American Favorite Ballads*. New York, Oak Publications, 1961.

Cecil J. Sharp. *English Folk Songs from the Southern Appalachians*. 2 vols. London, Oxford Univ. Press, 1932.

R. C. Shaw. *Across the Plains in Forty-Nine*. Farmland, Ind., W. C. West, 1896.

Frank Shay. *American Sea Songs & Chanteys.* New York, W. W. Norton & Co., 1948.

Sterling Sherwin and Harry A Powell. *Bad Man Songs of the Wild and Woolly West.* Cleveland, Ohio, Sam Fox Co., 1933.

——and F. Henri Klickmann. *Songs of the Roundup.* New York, Robbins Music, 1934.

Lee Shippey. *It's An Old California Custom.* New York, Vanguard Press, 1948.

Elie Siegmeister and Olin Downes. *A Treasury of American Song.* New York, Howell, Soskin & Co., 1940.

Sig Abecco's Sentimental Songster, containing all the most popular songs as sung by this favorite artist at Eureka Minstrel Hall. San Francisco, D.E. Appleton Co., 1864.

Irwin Silber. *Lift Every Voice! (The Second People's Songbook).* New York, Oak Publications, 1953.

——*Songs of the Civil War.* New York, Columbia Univ. Press, 1960. (Dover, 1995.)

C. Fox Smith. *A Book of Shanties.* London, Methuen & Co., 1927.

——*Small Craft; sailor ballads and chanteys.* New York, George H. Doran Co., 1919.

Songs of the Emerson Minstrels. San Francisco, S.S. Greene, n.d.

Songs of the Mormon Pioneers. With historical notations by Austin E. Fife and Alta S. Fife. Salt Lake City, Utah, Columbia Research Group.

Songs of the San Francisco Minstrels Birch & Backus, including all the continuously popular pieces that have been received with boundless applause from Maine to California when sung by this great troupe. New York, De Witt Pub., 1881.

Sigmund Spaeth. *A History of Popular Music in America.* New York, Random House, 1948.

——*Read 'Em and Weep.* New York, Doubleday, Page & Co., 1925.

Barrie Stavis and Frank Harmon. *Songs of Joe Hill.* New York, Oak Publications, 1955.

Rev. John Steele. *In Camp and Cabin; Mining Life and Adventures in California during 1850 and later.* New York, Citadel Press, 1962.

Bayrd Still. *The West: Contemporary Records of America's Expansion Across the Continent, 1607–1890.* New York, Capricorn Books, 1961.

Irving Stone. *Men to Match My Mountains: The Opening of the Far West, 1840–1900.* New York, Doubleday & Co., 1956.

John A. Stone. *Put's Golden Songster, containing the largest and most popular collection of California songs ever published.* San Francisco, D.E. Appleton Co., 1858.

——*Put's Original California Songster, giving in a few words what would occupy volumes, detailing the hopes, trials and joys of a miner's life.* San Francisco, D.E. Appleton Co., 1855.

Mary R. Van Stone. *Spanish Folk Songs of New Mexico.* Chicago, Ralph Fletcher Seymour, 1926.

John F. Stover. *American Railroads.* Chicago, Univ. of Chicago Press, 1961.

Howard Swan. *Music in the Southwest (1825–1950).* San Marino, Calif., The Huntington Library, 1952.

Robert E. Swanson. *Rhymes of a Western Logger.* Vancouver, Lumberman Prntg. Co., 1942.

William Targ. *The American West.* Cleveland and N.Y., World Pub. Co., 1946.

Mart Taylor. *The Gold Digger's Songbook, containing the most popular humorous and sentimental songs.* Marysville, Calif., 1856.

——*Local Lyrics and Miscellaneous Poems.* San Francisco, Hutchings & Rosenfield, 1858.

Ambrose A. Thayer. *Morris Bros., Pell and Trowbridge's Songs.* Boston, Russell & Tolman, 1860.

Stith Thompson. *Round the Levee.* Publications of the Texas Folklore Society, No. 1, Austin, Tex., 1916.

N. Howard Thorp. *Songs of the Cowboys.* Boston, Houghton Mifflin Co., 1908, 1921.

Thomas Henry Tibbles. *Buckskin and Blanket Days; Memoirs of a Friend of the Indians.* New York, Doubleday & Co., 1957.

Warren S. Tryon. *The Frontier Moves West.* Chicago, Univ. of Chicago Press, 1952.

Marjorie F. Tully and Juan B. Rael. *An Annotated Bibliography of Spanish Folklore in New Mexico and Southern Colorado.* Albuquerque, N. Mex., Univ. of New Mexico Press, 1950.

J. W. Turner. *100 Comic Songs, music and words.* Boston, 1858.

Elmore Vincent. *Lumberjack Songs.* Chicago, M. M. Cole, 1932.

Walking for Dat Cake Songster. San Francisco, S. S. Greene (circa 1872).

Kimball Webster. *The Gold-Seekers of '49.* Manchester, N.H., Standard Book Co., 1917.

Paul I. Wellman. *Glory, God and Gold.* New York, Doubleday & Co., 1954.

W. B. Whall. *Ships, Sea Songs and Shanties.* Glasgow, James Brown & Son, 1910.

C. S. White. *The People's Songster, for campaign purposes and a jolly time generally.* Indianapolis, Ind., Vincent Bros., 1892.

E. L. White. *The Boston Melodeon; a collection of secular melodies, etc.* Boston, Oliver Ditson Co., 1852.

Marguerite Wilkinson. *Golden Songs of the Golden State.* Chicago, A. C. McClurg, 1917.

Carl Wittke. *Tambo and Bones, a History of the American Minstrel Stage.* Durham, N.C., Duke Univ. Press, 1930.

John W. Work. *American Negro Songs*. New York, Howell, Soskin & Co., 1940.

The World's Best Cowboy Songs. New York, Amsco Music Pub., 1941.

Louis B. Wright. *Culture on the Moving Frontier*. Bloomington, Ind., Indiana Univ. Press, 1955.

Lionel D. Wyld. *Low Bridge! Folklore and the Erie Canal*. Syracuse, N.Y., Syracuse Univ. Press, 1962.

B. PERIODICALS

Adventure Magazine
Robert W. Gordon. "Old Songs That Men Have Sung." In every issue from July, 1923–Oct., 1927.

Arizona Highways
Katie Lee. "Folk Songs of the Colorado." May, 1954.

California Folklore Quarterly
Julia Cooley Altrocchi. "Folklore of the Old California Trail." Vol. 3, No. 1.
"Bibliography of California Folklore and Folksong." Vol. 2.
Sidney Robertson Cowell. "The Recording of Folk Music in California." Vol. 1, No. 1.
Jay Levette Davidson. "'Home on the Range' Again." Vol. 3, No. 3.
———"Songs of the Rocky Mountain Frontier." Vol. 2, No. 2.
Duncan Emrich "Songs of the Western Miners." Vol. 1, No. 3.
Rena V. Grant. "The Localized Vocabulary of California Verse." Vol. 1, No. 3.
Wayland D. Hand. "California Miners' Folklore: Above Ground." Vol. 1, No. 1.
———"The Folklore, Customs and Traditions of the Butte Miner." Vol. 5, Nos. 1 and 2.
James Murray. "Sailors' Songs with California Significance." Vol. 5, No. 2.
Hyman Palais. "Black Hills Miners' Folklore." Vol. 4, No. 3.

Heritage of Kansas
"Buffalo: Lord of the Plains." Vol. 1, No. 3.
"Fencing the Prairies." Vol. 4, No. 2.
"Free Range and Fencing." Vol. 4, No. 3.
"Kansans Talk Tall." Vol. 3, No. 1.
"Kansas History and Folksong." Vol. 5, No. 2.
"Some Place Names of Kansas." Vol. 4, No. 4.
"That A State Might Sing." Vol. 2, No. 2.

Hutchings Illustrated California Magazine
Published July 1856–June 1857. Contains considerable material of interest relating to life and culture of California in the period.

Journal of American Folklore
Contains many articles and song illustrations relating to the West.

The Midwest Journal
Philip Durham. "The Lost Cowboy." Vol. 7, No. 2.

Musical America
Susa Young Gates (a daughter of Brigham Young). "How Utah's Pioneers Carried Music Across the Rockies." Nov. 20, 1915.

The Musical Courier
Josephine Gro. "Music of the Pacific Coast During the Nineteenth Century." July 4, 1898.

Northwest Review
J. Barre Toelken. "Northwest Traditional Ballads." Winter, 1962.

Oregon Historical Quarterly
Joseph W. Ellison. "The Diary of Marie Parsons Belshaw, 1853." Vol. 33, No. 4.

Overland Monthly
Vols. 1–5 published in San Francisco 1868–1872. Contains many articles, first-hand accounts, original poetry, etc. relating to life and culture in California.

The Pacific Musical Gazette
Published in San Francisco 1867–1868, containing articles concerning musical activities, primarily in San Francisco.

The People's Songs Bulletin
Published in New York 1946–1949, continuing a number of songs relating to the West.

Sing Out!
Published in New York since 1950, containing many songs relating to the West.
John Greenway. "Songs of the Ludlow Massacre." Vol. 8, No. 3.

Southern Folklore Quarterly
Levette Jay Davidson. "Rocky Mountain Folklore." Dec., 1941.

Washington Historical Quarterly
"Narrative of James Longmire, A Pioneer of 1853." Vol. 23, Nos. 1 and 2.

Western Folklore
Alfred Adler. "Billy the Kid: A Case Study in Epic Origins." Vol. 10, No. 2.
Merton C. Babcock. "The Vocabulary of Social Life on the American Frontier." Vol. 9, No. 2.
"Folklore Aspects in Mormon Culture." Vol. 10, No. 3.
Joseph J. Cadlo. "Cowboy Life as Reflected in Cowboy Songs." Vol. 6, No. 4.
Earl H. Ellis. "'Idaho.'" Vol. 10, No. 4.
Austin Fife. "A Ballad of the Mountain Meadows Massacre." Vol. 12, No. 4.
———"Folk Songs of Mormon Inspiration." Vol. 6, No. 1.
Marshall W. Fishwick. "The Cowboy: America's

Contribution to the World's Mythology." Vol. 11, No. 2.

Edith Fowke. "American Cowboy and Western Pioneer Songs in Canada." Vol. 21, No. 4.

Wayland D. Hand (with Charles Cutts, Robert C. Wylder, Betty Wylder). "Songs of the Butte Miner." Vol. 9, No. 1.

Russell M. Harrison. "Folk Songs from Oregon." Vol. 11, No. 3.

Fred Kniffen. "The Western Cattle Complex." Vol. 12, No. 3.

Marvin Lewis. "Humor of Western Mining Regions." Vol. 14, No. 2.

Kenneth Lodewick. "The Unfortunate Rake and His Descendants." Vol. 14, No. 2.

C. Grant Loomis. "California Anecdotes from the East, 1849–1858." Vol. 7, No. 1.

————"Tough Californiana: 1849–1864." Vol. 6, No. 2.

Ben Gray Lumpkin. "Colorado Folk Songs." Vol. 19, No. 2.

Louise Pound. "Yet Another Joe Bowers." Vol. 16, No. 2.

Stanley L. Robe. "Some Hispanic Equivalents of the Big Rock Candy Mountains." Vol. 13, No. 1.

Kent L. Steckmesser. "Joaquín Murietta and Billy the Kid." Vol. 21, No. 2.

Muriel Sibell Wolle. "From 'Sailor's Diggins' to 'Miners' Delight.'" Vol. 13, No. 1.

DISCOGRAPHY

The original list was prepared for the 1967 edition of this book, when the LP record was common. Titles marked * are now out of print, but may be found in library and other collections of vintage LPs. In-print recordings are now available on audiocassette only, through the following sources:

FOLKWAYS recordings are available through: Smithsonian/Folkways Recordings, The Smithsonian Institution, 955 L'Enfant Plaza, Suite 2600, Smithsonian Institution MRC 914, Washington, D.C. 20560. Anthony Seeger is Curator of the Folkways Collection.

LIBRARY OF CONGRESS recordings are available through: M/B/RS Division, Library of Congress, Washington, D.C. 20540.

(Prestige-International and Riverside are now subsidiary labels of Fantasy Records, Inc., Berkeley, CA. Elektra's offices are in New York City. No current listing was found for Festival Records.)

American Ballads and Folksongs, sung by Joan O'Bryant. Folkways FA2338.

American Northwest Ballads, sung by Walt Robertson. Folkways FA2046.

Bunkhouse and Forecastle Songs of the Northwest, sung by Stanley G. Triggs. Folkways FG3569.

Canada's Story in Song, sung by Alan Mills. Folkways FW3000.

Corridos. Recorded in Mexico, traditional singers. Folkways FW6913.

The Cowboy: His Songs, Ballads and Brag Talk. Harry Jackson. Folkways FH5723.

Cowboy Ballads, sung by Cisco Houston. Folkways FA2022.

Cowboy Songs, Ballads and Cattle Calls from Texas. Field recordings, traditional singers. Archive of American Folksong, Library of Congress. L-28.

The Days of '49; Songs of the Gold Rush, sung by Logan English. Folkways FH5255.

Folksongs and Ballads of Kansas, sung by Joan O'Bryant. Folkways FA2134.

Folksongs of Idaho and Utah, sung by Rosalie Sorrels. Folkways FH5343.

Frontier Ballads, sung by Pete Seeger. Folkways FH5003.

Frontiers. Folkways FR10003.

*A Garland of American Folksongs, sung by J. Barre Toelken. Prestige–International 13023.

*The Great American Bum and other Hobo and Migratory Workers' Songs, sung by John Greenway. Riverside RLP 12-619.

Mormon Folk Songs, sung by L. M. Hilton. Folkways FA2036.

Music of the Sioux and Navajo Indians, collected and edited by Willard Rhodes. Field Recordings. Folkways FE4401.

*The Old Chisholm Trail. Traditional songs of the old west sung by Merrick Jarrett. Riverside RLP 12-631.

The Song of Men. Sam Hinton. Folkways FA2400.

Songs of a New York Lumberjack, sung by Ellen Stekert. Folkways FA2354.

Songs of Joe Hill, sung by Joe Glazer. Folkways FA2039.

Songs of Texas, sung by The Tex-I-An Boys. Folkways FH5328.

Songs of the Mormon Pioneers, sung by Rosalie Sorrels. Festival Records.

Songs of the Mormons and Songs of the West. Field recordings, traditional singers. Archive of American Folksong, Library of Congress. L-30.

Songs of the North Star State, sung by Gene Bluestein. Folkways FA2112.

*Songs of the Old West, sung by Ed McCurdy. Elektra EKL-112.

Songs of the Pawnee and Northern Ute, recorded and edited by Frances Densmore. Field recordings. Archive of American Folksong, Library of Congress. L-25.

Songs of the Sea, sung by Alan Mills. Folkways FA2312.

Songs of the West, sung by Dave Frederickson. Folkways FH5259.

Spanish and Mexican Folk Music of New Mexico, ed. John Donald Robb. Field recordings, traditional singers. Folkways FE4426.

The Unfortunate Rake: A Study in the Evolution of a Ballad. Ed. by Kenneth Goldstein. Folkways FS3805.

SUBJECT INDEX

Abilene, Kansas, 159, 164, 187
Abolitionism, 9, 213
"Acres of Clams," 153, 240
Aggression in Mexican-American War, 62
Alamo, the, 45, 47
Alaska, gold rush in, 311
Allen, George N., 200
"All Is Well," 73
American Federation of Labor, 299
American River, 3
Austin, Moses, 47

"Bad Girl's Lament, The," 279
Ballad, Anglo-American tradition of, 197
"Ballad of Sherman Wu," 280
Banjo players' instructions, 84
Barbary Coast
    entertainers of, 96
    saloons and music halls of, 4, 95, 120
Barker, Nathan, 9
"Barnyards of Delgaty," 304
Bass, Sam, 251, 276
"Battle Cry of Freedom," 39
Bean, Judge Roy, 276
Benton, Jessie, 30
Benton, Senator Thomas Hart, 30
Bernal, Heraclio, 270
"Beulah Land," 212, 233, 235
Bill, Pecos, 306
Billy the Kid, 251, 260, 276
Black Hills gold rush, 149
Blackface minstrels, 14, 27, 83, 142, 145, 229
"Boatman's Dance," 9
"Boatmen Dance," 27
Boise, Idaho, 145
"Border Affair, A," 203
Boston, Massachusetts, 5

Bowie, Jim, 47
Bowers, Joe, 18, 96, 120
Brewster, Higley, 221
Buckley, R. Bishop, 30
Buena Vista, Battle of, 52, 57
Buffalo, 169
"Buffalo Skinners, The," 173
Bunyan, Paul, 306
"Bury Me Not on the Lone Prairie," 206

California, 3-29, 95-141
    discovery of gold in, 3, 5
    dream and reality of, 115
    first generation of popular music in, 4
    first senator from, 30
    music in, 4
    gold rush in, 3, 9, 12, 14, 18, 23, 27, 100, 107, 111, 115, 120, 123, 125, 130, 132
    independence of, 3
    lice and, 117
    Spanish territory of, 36
    the trip to, 39
"Camptown Races," 27
"Canada-I-O," 169
"Canaday-I-O," 169
Canadian River, 164
Canales, Benito, 270
Cape Horn
    record trip around, 27
    voyage around, 3, 12, 39
"Caroline of Edinboro," 23
Carson, Kit, 30, 38
"Casey Jones," 298
Catholic missionaries, 36
Cattle industry, 159
Central America (steamship), 125
Central Pacific Railroad, 39, 138
Cerro Gordo, 52

Chapin, Reverend Edwin H., 200
Chapultepec, 52
Cherry Creek, Colorado, 142
Cheyenne, Wyoming, 149, 187
Chinese immigration to California, 138
Chisholm, Jesse, 164
Chisholm Trail, 159, 164
Christie, E. P., 27
Church of Jesus Christ of Latter-Day Saints, see Mormons
Civil War, 57, 252
Clark, Charles Badger, Jr., 203
Clayton, William, 73
Clipper ships, 12
Coal mining, 296
"Colley's Run-I-O," 169
Colorado
    gold strike in, 142
    Ludlow Massacre, 296
    settlements in, 3
Columbia River, 314
Conquistadores, 36
Cotton, Ben, 95
Cowboys, 159-168, 173-208, 262-269, 276-285
    ballad makers and, 206
    bragging by, 283
    girls of, 187, 195
    handling wild cattle by, 265
    horses of, 184, 262
    influence of the Spanish language and, 181
    love songs of, 203
    Mexican vaqueros as first, 181
    as myth and stereotype, 159
    Negro, 159
    stampedes and, 197, 206
    the trail ride and, 161, 177, 179
"Cowboy's Lament," 206, 279
Crazy Horse, Chief, 273
Crocker, Charles, 138

Crockett, Davy, 47
Crosboy, L. V. H., 27
Cultural diversity in San Francisco, 95
Custer, General George, 149, 273

"Daddy," 27
"Dakota Land," 235
"Dandy Jim of Caroline," 27, 130
Dawson City, Yukon Territory, 311
"Days of Forty-Nine, The," 99
Dean, John A., 233
"Dearest Mae," 27
"De Boatman Dance," 107
"Derby Ram, The," 265
Diaries, 23
Disease, 23
Dobie, Frank, 60, 187
Dodge City, Kansas, 159, 187
"Dodger Song, The," 132
Dreams and reality in California, 115

Earp, Wyatt, 276
Emerson, Ralph Waldo, 46
Emmett, Daniel, 9, 27, 107
England
    gold rush songs of, 5
    religious persecution in, 71
Ethiopian melodists, 14
"Ethiopian Serenaders," 27

Fancher Party, 77
Farmers, 233-247
    economic facts of life and, 236
    on Great Plains, 211
    political activity of, 240, 243, 245
    sod shanties of, 218
"Field of Monterey, The," 55
Finger, Charles J., 276
Fink, Mike, 306
Flying Cloud, The (ship), 27
Ford, Robert, 252
Fort Sumner, New Mexico, 38, 260
Foster, Stephen, 27, 164
Frémont, John Charles, 30

Gardner, Gail, 283
Garrett, Sheriff Pat, 260
"Girl I Left Behind Me, The," 243
Glover, Charles W., 115
Gold rushes, 3-29, 95-137
    Black Hills, 149
    California, 3, 5, 9, 12, 14, 18, 23, 27,
        100, 107, 111, 115, 120, 123, 125,
        130, 132
    Idaho, 145
    Klondike, 311
    mine names, 100
    minstrels of, 14, 95, 104, 132
    Pike's Peak, 142
    professional "sharpers" and, 125
    song authors and composers of, 14
"Good-Bye Old Paint," 179-180

"Good Old Days of '50, '1, and '2,
    The," 96
Grand Coulee Dam, 314
Gray, Maberry B., 60
"Greasers," 49
Great Plains, 211-247
    hardships of, 224, 233
    history of, 211
    homesteads on, 218
    legends of, 233
    slavery issue in, 213
Great Salt Lake, 72, 80
Greeley, Horace, 130
"Green Grow the Laurels," 49
"Grey Goose, The," 265
Griffin, G. W. H., 142
"Gringos," 49, 181
Guadalupe Hidalgo, Treaty of, 45
Guerra de la Intervencion Americana,
    La, 62
Guitar players' instructions, 84, 111,
    161, 184, 213, 280
Guthrie, Woody, 253, 256, 290, 296,
    314

"Hallelujah, I'm a Bum," 291
Hangtown, 123
Harte, Bret, 18, 100
Hatch, James, 60
Hays, William Shakespeare, 218
Henry, Frank, 153
Henry, John, 306
Hewitt, John Hill, 55
Hickok, Wild Bill, 276
Hill, Joe, 298-299
Hoboes, 289
"Home on the Range," 221
Homestead Act (1862), 211, 224
Homesteaders
    fight with cattlemen by, 231
    on Great Plains, 211
    westward movement of, 231
Houston, Sam, 47
Hutchinson Family Singers, 9, 46, 125,
    215
Hutchinson, Jesse, Jr., 9, 215

"I Ride an Old Paint," 206
Idaho gold rush, 145
Ike, see Pike County Ike
"I'm Off for California," 145
Immigration
    of Chinese to California, 138
    from 1820 to 1850, 215
"In the Sweet By and By," 298
Independence, Missouri, 3
Indians
    ancient civilizations of, 36
    boy skinned alive by, 33
    culture of, 38
    hostile, 4, 23
    plunder of, 273
    see also specific Indian tribes

Industrial era, the
    and the Mormons, 89
    in the West, 289
Industrial Workers of the World, see
    IWW
Interior, Department of the, 314
"Irish Molly, O," 111
"Irish Washerwoman," 224
IWW (Industrial Workers of the
    World)
    as anarcho-syndicalist organization,
        289
    jail, songs of, 302
    Joe Hill and, 298-299
    lumberjack strike, 308

Jacksboro, Texas, 169
"Jam on Gerry's Rocks," 304
James, Frank, 252
James, Jesse, 251, 252, 276
"Jeanette and Jeannot," 115
Jesus Christ, 253
"Jim Crack Corn," 27
Johnson, 4
Johnson's Comic Songs, 18
Johnson's Pennsylvanians, 18
"Jump Jim Crow," 27
"Just Before the Battle, Mother," 39

Kansas, settlements in, 3
Kansas-Nebraska Act (1854), 213
Kellie, Mrs. J. T., 243
Kellogg, Arthur L., 240
Kelly, Daniel E., 221
Kevess, Arthur, 62
"Kingdom Coming," 245
"King of the Cannibal Islands," 100
Klondike, 311

Labor movement, 289-310
Langtry, Lillie, 276
Laredo, Texas, 279
Latter-Day Saints, see Mormons
Lawrence, Kansas, 213
Lee, John, 77
Lice and California, 117
Lincoln, Abraham, 46
Little Bighorn massacre, 150, 273
"Little Old Log Cabin in the Lane,"
    206, 212, 218
"Little Old Sod Shanty on My Claim,
    The," 212
Little Red Songbook, 289
Loggers
    myths of, 306
    songs of, 304
Lomax, Alan, 184
Lomax, John A., 169, 173, 179, 197,
    221
Longfellow, Henry Wadsworth, 46
Los Pastores, 36
"Lost Jimmie Whalen," 304

Love, Captain Harry, 135
Lowell, James Russell, 46
"Lucy Neal," 27
Lumberjacks, see loggers
Luna, Miguel de la, 265
Lynch, Francis, 27
Lytle, James T., 60

McClintock, Mac, 291
McGrew, A. O., 142
"Maid of Monterey, The," 60
Mail for the miners, 111
Mains, J. Riley, 99
Manceras, Valentin, 270
Manifest destiny, 45
Marshall, James W., 3, 123
Mary Taylor (schooner-smack), 27
Massacres
    Little Bighorn, 150
    Ludlow, 296
    Mountain Meadows, 77
Meighan, Thaddeus W., 115
Mexican-American War, 3, 45-67
    as aggression, 62
    Battle of Buena Vista, 57
    Battle of Monterey, 55
    Irish-American troops in, 49
    peace treaty, 45
    Santa Anna in, 52
Mexico City, Battle of, 55, 57
"Michigan-I-O," 169
Migration westward, 3
Mining
    Ludlow Massacre, 296
    see also Gold rushes
Minstrels
    blackface, 14, 27, 83, 142, 145, 229
    of the gold rushes, 14, 95, 104, 132
"Mister Block," 298
Monterey, Mexico, Battle of, 52, 55, 60
Moore, Tom, 96
Mormons, 71-91
    cricket plague and, 75
    as converts from Europe, 80
    industrial era and, 89
    Mountain Meadows Massacre and, 77
    in Nauvoo, 71, 72, 73
    as persecuted sect, 71, 72
    polygamy and, 83
    in Salt Lake City, 72
    Smith as leader of, 71, 83
    transcontinental railroad and, 89
    Young as leader of, 15, 72, 73, 80, 83-84, 89
Morris, Pete, 120
Murieta, Joaquín, 135
"Mustang Gray," 55

Names of Mines, 100
Nauvoo, Illinois, 71, 72, 73
Navajo Indians, 38

Nebraska, settlements in, 3
Negroes
    as cowboys, 159
    as gold miners, 100, 145
    as trail-camp cooks, 177
    see also Abolitionism
New England Emigrant Aid Company, 213
New Spain, 47
New York, New York, 5
"New York Gals," 123
New York Jake, 96
Norteña, Alma, 135
Northern Pacific Railroad, 149
Northwest, the, 3
    mining in, 145

"Ocean Burial, The," 200
Oklahoma, 49, 164
"Old Chisholm Trail, The," 161
"Old Party Rallies," 243
"Old Put," 4, 14, 18, 23, 27, 95, 100, 107, 111, 117, 123, 125, 130, 135
"Old Rosin the Beau," 153
Oregon Territory, 30
    border issue, 46
Outlaws, 251-261
    Billy the Kid, 260
    Jesse James, 252
    Sam Bass, 257
    as symbols of defiance against law and landlord, 251
    Spanish, 270
Overland route, 23

Panama as route to California, 3, 23
Panic of 1873, 149
"Pathfinder, The," 30
Pauline (brig), 27
People's Party of the U.S.A., see Populists
Persecution
    of Chinese, 138
    religious, 71-72
Philadelphia Minstrels, 95
Philadelphia, Pennsylvania, 5
Piano players' instructions, 84, 111
"Pie in the Sky," 298
Pike County, Missouri, 15, 18
Pike County Ike, 96, 120
"Piker," 18
Pike's Peak, 142
Platte River, 15
Poker Flat, 100
Polygamy of the Mormons, 83
Pony Express, 39
"Popular sovereignty," 213
Populists
    activity of, 245
    in presidential election of 1892, 240
    songs of, 243

Prejudice
    against Chinese, 276
    against Indians, 276
    against Mexicans, 203, 276
    religious, 71-72
Presidential elections
    1848, 57
    1856, 30
    1892, 240
"Professor's Lament," 280
Promontory, Utah, 39
Put, see "Old Put"
Put's Golden Songster, 15
Put's Original California Songster, 14

Quantrill's Raiders, 252

Rackensack Jim, 96
"Raging Canal, The," 120
Railroad, first transcontinental, 39, 89, 211
"Rebel Girl, The," 298
Reed, Samuel B., 89
Religious persecution, 71-72
Republican Party, 240, 243
    first presidential candidate of, 30
Rhodes, Charles, 96
Rice, Thomas Dartmouth ("Daddy"), 27
Rio Grande River, 60
Riggs, Lynn, 49
Robin Hood, 135, 251, 252
Robinson, D. G. ("Doc"), 4, 95, 104, 107
Robinson, Earl, 117, 308
Rockefeller, John D., 296
Rock Island Railroad, 80
Root, George Frederick, 39, 276
"Rosin the Beau," 240

Sacramento Valley, 3, 95
"Sailor Cut Down in His Prime, The," 279
Salt Lake City, Utah, 72, 75, 80
San Antonio, Texas, 47, 164
San Diego, California, 36
San Francisco, California, 4, 27, 107, 115
    Chinese in, 138
    cultural diversity and, 95
    foremost minstrel composer of, 14
    stagecoach lines around, 130
    see also Barbary Coast
San Jacinto, Texas, Battle of, 45, 47, 52, 60
Sandburg, Carl, 236
Sankey, R. V., 5
Santa Anna, Antonio López de, 45, 47, 52, 57, 64, 107
Scott, General Winfield, 57
Seeger, Pete, 33
Service, Robert, 311

Shelley, Percy Bysshe, 236
Ships, sailing, 12
Shirley, J. T., 197
Sierra Nevada Rangers, The, 14
Simon, Bill, 283
Sioux Indians, 33, 273
Sitting Bull, Chief, 273
Slavery, *see* Abolitionism
Smith, Frank, 18
Smith, Joseph, 71, 83
Soldier songs, 62, 64
"Song to the Men of England," 236
"Song of the Texas Ranger," 60
Sonoma, California, 3
Southern Literary Messenger, 200
Stagecoaches, 130
Steamship companies in California gold
    rush, 125
Stevens, James L., 306
"St. James Hospital," 279
"St. James Infirmary," 279, 280
Stone, John A., *see* "Old Put"
"Storming of Monterey, The," 55
"Stung Right," 298
Sweet Betsy, 14, 96, 120

T-Bone Slim, 302
Taylor, General Zachary, 52, 107
    Battle of Buena Vista and, 57
    capture of Monterey and, 55
    Texas Rangers and, 60

Taylor, Mart, 4, 95, 132
Texas, independence of, 45, 47, 52, 60
Texas Rangers, 60
"They Go Wild, Simply Wild Over
    Me," 302
Thoreau, Henry David, 46
Thorp, N. Howard, 173, 200, 206
"Three-Fingered Jack," 135
"Tramp, The," 298
"Tramp, Tramp, Tramp," 39, 276
Transcontinental railroad, 39, 89, 211
Travis, Lieutenant Colonel William, 47
"Trooper Cut Down in His Prime,
    The," 279
Twain, Mark, 18

"Uncle Ned," 164
"Uncle Sam's Farm," 125
"Unfortunate Rake, The," 279, 280
Union Pacific Railroad, 39, 89
"Used Up Man," 104
"Utopia Dream," 291

"Van, Van, He's a Used-Up Man," 104
Velasco (schooner), 27
Vera Cruz, Mexico, Battle of, 57, 60
Vigil, Cleofes, 135
"Villikins and His Dinah," 14
Virginia Serenaders, The, 95

"Wait for the Wagon," 30

Washington, unofficial state song of,
    314
Washita Indians, 273
Washita River, 164
"Wearing of the Green," 138
Wells, Sam, 4
"We're A' Noddin'," 132
Whitney, C. S., 235, 245
Whittier, John Greenleaf, 46, 213
Whores of Hangtown, 123
Wichita Indians, 164
Willis, Charley, 179
Wilson, Woodrow, 299
Wobbies, *see* IWW
Woodward, John, 18, 95
Work, Henry Clay, 245
Wrangler, defined, 206
Wyoming, 3, 149

"Year of Jubilo," 212, 245
Yerba Buena, 95
    see also San Francisco
Young, Brigham, 15, 72, 73, 80
    as leader, 83-84
    polygamy and, 83
    transcontinental railroad and, 89
Younger, Cole, 276

"Zebra Dun," 161, 265
Zion (Salt Lake City), 71, 80

INDEX OF TITLES AND FIRST LINES

A bully ship and a bully crew, 13
A cowboy's life is a dreary, dreary life, 194
Across the Bighorn's crystal tide, against the savage Sioux, 274
A LA RU, 36
Año de mil ochocientos, 271
Aquí me siento a cantar, 266
As I sat down one evening, 307
As I walked out in the streets of Laredo, 282
As I was a-walking one morning for pleasure, 175

BIG ROCK CANDY MOUNTAIN, THE, 291
BILLY THE KID, 260
BRIGHAM YOUNG, 83
Brigham Young was a Mormon bold, and a leader of the roaring ram, 87
BUENA VISTA, 57
BUFFALO SKINNERS, THE, 169
BURY ME NOT ON THE LONE PRAIRIE, 200

CALIFORNIA AS IT IS, 114
CALIFORNIA STAGE COMPANY, 130
CLARIN DE CAMPAÑA, 62
Come all you Californians, I pray ope wide your ears, 25
Come all you sons of Liberty, unto my rhyme give ear, 79
COME, COME, YE SAINTS, 73
Come, come, ye Saints, no toil nor labor fear, 74
Come gather 'round me miners, I got something for to tell, 148
COMING AROUND THE HORN, 27
COMMONWEALTH OF TOIL, THE, 302
CORRIDO DE HERACLIO BERNAL, 270
CORRIDO DE JOAQUÍN MURIETA, 135
CORRIDO DE KANSAS, 181

Cowboys come and hear the story, 277
COWBOY'S GETTIN'-UP HOLLER, 177
COWBOY'S LIFE IS A DREARY, DREARY LIFE, 192
CROSSING THE PLAINS, 23
Cuando salimos pa' Kansas, 182
CUSTER'S LAST CHARGE, 273

DAKOTA LAND, 233
DAYS OF FORTY-NINE, THE, 96
DONEY GAL, 184
DREARY BLACK HILLS, THE, 149
Duérmete, Niño lindo, 37

ECHO CANYON, 89

FARMER IS THE MAN, THE, 236
FIFTY THOUSAND LUMBERJACKS, 308
Fifty thousand lumberjacks, fifty thousand packs, 310
FROZEN LOGGER, THE, 306

GAL I LEFT BEHIND ME, THE, 195
GIT ALONG, LITTLE DOGIES, 173
GOOD-BYE OLD PAINT, 179
Good-bye, old Paint, I'm a-leavin' Cheyenne, 180
GOOD OLD DAYS OF '50, '1, AND '2, 99
Green Douglas fir where the waters cut through, 317
GREEN GROW THE LILACS, 49
Green grow the lilacs, all sparkling with dew, 51

HANDCART SONG, THE, 80
HANGTOWN GALS, 123
Hangtown gals are plump and rosy, 124
HAYSEED, THE, 240

Hello girls, listen to my voice, 230
Here's luck to all you homesteaders, 232
HO! FOR CALIFORNIA, 9
HOMESTEAD OF THE FREE, THE, 213
HUMBUG STEAMSHIP COMPANIES, 125

I am looking rather seedy now while holding down my claim, 220
I am not American, 136
I heard of gold at Sutter's Mill, 102
I OFTEN THINK OF WRITING HOME, 111
I often think of writing home, but very seldom write, 113
I once was a tool of oppression, 242
I RIDE AN OLD PAINT, 161
I ride an old paint and I lead an old dan, 163
I struck the trail in seventy-nine, 196
I was a party man one time, 244
I'll sing you a song, though it may be a sad one, 34
I'll sing you a true song of Billy the Kid, 261
I'll sit down here and sing, 266
I'M OFF TO BOISE CITY, 145
In the Canyon of Echo, there's a railroad begun, 90
In the gloom of mighty cities, 302
In the year of eighteen hundred, 271
INDEPENDENT MAN, THE, 243
It was early springtime that the strike was on, 297
It was in the year eighty-three, 191
It's four long years since I reached this land, 119
I've been to California and I haven't got a dime, 116
I've wandered all over this country, 154

JESSE JAMES, 252
Jesse James and his boys rode that Dodge City Trail, 256
Jesse James was a lad that killed many a man, 254
JOE BOWERS, 18

KANSAS BOYS, 229
KANSAS FOOL, THE, 235
Kind folks, you will pity my horrible tale, 151

LANE COUNTY BACHELOR, THE, 224
LIFE IN CALIFORNIA, 104
LITTLE JOE, THE WRANGLER, 206
LITTLE OLD SOD SHANTY ON MY CLAIM, THE, 218
Little owl where do you come from, 67
Long-haired preachers come out every night, 301
LOUSY MINER, THE, 117
LUDLOW MASSACRE, THE, 296

MAID OF MONTEREY, THE, 55
Mientras tengan licor las botellas, 63
MOUNTAIN MEADOWS MASSACRE, THE, 77
MUSTANG GRAY, 60
My eyes look like dried up raisins, 305
My name is Frank Bolar, an old bachelor I am, 227
My name it is Joe Bowers, I've got a brother Ike, 21

Near Buena Vista's mountain chain, 58
Now I'll tell you of my history since eighteen forty-seven, 122
Now, miners, if you'll listen, I'll tell you quite a tale, 28

O workman dear, and did you hear, the news that's goin' round?, 141
Of all the mighty nations in the East or in the West, 216
"Oh, bury me not on the lone prairie," 202
Oh, don't you remember sweet Betsy from Pike, 16
Oh! give me a home where the buffalo roam, 222
Oh, here you see old Tom Moore, 97
Oh, I ain't got no home, nor nothing else, I s'pose, 105

Oh, it's Little Joe, the wrangler, he will never wrangle more, 207
Oh, kind friend you may ask me what makes me sad and still, 198
Oh sleep, Thou Holy Baby, 37
Oh, the good time is come at last, and each succeeding day, Sir, 7
OLD CHISHOLM TRAIL, THE, 164
OLD SETTLER'S SONG, THE, 153
One evening as the sun went down, 295

PACIFIC RAILROAD, THE, 39
PEOPLE'S JUBILEE, THE, 245
POKER JIM, 120
PREACHER AND THE SLAVE, THE, 298

RACE TO CALIFORNIA, THE, 5
REMEMBER THE ALAMO!, 47
Ring out, oh bells! Let the cannons roar, 41
ROLL ON, COLUMBIA, 314
ROOT HOG, OR DIE, 142
ROY BEAN, 276

SACRAMENTO, 12
SAM BASS, 257
Sam Bass was born in Indiana, it was his native home, 258
SANTY ANNO, 52
Say, workers, have you seen the bosses, 246
SEA GULLS AND CRICKETS, 75
SEEING THE ELEPHANT, 107
SIOUX INDIANS, 33
SONG OF HAPPINESS, 38
SPANISH IS THE LOVING TONGUE, 203
Spanish is the loving tongue, 205
STREETS OF LAREDO, THE, 279
SWEET BETSY FROM PIKE, 14

TECOLOTE, EL, 64
¿Tecolote de dónde vienes? 67
The greatest imposition that the public ever saw, 127
The moon was shining brightly, 56
The winter of Forty-nine had passed, 76
There was a brave old Texan, 61
There's a husky, dusky maiden in the Arctic, 313
There's no respect for youth or age, 131

Tom Moore has sung of '49, 99
TOO REE AMA, 304
TORO MORO, EL, 265
TRAIL TO MEXICO, THE, 187
'Twas in the town of Jacksboro in the spring of seventy-three, 171
TWELVE HUNDRED MORE, 138
TYING TEN KNOTS IN THE DEVIL'S TAIL, 283

UNCLE SAM'S FARM, 215
UTAH CARROLL, 197

Wake up, Jacob, 178
Way high up in the Sierry Peaks, 284
Way out upon the Platte, near Pike's Peak we were told, 143
WE ARE ALL A-PANNING, 132
We are all a-panning pan, pan, panning, 133
We cross the prairie as of old, 214
We have the land to raise the wheat, 235
We was camped on the plains at the head of the Cimmaron, 263
Well, come along boys and listen to my tale, 165
WE'LL GIVE 'EM JESSIE, 30
We're alone, Doney Gal, in the rain and hail, 185
We're sailing down the river from Liverpool, 54
WESTERN HOME, 221
We've formed our band, and we're all well manned, 10
We've reached the land of desert sweet, 234
When I left the States for gold, 109
WHEN I WENT OFF TO PROSPECT, 100
When on the wide-spread battle plain, 48
When the farmer comes to town, 239
WHEN THE ICE WORMS NEST AGAIN, 311
When we left for Kansas, 182
While there's wine in our glass let's be merry, 63
WYOMING NESTER, THE, 231

Ye friends of Freedom, rally now, 31
Ye Saints who dwell on Europe's shore, 81
Yo no soy americano, 136

ZEBRA DUN, THE, 262